MW00745482

MEXICO

Contents

Written by Robin Barton

Verified by Anto Howard

Project editor Karen Kemp
Designer Alan Gooch
Cartographic editor Anna Thompson
Managing editor Clare Garcia

American editor Greg Weekes

Published in the United States by AAA Publishing,
1000 AAA Drive, Heathrow, Florida 32746-5063
Published in the United Kingdom by AA Publishing

ISBN-13: 978-1-59508-241-1

Cover design and binding style by permission of AA Publishing
Color separation by Keenes, Andover
Printed and bound in China by Leo Paper Products

10 9 8 7 6 5 4 3 2 1

A03007
Maps in this title produced from:
mapping © MAIRDUMONT/Falk Verlag 2007
and map data © Footprint Handbooks Limited 2004

the magazine

THE PYRAMIDS

Nobody is quite sure why early Mexican civilizations built the number of pyramids that have been discovered all over the country. Some are built over burial tombs, while others appear to be central to ceremonies and sacrificial rituals. One thing is certain: the pyramid was the most important construction in their civilizations and they are no less enthralling today.

Teotihuacán and Chichén Itzá

Mexico boasts the biggest and most complex examples of pyramid building in the world. The largest, the Pirámide de Sol (Pyramid of the Sun) at Teotihuacán, has a floor area of 46,000sq m (55,000sq yards) and was built between AD 100 and 400, a time when this vast site was becoming an empire that rivaled Rome's in scale. The civilization was crumbling by AD 650 but the pyramid, and its partner, the Pirámide de la Luna (Pyramid of the Moon), remain.

Inset: The view across Teotihuacán from the Pyramid of the Moon

Chichén Itzá, in the Yucatán, recently named one of the "new seven wonders of the world," is the most famous of the Mayan pyramids, and holds further astronomical secrets, representing the Mayan calendar in the number of steps and panels in its design. It is now a must-see stop on any tour of the Yucatán's Mayan ruins.

Ritual Killings

But while sightseers clamber over the ruins, archaeologists are still trying to piece together the complete picture of how and why these pyramids were constructed. Many Mayan sites have yet to be rescued from the jungle that has enveloped them over the centuries and they too will reveal further secrets.

In 2006 it was discovered that people and wild animals were ritually killed or buried alive in the foundations of Teotihuacán's Pyramid of the Moon as a way of consecrating the pyramid. And in the same year a 1500-year-old pyramid was discovered under the outskirts of Mexico City.

Above: Temple of the Inscriptions, Palenque

Left: The ruined palace of Hachakum, Yaxchilán, with its distinctive roofcomb crowning the top

The Mexican authorities have been careful to protect the country's heritage, and the sites of the most popular ruins – including Chichén Itzá, Uxmal and Teotihuacán – are generally well managed, but it's always a good idea to visit them as early as possible in the day to avoid the crowds and the sometimes intense heat of midday.

If you get the chance, seek out some of the less well-known ruins, such as magical Palenque and Yaxchilán in the south of the country. In these places, where you might share an early morning walk with just a handful of people and a cacophony of birdsong, the impact of the pyramids and temples seems to be all the greater.

A TASTE OF MEXICO

**Below left to right: Hot jalapeno peppers; prickly pear cactus; edible grasshoppers; fast-food Mexico style
Bottom: Tequila**

Mexican food has the reputation of having all the subtlety of a tequila slammer – it's assumed by many first-time visitors to be fried, eye-wateringly hot or coated in cheese or all three. But while Mexican street food – *tacos*, *burritos*, *enchiladas* and *chile rellenos* – is never going to qualify as fine dining, the reality is that Mexican cuisine is far more varied and subtle than it is often given credit for. True, the flavors tend to be big and bold, but for anyone with an interest in food, Mexico will be a thoroughly delicious experience.

Staple Diet

Corn has long been a staple of Mexican cooking, with flat pancakes forming the basis of *enchiladas* and *tacos*. Indeed, corn was an important part of pre-Hispanic Mexican mythology and there was even a god of corn. Another source of carbohydrate is the black or pinto bean, often refried and served daily at all three meals. Adding flavor to this base are chilis, fruits (such as avocado for guacamole) and spices. While Mexican food is thought to be hot, you'll find that many of the hottest parts of the meal are the dips, which are optional.

Meat

There are also significant regional variations. *Carne asado* (grilled meat) is a staple of the ranching country of northern Mexico, while in the tropical Yucatán pork is marinaded in Seville

orange juice (or lemon and lime) to create the classic dish *cochinita pibil*, served in a banana leaf.

Seafood comes in a wide range of styles along the Caribbean and Pacific coasts.

In the cities and upscale tourist spots, a new restaurant movement is introducing a style described as *alta cocina Mexicana* to discerning diners: the portions are smaller, but the flavors are more distinct.

Desserts

Mexicans also have a sweet tooth; breakfast may simply be a sugary pastry while desserts tend to be very sweet. Flan, egg custard with caramel sauce, the equivalent of a creme caramel, and *churros*, like donuts, but in a long stick, are popular. And we have the Mexicans to thank for chocolate, which was first prepared as a drink flavored with cocoa beans and vanilla by the Aztecs.

Below left to right: Mexican beer (*cerveza*); fish in spicy red chili sauce; unusual fruit from Ocosingo; tacos (flour tortillas with meat sauce); mangoes; fresh fruit platter; beer and colorful cocktails; cocoa pod

Tequila and Mescal

If tequila is a fiery drink, its country cousin mescal is positively explosive. Tequila and mescal are both made from variants of the *agave*, a spiky plant from the family of succulents that is often seen planted in rows in field after field. While tequila comes from the blue *agave* plant and is distilled in Jalisco state, mescal has its roots in Oaxaca state and comes from the fleshy heart of the plant, which is roasted, crushed, fermented and distilled to produce the rough-edged spirit. Tequila is closely associated with nights out that are difficult to recall afterwards, and a pounding headache. However, try a fine, aged tequila and a whole new world opens up. The best tequilas are up to 15 years old and are never drunk with lime or salt, which are used to disguise the taste of cheap tequilas. Nor should a worm be in the bottle; this was a marketing gimmick when the drink was introduced to the United States. In Oaxaca, mescal aficionados ascribe a similar complexity to the spirit — there are *joven* (young, or white) mescals all the way up to *gran reserva* mescals (aged for a minimum of five years). The taste should be smoky but not fiery.

HOME-GROWN TALENT

featuring well-known names such as Sean Penn and Naomi Watts. *Babel*, starring Brad Pitt and Cate Blanchett, followed *21 Grams*.

After hitting the headlines with his performance in *Amores Perros*, Guadalajara-born García Bernal's next job was in *Y Tu Mamá También* (*And Your Mother Too*), a warmly received coming-of-age movie also set in Mexico. It was directed by Mexican filmmaker Alfonso Cuarón. Bernal's role in *Y Tu Mamá También* brought him to the attention of Hollywood's casting directors. The London-trained actor was selected to play Che Guevara in the biopic *The Motorcycle Diaries* (2004).

Mexican cinema has come a long way since the 1960s and 1970s when the desert around Durango (► 72) stood in for the Wild West in films such as Sam Peckinpah's *Pat Garrett and Billy the Kid* (1973). Today, Mexican actors and directors are fêted by Hollywood and the range of movies produced in Mexico or with Mexican talent has expanded to include road movies, horror films, love stories and sophisticated dramas such as the 2006 Oscar-nominated film *Babel*, directed by Alejandro González Iñárritu.

Iñárritu, one of the leading lights of the new wave of Mexican cinema, was born in Mexico City in 1963. He came to the attention of Hollywood with the fast-paced drama *Amores Perros* (*Love's a Bitch*), which followed three interwoven stories, all connected to a car crash in Mexico City. The film's Mexican cast included Gael García Bernal, who has also moved onto the Hollywood A-list.

But back to Iñárritu. After *Amores Perros* was released in 2000, Iñárritu was offered the Hollywood-funded film *21 Grams*, another drama, this time

The success of *Y Tu Mamá También* also brought Alfonso Cuarón into the mainstream and he accepted the job of directing the third instalment of the Harry Potter movies, *Harry Potter and the Prisoner of*

Above: Alejandro González Iñárritu

Right: Gael García Bernal

Below: Villa del Oeste film set, Durango

Azkaban (2004), to which he added an extra air of menace.

Iñárritu, Bernal and Cuarón are just three of the latest Mexicans to be celebrated in Hollywood, and several of their predecessors have gone on to become household names. Salma Hayek, born in the Caribbean coastal state of Veracruz, played Frida Kahlo in *Frida* (2002) after parts in *Dogma*, *Traffic*, *From Dusk Till Dawn* and *Desperado*. Her co-star in the violent thriller *Desperado* (1995), a re-working of Robert Rodriguez's low-budget classic *El Mariachi*, was

Antonio Banderas. The Spaniard starred in one of the most recent Hollywood-funded movies to be filmed in Durango: *The Mask of Zorro* (1998).

Mexican cinema's relationship with Hollywood, it seems, will only get closer, as both seek to reach each other's markets. And that's good for film fans because there is no shortage of talent south of the U.S. border.

Above left: Salma Hayek as Frida Kahlo
Above right: Antonio Banderas, Salma Hayek and director Robert Rodriguez in the action movie *Desperado*

Below: Movie poster along Mexico City's Paseo de la Reforma

Mexico's Indigenous People

When the Spanish arrived in Mexico in the 16th century they found a country that was made up of a tapestry of separate tribal groups: Mayans, Aztecs, Mixtecs, Totonacs and Zapotecs, among others. During the colonial period many of the *indígenas* (indigenous groups) had to form alliances with the Spanish or be wiped out – and many perished as a result of imported diseases. In the first century of Spanish occupation up to 90 percent of the indigenous population vanished. Many ethnic groups did survive after Spanish rule petered out and today there remain about 50 distinct indigenous groups around the country. They have learned to adapt to a modern Mexico, which sometimes seems more interested in economic development than maintaining its heritage.

Preserving Cultural Identity

About 13 percent of the Mexican population is classed as indigenous, and the states with the highest proportion are the Yucatán and Oaxaca. Quintana Roo, Campeche and Chiapas, also in the south of the country, have high proportions of indigenous people. It's no coincidence that, outside of the tourist areas, these states are also among Mexico's least developed and most remote. Many of these groups have preserved their own languages, such as the many dialects of Mayan, and this is an important step in maintaining their own cultural identity. The Law of Linguistic Rights, passed in 2003, has helped to support indigenous tongues, and initiatives, such as bilingual road signs, are spreading. However, to the north, the story isn't so positive. Groups such as the Tarahumara in the highlands around Barranca del Cobre (Copper Canyon) are struggling, caught between a basic, subsistence existence and the pressures of a fast-encroaching modern world. Famed as fast, long-distance runners, a skill once used to hunt wild animals, many now make a living selling trinkets to tourists, but for how much longer will they be able to preserve their way of life?

One answer may be found in the southern states of Chiapas and Oaxaca. In towns such as San Cristóbal de las Casas, the Zapatista Army of National Liberation has been demanding a better deal for the local poverty-stricken indigenous groups and they have a largely peaceful presence across the area. In the churches of San Cristóbal de las Casas Catholicism has been blended with local traditions and beliefs. In the villages surrounding the city of Oaxaca, local groups manufacture and sell crafts to visitors and, to an extent, have a greater degree of control over their destiny. And in the Yucatán, the Mayan cause, already an important tourist attraction, was delivered a boost by the 2006 Mel Gibson movie *Apocalypto*, which was filmed entirely in the local Mayan language.

Many people still wear traditional costume
Left: Mother and daughter, San Cristóbal de las Casas
Above: Huichol man
Right: *Conchero* dancer
Far right: Tarahumara children
Bottom right: Mayans from Ocosingo
Bottom far right: Lacandon children

From the world's most delicate insects to some of its largest mammals, Mexico's wildlife is as diverse as the country itself. But it is Mexico's oceans that are home to its biggest animals. Every year gray whales migrate from the lagoons of the Baja peninsula up the Pacific coast of Mexico and the United States to their summer Arctic feeding grounds, a distance of up to 8,000km (5,000 miles). They can be seen calving in the Baja lagoons from around January to April.

Another creature also makes a remarkable migration to Mexico, but this time its strength is in numbers, not size. It is the orange and black Monarch butterfly, which gathers in vast quantities in the wooded mountains of central Mexico during the winter (➤ 97–98).

Top to bottom: Grasshopper; hyacinth macaw; Mexican deer; jaguar; diamond-backed snake; Monarch butterfly
Background: Celestún is famous for its colony of flamingos

Mexico's Wildlife

They return to the north United States each spring, breeding along the way. The adults die before they complete the journey but the next generation continues the epic migration.

Other creatures are also found in abundant numbers in Mexico. In the Sea of Cortéz, between Baja and the mainland, Humboldt squid can grow to 1.2 or 1.5m (4 or 5 feet) in length. These voracious predators will try to eat anything they can lay their tentacles on. This makes it very easy for local fishermen to catch them.

Not all Mexican wildlife is so common, however. Habitat loss has forced many of the larger herbivores and carnivores out of northern Mexico and into ever smaller parcels of land in the south. The rain forests and jungles of southern Mexico were once home to elegant jaguars – as demonstrated by the jade carvings found at many Mayan sites – but these big cats are now limited to the eco-theme parks of the Yucatán. Their prey would have included the tapir, now a very elusive forest resident. Howler and spider monkeys are easier to spot, or at least hear, at the less-frequented Mayan sites of southern Mexico. Birdlife is in a slightly stronger position and bird-watchers won't be disappointed with the variety of indigenous and migratory birds in places such as Puerto Vallarta on the Pacific coast and Celestún in the Yucatán. Reptiles, too, are numerous and varied, with more than 700 species in evidence, from monstrous pythons to delicate geckos.

PLIGHT OF THE TURTLES

Turtles are endangered. Several species attempt to use the beaches of both the Caribbean and Pacific coasts in which to lay their eggs, but increasing beachside development and illegal poaching has made this an uphill struggle for the leatherback and loggerhead turtle. Conservationists are fighting to preserve some hatching grounds, but the turtles also face threats at sea from fishing boats and pollution.

Spain Rules

The conquistador Hernán Cortés set out for Mexico from Cuba in January 1519 with just 11 ships, 100 sailors and 600 soldiers. His patron, Diego Velázquez de Cuéllar, governor of Cuba, had a last-minute change of heart about the expedition when he realized that Cortés would seize the glory and fortune by conquering Mexico. But as he hurried to the dock, it was clear that nothing was going to stop Cortés.

Cortés landed on the Yucatán peninsula and did indeed prove unstoppable, but more through strategy and good fortune than strength of arms. With translation skills provided by an Aztec princess, Dona Marina, or La Malinche, who spoke Aztec and Mayan, Cortés was able to play one indigenous group off against another. He formed strategic alliances, to the extent that the Totonacs helped build the settlement that would become Veracruz, and soon Cortés had a formidable force at his command.

On learning that the powerful Mexican empire was ruled from a city called Tenochtitlán, which later formed the foundations of Mexico City, Cortés set off for central Mexico. He arrived in November 1519 and his welcome may have surprised him: Moctezuma II, the Aztec ruler, appears to have believed that Cortés was the the god Quetzalcóatl, returning to his people. Not one to ignore a gift-wrapped opportunity, Cortés soon stamped his authority on the city, imprisoning Moctezuma.

Cortés had already scuttled his ships to prevent deserters slipping back to Cuba, and he declared himself independent of Velázquez. His greatest test, however, was when a force led by Pánfilo de Narváez was ordered by Velázquez to bring Cortés back for trial. Cortéz intercepted Narváez, defeated his much larger force and then returned to rescue the Spaniards he had left in charge of Tenochtitlán. Wars between the Spanish invaders and indigenous Mexicans raged for decades, but Cortés had made his name. He was a wealthy man when he died in Spain in 1547.

But for all the stories of battles against the odds and gruelling expeditions, the conquest of Mexico by the Spanish was a bloody and brutal time. Those indigenous people who didn't ally themselves with the conquistadors were often slaughtered. Others died from diseases against which they had no immunity. The Spanish tried to ban traditional beliefs and languages and introduced Catholicism; churches were built on the sites of temples and Aztec priests were persecuted. The Spanish extracted vast amounts of gold and silver from Mexico, sending it back to Spain in galleons that were obvious targets for pirates. But the conquest of Mexico also formed the building blocks of modern Mexico. Many of the Spanish who ventured to Mexico to seek their fortunes married Mexican women and had families.

Spanish rule over Mexico couldn't last forever. The Mexican war of independence was concluded in 1821 with the Treaty of Córdoba and Mexico embarked on a period of uncertainty that continued into the 20th century.

Above: Detail of a relief showing Cortés entering Mexico City on horseback
Right: Diego Rivera mural in the Palacio Nacional depicting the arrival of Cortés

Mexican Art

Frida Kahlo and

You could be excused if you thought that Mexican art began and ended with Frida Kahlo (1907–54). But the Mexican artist, although the nation's most famous thanks to the 2002 biopic starring Salma Hayek, is just one figure in a much larger picture.

Before the arrival of the Spanish in the 16th century, Mexico already had a fascinating arts tradition. Mayan sites such as Bonampak have some superb examples of Mayan art, including frescoes, mosaics and sculptures. The Museo Nacional de Antropologia in Mexico City also has some fine exhibits, from gigantic Olmec sculptures to delicate jewelry and ceramics. The Spanish brought with them a tradition of ornate, Catholic iconography which, in time, was woven into Mexico's artistic fabric. But it wasn't until Mexican independence and the arrival of ground-breaking artists such as Frida Kahlo and her husband the muralist Diego Rivera (1886–1957), that these separate strands were pulled together.

Public Murals

Politically radical, Rivera was at the forefront of a wave of creativity that swept Mexico in the 1920s. With fellow muralists José Clemente Orozco (1883–1949) and David Alfaro Siqueiros (1896–1974), he was commissioned to paint a series of vast murals, in or on public and state buildings, depicting events from Mexico's history. As an expression of what it was to be a Mexican, the project had a huge impact. You can see many of the murals today, particularly in cities such as Mexico City and Guadalajara and several American museums.

Inspiration

At the end of the decade, in 1929, Rivera married Frida Kahlo, who was 20 years his junior. Kahlo had suffered terrible injuries, including a broken spine, a broken pelvis and a broken leg, in a bus crash in 1926 and remained in pain for the rest of her life. This, together with a difficult childhood and a politicized outlook, became the source of many of the themes of her work. Her tempestuous relationship with Rivera was also a source of anguish and inspiration. Both had extra-marital affairs; they divorced then remarried, living together in the Coyoacán suburb of Mexico City close to fellow Communist Leon Trotsky. Kahlo's achievement, recognized by Rivera, was to imbue her work with the presence of Mexico's indigenous groups, but her paintings, frequently self-portraits, also contained references to Christianity and feminism.

Hip City

The last of Mexico's great muralists to die was Alfredo Zalce (1908–2003), who is commemorated by the Museo de Arte Contemporáneo Alfredo Zalce in Michoacán. But in recent years, trendy new galleries have been springing up in Mexico City's gentrified neighborhoods and the capital is supporting several successful new artists such as Gabriel Orozco and Miguel Calderón. In 2006, Mexico City's Hilario Galguera gallery hosted an exhibition by British artist Damien Hirst and the occasion was perhaps the catalyst for reappraisal of Mexico City as one of the hippest cities for art lovers.

Top left: Diego Rivera
Top right: Rivera's studio in Coyoacán
Above: Museo de Frida Kahlo

Left: Rivera mosaic on Teatro de los Insurgentes, Coyoacán
Right: Juan O'Gorman mural at the University of Mexico

The Sporting Life

Mexican sporting attention is focused on the football (soccer) pitch, the boxing ring and the bullring. *Lucha Libre* wrestling (free wrestling or fighting), while enormously popular, is treated more as a branch of showbiz rather than a sporting endeavour.

World-class Fighters

The boxing ring is a venue where Mexicans have proved particularly successful over the years. The country has produced several world-class fighters, boxing in the light-weight classes and earning a reputation as tenacious, tactical boxers. None has eclipsed the great **Julio César Chávez** (pictured), who turned professional in 1980 and won his first 90 fights, gaining 5 world titles in the process. He remains a national hero in Mexico. His contemporary counterpart is probably Marco Antonio Barrera, nicknamed "The Baby-Faced Assassin." Although Barrera fights in the super featherweight class, he's inflicted more than 40 knockouts. Boxing matches attract huge crowds in stadiums in Mexico City and other cities.

Lucha Libre

Another crowd puller in Mexico is the country's *lucha libre* (wrestling). With an atmosphere somewhere between a pop concert and pantomime, matches are staged between masked wrestlers who assume various personas, and are usually between a "good" clean-fighting wrestler and a "bad" (*rudos*) character. As with any good story, there is usually a background to the confronta-tion, and the good guy usually wins. Mexico's *lucha libre* wrestlers, such as El Santo, are often folk heroes who wear their masks in public until they retire.

The Beautiful Game

For many years now, Mexico has fielded a formidable national football team; what they lack in stature they make up for with tireless, fast-paced football. In the 2006 World Cup the Mexican team was knocked out by Argentina after one of the tournament's best games. Their fans, clad in the national colors of green, white and red, are always a friendly, lively presence in World Cup stadiums – indeed the country has twice hosted the World Cup finals, in 1970 and 1986.

The Mexico team dominates the regional league, the Confederation of North, Central and Caribbean Association Football (CONCACAF), but it is the domestic league, the Primera División, that really gets the fans going. Matches between the 20 leading teams in the country attract massive audiences on TV, with rivalries between cities such as Guadalajara and Mexico City fueling the passion. You can catch a game at weekends during the season (August to December and January to June).

Bullfighting

A less sporting weekend activity is the tradition of bullfighting. There are bullrings, such as Mexico City's Plaza México, the world's largest bullring, in many towns and cities across the country. Fights usually take place on Sundays and are as much about the ritual and performance of the matadors as the sporting spectacle itself. After the bull has been softened up by mounted *picadores* and daring *toreros*, the *coup de grâce* is delivered by the matador, who has to kill the bull with his sword in less than 16 minutes. Most matadors are Mexican, although occasionally visiting Spanish matadors will put in an appearance. Fighting spirit is applauded in bulls and particularly spirited bulls may have their lives spared.

The best of Mexico

The best ruins

- Uxmal (➤ 164–165), in the Yucatán, is a low-key but utterly absorbing alternative to the area's star Mayan site, Chichén Itzá (➤ 160–161).
- Tulum (➤ 158–159), may not be the most elaborate Mayan ruin, but it has the most spectacular setting, overlooking the aquamarine Caribbean.
- Palenque (➤ 140–141), in the south of the country, is shrouded in jungle, which makes the experience all the more exciting.
- The scale of Teotihuacán (➤ 114–115), built almost 2,000 years ago, will amaze even the most jaded city-dweller.

Best towns and cities

- Guanajuato (➤ 92–94), for its colonial charm and restored historic heart, best explored on foot.
- San Cristóbal de las Casas (➤ 142–143), for its beautiful white-washed buildings.
- Puerto Vallarta (➤ 100), for proving that even resorts can retain their character.

The best journeys

- Take the Copper Canyon railway to or from Chihuahua and you will pass through some of the most stunning scenery in the country (➤ 75).
- Rent a car and drive the Mayan Riviera (➤ 185–188), stopping at beaches, Mayan ruins and eco-parks.
- Take the boat to Yaxchilán (➤ 145–146), a Mayan site only accessible by river.

Top: The Pyramid of the Magician, Uxmal
Above: The old port town of Puerto Vallarta

The best nights out

- Party with the capital's beautiful people in Condesa's bars (➤ 58).
- Scream along with the crowd at a *lucha libre* wrestling match.
- Dip your feet in the surf at Cabo San Lucas (➤ 66), a Baja playground that rivals Cancún for nightlife.

Best activities

- Swim with sea lions on a kayaking trip in the Sea of Cortéz (➤ 180–181).
- Surf the Pacific waves of Puerto Escondido, a popular hotspot south of Acapulco (➤ 135).
- Learn to rock climb at the walls of Potrero Chico in northern Mexico.
- Try your hand at cooking some of the local specialties in Oaxaca (➤ 150).

Best buys

- Leather cowboy boots from Chihuahua (➤ 81).
- Handicrafts from the villages surrounding Oaxaca (➤ 139).
- Silver jewelry from Taxco, a city built on a silver mine (➤ 128).

Finding Your Feet

First Two Hours

Mexico has many ports of entry, including 60 airports. The principal international ones are Mexico City's Benito Juárez airport (MEX), Cancún (CUN), Puerto Vallarta's Ordaz airport (PVR), Acapulco's General Juan N. Alvarez airport (ACA), Guadalajara's Miguel Hidalgo y Costillo airport (GDL) and Monterrery's General Mariano Escobedo airport (MTY). Visitors can also enter Mexico overland via more than 40 border crossings with the United States (such as San Diego-Tijuana and El Paso-Ciudad Juárez). There are also border crossings with Guatemala and Belize. Passengers on cruise ships enter Mexico at terminals such as Cancún on the Caribbean coast and Acapulco or Puerto Vallarta on the Pacific Coast.

Arriving By Air

- Mexico City's **Benito Juárez Airport** (MEX) is located in the suburbs 13km (8 miles) east of the city center (www.aicm.com.mx). A second terminal opened in 2007. Both terminals have domestic and international arrivals and departures, left-luggage lockers, tourist information desks and car rental agencies.
- When taking a **taxi** to your hotel ensure you buy a **pre-paid ticket** from the offices on the main arrivals concourse. The tickets are priced according to zones. Hand the ticket to the uniformed airport staff who marshall the taxi rank, and they will direct you to the next available taxi in the rank. The driver will take a stub ensuring there will be no negotiations for further payment. Use only the official yellow and white airport taxis.
- **Cancún Airport** (CUN) is 16km (10 miles) south of central Cancún (no telephone enquiries; contact the airline; www.cancun-airport.com).
- Buy a pre-paid ticket for **taxis** and *colectivos* (shared minibuses) to the hotel zone.
- Puerto Vallarta's **Ordaz Airport** (PVR) is 6km (4 miles) north of central Puerto Vallarta (www.cancun-airport.com).
- Buy a pre-paid ticket for **taxis** and *colectivos* (shared minibuses) at a small kiosk outside the terminal building exit.
- Most **international airports** in Mexico have money-changing facilities and an information desk.
- Mexican **customs regulations** permit the importation of no more than 400 cigarettes and 3 liters of wine, beer or liquor.
- At airports such as Cancún the customs desks operate a lottery-style traffic light system – if the **light flashes red** you will be searched.

Arriving By Land

- Crossing the **U.S.-Mexico border** on foot is easy and speedy, although returning to the U.S. takes much more time.
- If traveling beyond the immediate vicinity of the border, foreign visitors require a **Mexican Tourist Card**, available around the clock at most border crossings. A fee, payable in US$, is charged.
- To bring a **vehicle** across the border you will need a vehicle permit, driving license, insurance and car rental details.
- Many **American car rental agencies** allow their vehicles to be driven in Mexico within a few miles of the border, with the purchase of extra insurance.
- All persons, including U.S. citizens, traveling to and from Mexico are required to **carry their passport** (visit www.travel.state.gov/).

Getting Around

Mexico is a vast country with challenging environmental conditions – altitude, desert and jungle – so prepare for a degree of unpredictability when making travel arrangements. Modes of travel include airlines, buses, rental cars and ferries (from Baja to the mainland and from Cancún to Isla Mujeres and Cozumel). Train travel, apart from the Copper Canyon railway (▶ 70–71), isn't an option.

Domestic Flights

- With such **large distances between cities**, and as many small towns have their own airport, air travel is a popular way of getting around.
- Air travel has come down in price with the arrival of **low-cost airlines**: Volaris (www.volaris.com.mx), Alma (www.alma.com.mx), and Avolar (www.avolar.com.mx), among others, challenging the dominance of **national carriers** Aeromexico (tel: 800 021 4010; www.aeromexico.com) and Mexicana (tel: 55 54 48 09 90; www.mexicana.com).
- The **national carriers** still have the most comprehensive networks and highest reliability, while the **budget airlines** tend to specialize in particular regions. Mexicana flies to more than 20 domestic destinations and Aeromexico, Latin America's largest airline, flies to more than 40 destinations within Mexico.
- Tickets can be **booked online** with the national carriers and the low-cost airlines. However, you may have trouble paying with a **credit card** if the card is registered outside Mexico or the U.S. You can use credit cards or cash to pay for tickets at the airline's counter in the airport.

Driving

- A **rapidly improving road infrastructure**, including uncrowded toll roads, means that traveling by bus or car is relatively safe and speedy.
- **Caution** is still required. Avoid driving a car by night because there is still a risk from bandits in some states and the unlit roads may also have hazards such as livestock and *topes* (speed bumps). Driving in cities, especially Mexico City, is not recommended for nervous drivers.
- **Car rental** rates are moderately expensive. All the major international rental agencies have offices in the main tourist destinations. Ensure that your insurance is fully comprehensive.
- **You will need** a credit card, driving license and passport to rent a car.
- Leaded (*Nova*) and unleaded (*Magna Sin*) fuel are sold by the liter. Fill up the fuel tank at every opportunity on **long car journeys**, and take plenty of drinking water. Breakdowns in remote places can mean a long wait for assistance. The Mexico Tourism ministry has a fleet of **Green Angels** – bilingual mechanics – who patrol the roads and help tourists.
- Drive on the **right side** of the road.
- Seat belts are **compulsory for front seats**.
- **Breath-testing** is not widespread in Mexico.
- Speed limits on motorways: **110kph (68mph)**.
- Speed limits on country roads: **70–80kph (43–50mph)**.
- Speed limits in towns: **40–60kph (25–37mph)**.

Taxis

- In Mexico City, **avoid hailing a taxi** on the street, even if they have the green and white livery and registration details of the capital's other taxis. Cases of robbery and abduction persist in the city. Instead, ask your hotel to call you a taxi. The hotel can also provide you with the number of the private taxi firm they recommend, such as Servitaxis (tel: 55 5516 6020; www.servitaxis.com.mx).

■ In other places you may need to agree a price with the taxi driver before setting off. Many major airports and bus stations operate a **pre-paid fixed price ticket system** which is always worth using.

Buses

■ Bus travel is best for **short distances** (of up to six hours) between cities. Don't underestimate distances: in Mexico bus routes of more than 12 hours are not uncommon.
■ Bus services to **mainstream destinations** are regular and reliable.
■ For comfortable, air-conditioned, **long-distance buses**, buy a ticket for the first-class or deluxe service. Most of these buses will have a restroom. These classes of bus tend to use toll roads, which are quicker and safer than other highways, especially at night.
■ Mexico City has four **bus terminals**: Norte (for northern Mexico), Sur (for southern states), Oriente (for the Caribbean coast and the Yucatán) and Poniente (for the west and Pacific coast).
■ Each region is served by competing **private bus** companies. Their schedules and frequency of departures may differ slightly but prices will be similar.

Métro

■ Mexico City's Métro consists of **11 lines**, predominantly running north to south and east to west.
■ In the **Centro Histórico**, the stations are at frequent intervals but become more spaced out the further you go into the suburbs.
■ Most of the **capital's attractions**, including Coyoacán, Bosque de Chapultepec and the Zócalo, can be reached by Métro. The airport and some of the main bus stations are also served by the Métro.
■ Tickets are **priced per trip** and are cheap. They can be bought at machines and manned counters before you go through the turnstiles.
■ The Métro **attracts pickpockets**; take care of your possessions.

Admission Charges
The cost of admission for museums and places of interest mentioned in the text is indicated by the following price categories:
Inexpensive under US$5 **Moderate** US$5–10 **Expensive** over US$10

Accommodations

There is an enormous variety of accommodations in Mexico to suit all budgets, from international hotel chains to backpacker hostels. During the peak holiday seasons and festivals such as the Day of the Dead it is advisable to reserve well in advance. At other off-peak times, it may be possible to negotiate a lower rate.

Hotels

■ In the major resorts, on both coasts, you will find **world-class hotels**, including vast chain hotels with hundreds of rooms which are typically used by package holidaymakers on all-inclusive holidays.

- In the resorts and at other key destinations, you may find **small boutique hotels** which offer an interesting and personal experience. They often occupy restored colonial houses (www.mexicoboutiquehotels.com).
- One of the largest **international hotel chains**, with a good selection of mid-range hotels and motels in towns and cities across the country, is Best Western (www.bestwestern.com). Other **major hotel groups** include Westin and Sheraton (www.starwoodhotels.com), Howard Johnson (www.hojo.com), Iberostar (www.iberostar.com), NH Hotels (www.nh-hotels.com), Camino Real (www.caminoreal.com) and Sol Melia (www.solmelia.com).
- Prices in the international hotels are often quoted in US$. Mid- and upper range hotels will accept **credit cards**, but check before booking at the cheaper hotels. **Taxes**, which vary slightly from state to state, will be added to the final bill.
- **Air-conditioning** should be available at mid- and upper-range hotels, but a fan is common in out-of-the-way places. In highland areas it can get very cold at night so check whether the hotel provides heating.
- Mid- and high-end hotels will have **modern facilities**, including a TV, electrical supply and amenities such as a gym and restaurant. Business-class hotels usually offer broadband internet and other services.
- Tap water in the top hotels is likely to be purified, but many guests use **bottled water** (usually provided in most good-quality hotels) to minimize the chance of illness.
- Some **hotels around bus stations** and at stops along the **highways** can be seedy. Use your discretion.

Alternative Accommodations

- Smaller places offering accommodations include *posadas* (inns), *paradores* (basic hotels) and *casas de huéspedes* (often upscale B&Bs).
- *Cabañas* (cabins) at beaches are usually very basic, with just a palm-frond roof and shared facilities. **Campsites** are not common.
- In popular tourist areas, renting a **self-catering apartment** can, for groups, be a cost-effective alternative to staying in a hotel. Local tourist offices may be able to provide a list of available apartments or book in advance with an agency. A minimum stay of several days will be expected.

Diamond Ratings

AAA tourism editors evaluate and rate lodging establishments based on the overall quality and services. AAA's diamond rating criteria reflect the design and service standards set by the lodging industry, combined with the expectations of our members.

Our one (❧) or two (❧❧) diamond rating represents a clean and well-maintained property offering comfortable rooms, with the two diamond property showing enhancements in decor and furnishings. A three (❧❧❧) diamond property shows marked upgrades in physical attributes, services and comfort and may offer additional amenities. A four (❧❧❧❧) diamond rating signifies a property offering a high level of service and hospitality and a wide variety of amenities and upscale facilities. A five (❧❧❧❧❧) diamond rating represents a world-class facility, offering the highest level of luxurious accommodations and personalized guest services.

Prices
Expect to pay for a double room per night:
$ under US$50 $$ US$50–150 $$$ over US$150

Food and Drink

Mexican cuisine is famous the world over and is the result of years of foreign influence, from the Spanish colonial recipes to American fast-food. As varied as the country's scenery, the food of Mexico covers every budget, from street-corner *tacos* to sophisticated pre-Hispanic recipes.

Mexican Cuisine

■ Much of Mexico's cuisine is associated with fast-food or snack food – *tacos*, *fajitas*, *enchiladas* – and is **based around the *tortilla***, a flat, unleavened corn pancake.

■ A new wave of **Mexican chefs** has introduced a more sophisticated take on Mexican food, *alta cocina Mexicana*. This brings Mexican cooking into contemporary restaurants in the major cities and resorts.

■ Certain ingredients and dishes from pre-Columbian Aztec Mexico survive and can be tried at restaurants such as Los Girasoles in Mexico City (► 56). Specialties include *chapulines* (smoked and fried grasshoppers) and *jumiles* (stink beetles sometimes served live) – the first is edible, the second an acquired taste. *Chapulines* have a high lead content and may not be suitable for children or pregnant women.

■ One Mexican ingredient that most people love is **chocolate**; the Mayans and Aztecs cultivated and developed cocoa, and chocolate is used in recipes such as the savoury *mole* sauces of Puebla and Oaxaca.

■ Not all Mexican food is spicy or hot. There are several distinct **regional styles**, such as the Afro-Caribbean flavors of Veracruz, the Mayan dishes of the Yucatán and the barbequed meats of Northern Mexico.

Eating Out

■ Meal times hardly vary across the country. Most Mexicans will have **breakfast** (*desayuno*) early, eating anything from sweet pastries with coffee to a large meal of *huevos rancheros* (fried eggs, tortillas and refried beans). **Lunch** (*comida*) is often the largest meal of the day and is eaten around 2pm, while **supper** (*cena*) is often eaten relatively early (by 8pm).

■ **Reservations** are recommended for the best Mexican restaurants, but outside the capital's trendiest dining spots you can usually find a table on the spot. At the top end, expect to pay up to $50 a head.

■ **Wine** can be expensive. Most is imported from Chile or Argentina, although Mexico has its own wine region (northern Baja).

■ A **service charge** of 10–15 percent is often included in the bill. Check before adding your tip. Most restaurants in popular tourist areas will accept **credit cards**.

■ With a rigorous and cautious approach, **stomach upsets** can be avoided. Avoid all water, including ice, unless it comes out of a freshly opened bottle. Avoid vegetables that haven't been cooked or peeled. Use your discretion when ordering food with shellfish, eggs (including mayonnaise) and other perishable ingredients.

■ Don't expect to find many **non-smoking restaurants**.

■ **Children are welcomed** in most restaurants.

Alcohol

■ Mexican **beers** are very good – the best are produced according to Germany's purity laws and there are significant variations between brands, including light lagers and dark, malty beers. Try Dos Equis (double X), Modelo, Pacifica, Tecate and Bohemia.

- Mexican **spirits** – tequila, mezcal and pulque – vary greatly in quality. The best aged tequilas offer a completely different experience to the cheap, chemically infused version served in tourist areas.
- Local **wine** is inexpensive and improving in quality – look for Domecq, Casa Madero and Santo Tomás. Some of the best wines come from Monte Xanic, near Ensenada, in Baja California, but they are expensive.

Diamond Ratings

As with the hotel ratings (▶ 29), AAA tourism editors evaluate restaurants on the overall qulaity of food, service, décor and ambience – with extra emphasis given to food and service. Ratings range from one diamond (❤), indicating a simple, family-oriented establishment to five diamonds (❤❤❤), indicating an establishment offering superb culinary skills and an ultimate dining experience.

Prices
Expect to pay per person for a meal, excluding drinks:
$ under US$10 **$$** US$10–20 **$$$** over US$20

Shopping

Mexico has retail opportunities that will excite every shopper, from the chic boutiques of Mexico City and the major resorts to the weekly markets (*mercados*) in plazas around the country. There are department stores in cities and large malls that stock many items under one roof.

Opening Hours

- Opening hours vary according to the type of shop. Most shops open at 9am and close as late as 7pm. **Smaller shops** may **close** for an hour or two at lunch; most will stay open. Many shops close Sunday or Monday.

Payment

- Credit cards are widely accepted in major stores and boutiques in the tourist areas. In local shops in remote areas expect to **pay in cash**.

What To Buy

- Mexican **crafts** have several regional specialties. **Silver jewelry** is very popular in the highland silver towns such as Taxco.
- **Ceramics** are widespread and include the famous Talavera tiles of Puebla.
- **Tribal masks** also have regional variations.
- **Leather** (including colorful cowboy boots from Chihuahua), **lacquerware** and **textiles** such as blankets are also good purchases.

Where To Buy It

- **Handicraft shops** will usually stock items produced nationally, although the best will specialize in local crafts, such as those around Oaxaca.
- **FONART shops** in many towns and resorts are government-run outlets that stock a range of good-quality, traditional crafts, at a price.
- **Street markets** are commonplace in Mexican towns and villages. In areas with lots of visitors there may also be a section devoted to **crafts** (*artesanías*); otherwise the markets typically sell food and household items.

Entertainment

Many towns have a theater showing drama, dance and other live performances. Some theaters are in beautiful colonial buildings which alone make the price of a ticket worthwhile. Remember that performances are usually in Spanish.

Information

- Cities have **listings magazines** or **leaflets** distributed in hotels, restaurants and shops detailing the forthcoming events. For information on Mexico City try www.codigo06140.com and www.tiempolibre.com.mx.
- Many mid-range and luxury hotels offer **internet access**, either through their own computers for guests or via wireless broadband for laptops. Some cafés in popular tourist areas also offer wireless broadband.

Movies

- **Movies** are very popular in Mexico and the country has produced several actors and directors who have gone on to have great success in Hollywood (► 12–13). Most towns and all cities have at least one cinema screen and films made in **English** have **Spanish subtitles**.
- As well as American films, there is also high demand for **art-house** and **independent movies** from Mexico and elsewhere.
- One of the largest movie chains is **Cinemex** (tickets can be bought online, www.cinemex.com.mx).

Music

- Mexican music isn't limited to the *mariachi* **bands** that stroll the plazas and restaurants of the tourist areas, although these are by far the most visible Mexican musicians.
- There is a rich tradition of Mexican **folk music** (called *son*), and dance and shows can be seen in a variety of places. In the east, around Veracruz, folk music has an Afro-Caribbean sound, while in the ranching areas of the north it is closer to a form of **country and western** music.
- In the major cities, such as Mexico City, Monterrey and Cancún, venues host **rock and pop bands** and **nightclubs** book international DJs.

Festivals

Mexicans need little excuse for a fiesta and most villages, towns and cities celebrate a variety of festivals – mostly religious in inspiration – throughout the year. The largest festivals may cause hotels in the area to be booked far in advance so make reservations early if you aim to attend. Nationally, the year's biggest events are Semana Santa (Holy Week), which culminates on Easter Sunday, and Día de los Muertos (Day of the Dead) in early November. Important festivals and events include:

- **Carnaval** (late Feb): A Latin American fiesta before Lent, celebrated especially hard in Veracruz.
- **Semana Santa** (Palm Sunday to Easter Sunday): Holy Week sees parades and events in every town. Traffic tends to be atrocious.
- **Día de la Independencia** (Sep 16): Independence Day marks Mexico's fight for independence, which began on September 16 1810.
- **Día de los Muertos** (Nov 1 and 2): the Day of the Dead is not as macabre as it sounds; it's about celebrating life and acknowledging the dead.
- **Día de Navidad** (Dec 25): in this predominantly Catholic nation, Christmas Day is ushered in with a midnight Mass.

Mexico City

Getting Your Bearings

Mexico City is one of the world's most densely populated cities; its population increased from 400,000 to 24 million during the 20th century and today it sprawls as far as the eye can see across what was once a lake bed. Latin America's oldest capital city was founded by the Aztecs almost seven centuries ago where, according to legend, an eagle was witnessed eating a snake while perching on cactus; this was the signal mystics were waiting for and the building of the pyramids of Tenochtitlán swiftly began.

After conquering Mexico City's original incarnation, the heart of the Aztec empire Tenochtitlán, the Spaniards rebuilt the city as New Spain. The colonial design can still be seen in the wide avenues and boulevards of the historic heart of the city (the Centro Histórico), around the vast Zócalo. Due to the capital's rapid and chaotic expansion, there is little organization to the layout.

The historic center, where the Templo Mayor is located, is connected to the Bosque de Chapultepec, an expansive park containing the unmissable Museo Nacional de Antrolopogía, by the Paseo de la Reforma.

Page 33: Busy market outside the Catedral Metropolitana

Right: The ubiquitous VW

★ Don't Miss

At Your Leisure

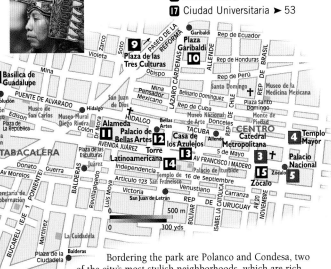

Bordering the park are Polanco and Condesa, two of the city's most stylish neighborhoods, which are rich hunting grounds for bars, restaurants and good hotels. Between Condesa and the Centro Histórico, the Zona Rosa and Roma are two slightly more commercial neighborhoods.

Coyoacán and San Angel, south of the city center, should also be included on any itinerary – they are attractive, genteel quarters where colonial mansions and cobbled streets have been diligently preserved. Further south still, Xochimilco is noted for its waterways and boat trips; it's a popular destination for weekending office workers.

With such a large city to explore, it is best to focus on one or two neighborhoods at a time, and you'll need to take a taxi or use the Métro since Mexico City is not a place in which to get lost.

Top: *Conchero* dancer
Left: Monumento a Los Niños Héroes

One of the world's largest and most chaotic cities still has small pockets of calm in the southern suburbs of Coyoacán and San Angel. But first venture into the giant Plaza de la Constitución, the Zócalo, at the heart of Mexican culture, with ancient Aztec sites, museums and a cathedral.

Mexico City in Three Days

Day One

Morning

Take a taxi or the Métro to the Centro Histórico. The central **15 Zócalo** (➤ 52), the Plaza de la Constitución, is dominated by the twin towers of the **3 Catedral Metropolitana** (➤ 43), and flanking its eastern side is the **5 Palacio Nacional** (below; ➤ 46). The Zócalo, the largest in the country, is the venue for many state occasions, and wide avenues radiate outwards: the 5 de Mayo leads to the **13 Casa de los Azulejos** (➤ 52)and the eye-

catching **12 Palacio de Bellas Artes** (➤ 51), while following Seminario northeast of the Zócalo will lead you to the **4 Templo Mayor** (➤ 44–45), once the heart of the Aztec empire. For lunch, stop at Los Girasoles on Tacuba (➤ 56).

Afternoon

Make your way west toward the Alameda Central via Avenida Hidalgo. The **11 Alameda** (➤ 51) is a peaceful park flushed with ornamentation – you can spend some time people-watching here, or enter the **12 Palacio de Bellas Artes** (➤ 51) for a glimpse of its art deco interior.

Evening

Head down the **7 Paseo de la Reforma** (➤ 50), left at the corner of the Alameda, to the bars and restaurants of Polanco and Condesa (➤ 58). You may wish to take a taxi if it is dark.

Day Two

Morning

Make your way to the central Plaza Hidalgo in **6 Coyoacán** (➤ 47–48). From here you can walk to the **Museo de Frida Kahlo** and **Leon Trotsky's house**, also a museum (portrait of Trotsky left). On the way don't forget to try the sidewalk street cafés of Coyoacán and look around the excellent *mercado* (market). On weekends, the central plaza also becomes a popular, open-air market place. There is no shortage of places to stop for a bite to eat, with the *chile rellenos* stands offering particularly good sweets in Coyoacán, but you might like to sit down at Los Danzantes (➤ 56), overlooking a leafy plaza.

Afternoon

In the afternoon, take a taxi to **6 San Angel** (➤ 48–49), where you will find the **Museo Estudio Diego Rivera y Frida Kahlo**, a bold modernist house transformed into a museum. The **Museo de Arte Carrillo-Gil** is another inspiring modern art gallery.

Evening

End the day on a high note at the San Angel Inn (➤ 57), a highly regarded restaurant in a beautiful colonial building.

Day Three

Morning

This is the day for shopping and snacking in two of Mexico City's most stylish districts – Polanco and Condesa. If you're staying in either of these neighborhoods you can walk from one to the other via the **1 Bosque de Chapultepec** (➤ 38–39), but don't underestimate the time it will take. Both areas are packed with delightful boutique shops, designer hotels, cosy cafés serving mid-morning coffees to Mexico City's hip young things, and smart restaurants.

Afternoon

After lunch visit the **2 Museo Nacional de Antropología** (statue outside, right; ➤ 40–41) in the northern part of the Bosque de Chapultepec. Alternatively, explore the streets and shops of Polanco and Condesa and give the museum the attention it deserves on another day.

Evening

Eat at Bistro Mosaico (➤ 55), a charming French restaurant in Condesa.

MUSEO NACIONAL DE ANTROPOLOGIA

⬛ Bosque de Chapultepec

Plant a handful of world-class museums in one of the largest city parks in the world, add water, entertainment and sunshine and what do you get? The amazing Bosque de Chapultepec. One of the largest city parks in the world, the Bosque de Chapultepec (forest of Chapultepec, named for the grasshoppers that populated the area) performs the vital function of providing fresh air and green space for the capital's residents. More than that, however, it is also home to one of the finest museums in the world, the Museo Nacional de Antropología (▶ 40–42) and a host of other attractions.

Chapultepec's boundaries extend south and west from the Paseo de la Reforma to Avenida Constituyentes. The bordering neighborhoods are Polanco and Condesa, and you can walk to the park from them, though most people enter the park via the main entrance, marked by the Monumento a los Niños Héroes (monument to Mexico's child-heroes), adjacent to the Chapultepec Métro station. Once inside, you'll find broad boulevards filled with joggers, sightseers, stallholders and snack vendors. There are signposts on the main

thoroughfares to help you find your way around.

One of the highest viewpoints is the Castillo (Castle) de Chapultepec, to the south of the main entrance. The park has its origins in the 16th century and the castle was originally an Aztec fort. Today it is the **Museo**

Left: The Castillo de Chapultepec
Below: A family day out in the park

The gates of the Castillo de Chapultepec

Nacional de Historia, covering Mexican history from the arrival of the Spanish to the Mexican revolution. To the north of the castle is the Lago Chapultepec where rowing boats can be hired. Children will also enjoy La Feria de Chapultepec, a funfair near the center of the park. A children's museum, **El Papalote**, features interactive exhibitions on science, art, communication and other subjects. It also has an IMAX cinema screen.

Adults may prefer the **Museo de Arte Moderno**, which exhibits a wide range of contemporary work by Mexican artists including Frida Kahlo, Diego Rivera, José Clemente Orozco and David Alfaro Siqueiros, and also has sculpture in the gardens. Top marks go to the **Museo Rufino Tamayo**, on the north side of the Paseo de la Reforma, for the award-winning, blocky, modernist building. Inside, Rufino Tamayo's personal collection includes paintings, sculpture and some of the biggest names in modern art. A short walk along the road is the **Museo Nacional de Antropología** (➤ 40–42).

Right: The popular Feria (funfair) in the Bosque de Chapultepec

(➤ 40–42).

TAKING A BREAK

Many of the museums in the Bosque de Chapultepec have cafés or restaurants. **El Papalote** has a food court.

Bosque de Chapultepec
🚇 210 A1 🅜 Auditorio, Chapultepec, Constituyentes

Museo Nacional de Historia
☎ 55 5241 3100; www.mnh.inah.gob.mx
🕐 Tue–Sun 9–4:30 💷 Inexpensive

Museo de Arte Moderno
☎ 55 5211 8331; www.conaculta.gob.mx/mam
🕐 Tue–Sun 10–6 💷 Inexpensive

El Papalote, Museo del Niño
☎ 55 5237 1781; www.papalote.org.mx
🕐 Mon–Wed, Fri 9–1, 2–6, Thu 9am–11pm, Sat–Sun 10–2, 3–7 💷 Moderate

Museo Rufino Tamayo
☎ 55 5286 6519; www.museotamayo.org
🕐 Tue–Sun 10–6 💷 Inexpensive

BOSQUE DE CHAPULTEPEC: INSIDE INFO

Top tips Rent a **rowing boat** on the large lake south of the Paseo de Reforma and the Museo Nacional de Antropología. Mind the geese!
• The **Auditorio Nacional** (➤ 58), on the north edge of the park, has a free art gallery and exhibition of musical memorabilia.

Hidden gem There is an excellent view over the **Monumento a los Niños Héroes** down the Paseo de Reforma and into the Zona Rosa from the Castillo de Chapultepec.

2 Museo National de Antropología

Few countries have such an enthralling history as Mexico and even fewer can present it as beautifully as the National Museum of Anthropology in the Bosque de Chapultepec. Aztecs, Olmecs, Toltecs: they're all represented in this incomparable museum by an extraordinary collection of objects organized by period and geography and categorized according to purpose (music, society, religion and sacrifice).

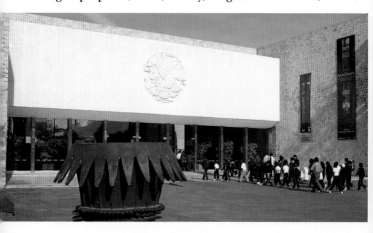

For some, seeing Pedro Ramírez Vázquez's angular building – a masterpiece of 1960s architecture – is reward enough for the price of admission, with what appears to be a showerhead 15m (50 feet) wide underneath the concrete canopy in the courtyard. From any vantage point, the building's lines collide and intersect: an example of bold, modernist architecture done well.

The entrance to the National Museum of Anthropology

When you've finished admiring the exterior, start your immersion into ancient Mexico at any point around the horse-shoe-shaped building, which is divided into 12 clearly labeled galleries. The first seven from the left are organized chronologically, the final five cover Mexico from a geographical perspective. The lower floors exhibit archaeological finds and relics, while the upper level illustrates the lifestyles and customs of the various cultures today, including displays on traditional costumes, dances, ceremonies and food preparation. If you have the time, start at the beginning, although the content is so absorbing that you could well lose track of time.

Exhibits in the museum

Below: Detail of a golden mask

Bottom: Carving from a Zapotec temple from the state of Oaxaca

The first three galleries to the right of the entrance intro-
duce the Preclassic, Teotihuacán and Toltec periods. Given the
fact that Mexico's Preclassic era began in 2300 BC, the level of
artistry in the figurines unearthed is incredible. By the time
Teotihuacán (➤ 114–115) had been built, Mexican civilization was racing along and producing complex and beautiful
items such as funeral masks. The Toltecs, whose civilization is
thought to have peaked from AD 1000–1200, began to display
more of a martial interest and the exhibits in this gallery
include towering stone statues of warriors, known as Atlantes.
Next, you discover the México peoples, the southern state of
Oaxaca and the Gulf of Mexico. The highlight of the museum,
and the gallery to focus on if your time is limited, is that of
the Aztecs, in the México gallery. The wealth of exhibits in
here, from the stone jaguar with a scoop out of its back in
which to place human hearts to the 24-ton Sun Stone, which
encapsulates the Aztec's understanding of their world, is
breathtaking.

Of a completely different scale, but just as impressive, is
the glossy black stone vase crafted by an Aztec artist. Small,
shiny and made from obsidian (a hard, glass-like volcanic
rock), it features the image of a monkey. In the next gallery,
that of the Maya, there are some outdoor reproductions of
Mayan buildings, also visible from the Paseo de la Reforma.
Another highlight of the Maya gallery is the sunken replica of
King Pakal's tomb, discovered at Palenque (➤ 140–141) – you
can go around the tomb on a walkway with each part of the
tomb clearly explained. A final treat awaits visitors outside
the front terrace where, on a pole 20m (65 feet) high, the
Voladares de Papantla perform their dizzying routine,
swinging upside-down from ropes attached to the top.

Mayan bas-
relief from
Yaxchilán

TAKING A BREAK

The canteen-style **restaurant** is on the first floor, although
the most popular spot for a break is around the water feature
in the main courtyard: you can bring your own snacks.

➕ 210 A2
✉ Paseo de la Reforma and Calzada Gandhi, Bosque de Chapultepec
☎ 55 5553 6381; www.mna.inah.gob.mx 🕒 Tue–Sun 9–7 💷 Moderate
🚇 Auditorio, Chapultepec

MUSEO NATIONAL DEL ANTROPOLOGÍA: INSIDE INFO

Top tips All bags have to be **checked into the cloakroom**, so make sure you
remove all valuables. Cameras can be used in the museum with a special pass.
• **English-language labeling** in the museum is generally good, with English
guides, audioguides and guidebooks available (you should book an English-
speaking guide in advance if required).

Hidden gem Unraveling the symbolism of the 6m (12-foot) diameter **Sun
Stone** is an absorbing task. The disc has the sun god Tonatiuh at its center,
surrounded by four squares to represent the four lost worlds the Aztecs believed
pre-dated their civilization. The next ring of 20 image-filled squares refers to
the 20 days of the Aztec month.

③ Catedral Metropolitana

The venerable Catedral Metropolitana in the Zócalo is the focal point for the largest Catholic diocese in the world. Its vast proportions can't fail to inspire awe.

Mexico City is a city of superlatives, and its cathedral is no exception. It's the biggest and oldest church in Latin America, sprawling across the northern side of the Zócalo.

Construction began in 1525 and wasn't completed until 1813, so what you will see is an elaborate hybrid of architectural styles, featuring baroque, classical, neo-classical and a late form of baroque architecture known as Churriguersque – for an example of this style, see the facade of the 18th-century Sagrario chapel on the west side of the cathedral. There are two towers, four domes, five altars and a further fifteen chapels.

You can go inside to explore the magnificent interior where no expense has been spared on gold leaf and stone masonry. Tours also climb the bell tower to see the 13-ton Santa Maria de Guadalupe bell. However, the bell is contributing to a problem affecting the cathedral: its immense weight has caused the building to subside in the soft soil, although measures to halt this seem to be working.

The main entrance, facing the Zócalo and flanked by the cathedral's bell towers, leads to the Metropolitana's highlight, the choir, which contains some beautifully carved stalls and two organs.

TAKING A BREAK

The street behind the cathedral, Tacuba, has several restaurants, including a branch of **Los Girasoles** (▶ 56), serving traditional Mexican dishes. As you walk toward the Alameda Central on Avenida 5 de Mayo you will also pass cafés and restaurants, including the venerable **La Nueva Opera Bar** at No. 10.

➕ 210 E2
✉ Plaza de la Constitución
☎ 55 5510 0440
🕐 Daily 7–7
Ⓜ Zócalo

The Catedral Metropolitana dominates the vast Zócalo

4 Templo Mayor

Blood, sweat and tiers: 14th-century Tenochtitlán, the fore-
runner to Mexico City, revolved around the pyramid at this
site. It was central to the Aztec universe and the temple's
intriguing ruins are being carefully preserved today, aided
by a small but enthralling on-site museum.

Templo Mayor was the temple at the heart of the Aztec
Empire and the ceremonial centerpiece of the Aztec capital,
Tenochtitlán. It lay undisturbed for 600 years until unearthed
in 1978, but archaeologists are carefully excavating the site,
to the northeast of the Zócalo. Most of the ruins are below
ground, but the pyramid at the core of the site would have
towered above the modern buildings surrounding the site.

Deep inside the pyramid was a *chacmool* (➤ 161) and a
sacrificial stone: human sacrifice was essential to the Aztecs'
belief system and few places saw as many sacrifices as Templo
Mayor. Experts believe that during the dedication of the
temple, some time after 1325, around 20,000 people were
sacrificed here. Business as usual, for the Aztecs, meant sacri-
ficing up to 10,000 people at a time in the Templo Mayor,
many of them captured enemy soldiers.

Macabre mementos of this obsession with death include a
wall of skulls, re-created in the **Museo del Templo Mayor**,
which adjoins the Templo Mayor site and should be entered
via the main plaza, near the cathedral. This bloodthirstiness
had a point: the Aztecs believed it would appease two of their

**View across
the partially
excavated ruins
of the Aztec
Templo Mayor**

most important gods, Huitzilopochtli, the god of war, and Tlaloc, the god of rain and water.

Evidence of the pyramid's sacred role can be seen in the stone snake heads at the base of the main staircase. Temples dedicated to the two gods would have crowned the pyramid.

Above: The tzompantli (wall of skulls)

Below: Life-size eagle warrior in the museum

Museo del Templo Mayor

The first room in the onsite museum explains how the site is being excavated, while subsequent rooms detail many of the finds. The star attraction is the 8-ton stone disc, exhibited in the museum's vestibule, depicting the dismembered body of the Aztec goddess Coyolxauhqui, who was killed by her brother, Huitzilopochtli. Coyolxauhqui is always shown in this manner at temples dedicated to Huitzilopochtli.

The wall of skulls found at Templo Mayor, a common feature of Aztec sacrificial sites and known as a *tzompantli*, is replicated in the vestibule. Room 8 of the museum describes the arrival of the Spanish conquistadors; members of Hernán Cortés's expedition recorded that the entire complex was decorated with frescoes illustrating great battles, while the pyramid itself was finished in white stucco. However, once the Spanish arrived, it was the beginning of the end for the Aztecs as the city was sacked.

TAKING A BREAK

The **Centro Cultural de Espana**, opposite the Templo Mayor on Republica Guatemala (tel: 55 5521 1925 ext. 118; www.ccemx.org) has a rooftop terrace where you can enjoy freshly cooked Mexican and Spanish meals, along with splendid views of the Catedral Metropolitana (►43).

🕂 210 E2 (off map)
Museo del Templo Mayor
✉ Seminario 8 ☎ 55 5542 4784
🕐 Tue–Sun 9–5
💲 Inexpensive 🚇 Zócalo

TEMPLO MAYOR: INSIDE INFO

Top tip Entry to the eight-room **Museo del Templo Mayor** is included in the admission price and it is worthwhile since only the foundations of the Templo Mayor are visible at the excavation site itself.

5 Palacio National

A symbol of colonial dominance, the Palacio Nacional is notable not only for its size, but also for the fascinating murals created by Diego Rivera, depicting the progress of Mexican civilization.

Once the Spanish had swept away the Aztec city of Tenochtitlán, they set about building their own state buildings. In a demonstration of supremacy, the Palacio Nacional was built on the site of Emperor Moctezuma's palace by Hernán Cortés. Additional layers were added to the palace by subsequent rulers, the most recent modifications being the third tier of arches around the main courtyard, added by President Calles in the 1920s.

Flanking the eastern side of the Zócalo (▶ 52), the Palacio Nacional is today the workplace of the Mexican President and the Treasury. However, parts of it are open to the public and include some spectacular murals by Diego Rivera, commissioned after the Mexican Revolution (1910–20) in the hope of inspiring a sense of national cohesion. Enter the palace through the central door, over which hangs the Liberty Bell rung by Padre Miguel Hidalgo in 1810 at the start of the Mexican War of Independence.

Rivera's murals (1929–35), surround the staircase in the main courtyard. The main mural is vast and depicts nothing less than the history of Mexico, from the arrival of Quetzalcóatl (an Aztec god) and an idealized vision of pre-

Hispanic tribal Tenochtitlán on the right to the wars for freedom and independence on the left side. Rivera's left-leaning politics are hinted at in his treatment of workers, industrialization, revolution and war. Historical figures, including Cortés(▶ 18–19), Hidalgo and Zapata, are recognizable. The final fresco, on the left, is called *El Mundo de Hoy y de Manana* (*The World Today and Tomorrow*) and looks into post-Revolution Mexico's future as a free and industrious country.

Spectacular Diego Rivera mural depicting Mexican history

TAKING A BREAK

Make your way to Avenida Tacuba, on the north side of the cathedral, where there are several cafés and restaurants, or try the **Centro Cultural de Espana** (▶ 45).

➕ 210 E2 ✉ Plaza de la Constitución ☎ 55 9158 1259 🕐 Mon–Sat 9–6, Sun 9–2 💷 Free
🚇 Zócalo ❓ ID required for entry

⑥ Coyoacán and San Angel

Coyoacán, a genteel, pretty suburb south of the city center, and its neighbour San Angel, are closely associated with Frida Kahlo and Diego Rivera. It's hard to believe you're still in one of the world's largest cities as you walk their streets.

Above: Outside the Palacio de Cortés

Below: Casa de León Trotsky

Coyoacán

Escape the hectic city center in this charming neighborhood of paved, tree-lined roads and colorful colonial mansions. Its roots are in the Toltec period of the 10th century and Hernán Cortés based himself here when fighting for the city of Tenochtitlán in the 16th century. Now the area is home to many of Mexico City's wealthy elite and has had many notable residents occupying its private villas, including Leon Trotsky (who was murdered in his house here), previous presidents of Mexico and artists such as Frida Kahlo and Diego Rivera. Trotsky and Kahlo's homes are now museums.

Start your exploration of Coyoacán at the far end of Avenida Francisco Sosa, thought to be the first paved road laid in Spanish America. After passing the street's 16th- and 17th-century mansions (and a funky little bookshop and café at No 287), you'll reach the Jardin del Centenario and the Plaza Hidalgo. Together they form the central plaza in Coyoacán, which buzzes with activity, including musicians and performers, at weekends. Cross the Jardin del Centenario, then cross the road and follow the plaza round to the right past the 16th-century Iglesia de San Juan Bautista on your right. There are lots of stalls to browse here at the weekend

market, but to reach the Jardín Frida Kahlo take Calle Higuera (just before a large American delicatessen) and follow it past several tempting cafés to the peaceful Plaza de la Conchita.

The Jardín Frida Kahlo, with its statue of the artist, is at the southeast corner of the plaza. Her house, where she was born in 1907 and died in 1954, is in the residential streets north of the Plaza Hidalgo. A highly regarded food market is on Calle Allende, before you reach **Museo Frida Kahlo** at the junction with Londres. The museum includes examples of her work, including unfinished sketches, in addition to personal items such as her wheelchair and folk costumes. One of Kahlo's circle of friends in Coyoacán was the Marxist politician Leon Trotsky, who lived two blocks north on Viena. Now surrounded by modern apartments, Trotsky's house, **Casa de León Trotsky**, is a carefully curated museum of his life and work. He survived one assassination attempt here (you can see the bullet holes) but was killed in his study with an ice axe by a Stalinist agent in 1940. His grave is in the walled garden. The museum's entrance is on the far side of the building, on the main road.

Coyoacán's other delights include the Museo Nacional de Culturas Populares, just east of Plaza Hidalgo. It hosts some quirky and interesting exhibitions on popular Mexican culture. But the best way to appreciate Coyoacán and San Angel is to stroll the cobbled streets and take it all in at your own pace.

🗺 206 C4

Museo Frida Kahlo
✉ Londres 247 ☎ 55 5554 5999
🕐 Tue–Sun 10–6 💷 Inexpensive 🚇 Viveros

Casa de León Trotsky
✉ Rio Churubusco 410 ☎ 55 5554 0687
🕐 Tue–Sun 10–5 💷 Inexpensive 🚇 Viveros

TAKING A BREAK

There are numerous cafés and restaurants in this student-filled neighborhood, with Coyoacán's central Plaza Hidalgo being the best place to take time out to have a coffee. Or follow Higuera or Allende to find other chic options.

San Angel

San Angel, a smaller but similarly charming neighborhood to the west of Coyoacán, is centered around the Plaza de San Jacinto, which hosts a craft market on Sundays. A 16th-century church, the Iglesia de San Jacinto, is just to the east of the square. Continue east for the **Museo Colonial del Carmen** on Avenida Revolución. Now a museum of folk art and furniture, the domed 17th-century building was once a monastery. A much more contemporary building is the **Museo Estudio Diego Rivera y Frida Kahlo**, in the opposite direction. This angular modernist masterpiece was designed by

Top: Frida Kahlo's former home contains memorabilia of one of Mexico's greatest artists

Juan O'Gorman as a pair of houses for Diego Rivera and Frida Kahlo, but it now houses a collection of Rivera's personal items. The **Museo de Arte Carrillo-Gil**, to the north of Plaza de San Jacinto, contains a private collection of murals by the likes of Rivera, Orozco and Siqueiros, as well as work European and American modern artists; it's one of the most influential modern art galleries in the city.

Left: Fountain in the shape of a cross outside San Jacinto Church
Below: The Museo Estudio Diego Rivera y Frida Kahlo

➕ 206 C4

Museo Colonial del Carmen
✉ Avenida Revolución 4 ☎ 55 5516 1504
🕐 Tue–Sun 10–4:45 💷 Inexpensive

Museo Estudio Diego Rivera y Frida Kahlo
✉ Calle Diego Rivera (corner of Avenida Altavista) ☎ 55 5616 0996
🕐 Tue–Sun 10–6 💷 Inexpensive

Museo de Arte Carrillo-Gil
✉ Avenida Revolución 1608
☎ 55 5550 1254; www.macg.inba.gob.mx
🕐 Tue–Sun 10–6 💷 Inexpensive

COYOACÁN: INSIDE INFO

Top tip Take a **taxi to Coyoacán** if you don't fancy walking too far – the Métro stop is at the edge of the neighborhood. Pre-arrange a pickup time and place for returning to your hotel.

One to miss Viveros de Coyoacán is a plant nursery and park between the Métro stops of Viveros and Coyoacán. It's a pleasant respite from the urban jungle but it doesn't have the safest reputation and is best not visited after dark or while carrying valuables.

At Your Leisure

7 Paseo de la Reforma

The Paseo de la Reforma is the grand, arterial avenue linking the Centro Histórico with the Bosque de Chapultepec (► 38–39). It's a pleasant stretch of road to walk, almost 5km (3 miles) long, punctuated by a series of monuments commemorating Mexico's history.

From north to south, the first monument is a statue of Christopher Columbus at Glorieta Colón, followed by a statue of the last Aztec ruler, Cuauhtémoc, at Avenida Insurgentes. Finally, a marble column, marooned on a busy roundabout at Tiber and Florencia, supports a winged figure known as "El Angel," representing independence (from Spanish colonialism).

🚇 210 A1–E3 🚇 Hidalgo, Auditoria

8 Basílica de Guadalupe

Ever since an Indian named Juan Diego claimed to have had a vision of the Virgin Mary on this site in 1531, this has been the holiest shrine in Mexico. Diego is said to have received a cloak from the Virgin Mary, imprinted with her image, and in 2002 he was made the first Latin American saint by the Catholic Church.

Thousands of devout pilgrims make the journey to the Antigua Basílica every year on December 12. A new basilica was built in 1976 to relieve the pressure on the 16th-century original – one of the finest examples of baroque architecture in Mexico. You can see Diego's cloak encased in an altar in the new building from a moving walkway (shorts may not be worn inside the building).

The Antigua Basílica is at the foot of Cerro de Tepeyac and you can climb this hill for good views of northern Mexico City. The Basílica de Guadalupe is two blocks north of the Métro station.

🚇 210 C3 (off map) ✉ Plaza de las Americas ☎ 55 5577 6022 🕐 Daily 6–8 🚇 La Villa Basílica

9 Plaza de las Tres Culturas

North of the Centro Histórico, the Plaza de las Tres Culturas is where the strands of Mexico City's heritage interweave: Aztec, colonial and contemporary. This square, the second oldest in the city (after the Zócalo), is where, on August 13, 1521, Hernan Cortés defeated Cuauhtémoc, the last Aztec emperor, at the Aztec

Plaza de las Tres Culturas (Square of Three Cultures)

settlement of Tlatelolco. As the inscription on a plaque in the plaza reads, "it was neither a triumph nor a defeat, but the painful birth of the *mestizo* race that is Mexico today."

Arguably, this is where modern Mexico was born, but it also refers back to the pre-Hispanic Aztec empire, with the remains of Tlatelolco's Aztec pyramid and other ceremonial buildings visible from a walkway. Tlatelolco was the largest market place in Aztec Mexico and the Spanish built the Templo de Santiago here using stones from the Aztec buildings. The plaza also has a more somber connection to modern Mexico: shortly before the 1968 Olympics, between 300 and 400 demonstrating students were massacred here by police. A memorial outside the church marks the event.

➕ 210 E3 (off map)
✉ Eje Central Lázaro Cárdenas and corner of Flores Magón ☎ 55 5583 0295 ⏰ Daily 8–6
Ⓜ Tlatelolco

🔟 Plaza Garibaldi

If you are a *mariachi* fan, or simply want to see the musicians clad in their tight black silver embroidered trousers, then this is the place for you. Six blocks north of the Alameda, Plaza Garibaldi is *mariachi* mecca, with prowling bands looking for victims to serenade. Once you have paid for your musical entertainment, try some of the taco-and-tequila joints around the square. It is advisable to take a taxi or the Métro to Plaza Garibaldi, which has a less than savory reputation particularly in the evening, and to keep an eye on your possessions in the crowds.

➕ 210 E3 Ⓜ Garibaldi

🈁 Alameda

The Alameda, a neat and verdant city park with heroic statues, fountains

Classical sculpture in the Palacio de Bellas Artes

and a bandstand, is a pleasant place where families and couples promenade at weekends. There are plenty of benches and you can buy snacks and drinks from vendors in the park. But it hasn't always been such a happy place: during the colonial period it was where the Spanish Inquisition staged executions. Its transformation to sedate civic space took place in the 18th and 19th centuries when the statues and lighting were added.

Diego Rivera's famous 1947 mural of the *Sueno de una Tarde Dominical en la Alameda* Central (*Dream of a Sunday Afternoon in the Alameda*) was moved into the **Museo Mural Diego Rivera** on Balderas and Colón to the west of the Alameda after its original venue, the Hotel Prado, was damaged in the 1985 earthquake.

➕ 210 D3
Museo Mural Diego Rivera
✉ Balderas and Colón
☎ 55 5512 0754
⏰ Tue–Sun 10–6
💵 Inexpensive
Ⓜ Bellas Artes, Hidalgo

🈁 Palacio de Bellas Artes

This theater and museum is a stunning building on the east side of the Alameda. The exterior was designed in 1905 by the Italian architect Adamo Boari in his preferred neo-classical and art nouveau style. He was interrupted in his work by the Mexican Revolution and it wasn't until the 1930s that the interior was completed by architect Federico Mariscal – in the art deco style.

The outstanding feature of the Bellas Artes theater, a stained-glass curtain by Tiffany, can only be seen by attending a performance, but you are free to roam around the rest of the building. Murals by Rufino Tamayo, José Clemente Orozco,

David Alfaro Siqueiros and Diego Rivera can be found on the second and third floors. On the fourth floor is the Museo Nacional de Arquitectura, which describes the history of the palace.

➕ 210 D3 ✉ Eje Central Lázaro Cárdenas and Avenida Juárez ☎ 55 5512 3633 🕐 Tue–Sun 10–6 💲 Inexpensive 🚇 Bellas Artes

The Mudejar-style Casa de los Azulejos

13 Casa de los Azulejos

The Casa's name translates as House of Tiles, which gives away the unique selling point of this 16th-century building: it is covered in an elaborate pattern of blue and white tiles. The tiles were made in 1653 in a factory managed by Dominican friars, and have been carefully maintained ever since. A fine example of baroque architecture, the house is now occupied by a restaurant chain, Sanborns.

➕ 210 E2 ✉ Francisco Madero 4 ☎ 55 5518 9820 🕐 Daily 7 am–1 am 🚇 Bellas Artes

14 Torre Latinoamericana

A welcome landmark to many visitors, the Latin American Tower is a 182m (600-foot) skyscraper in the south-east corner of the Alameda. There are observation points and cafés on the 42nd, 43rd and 44th floors, and a museum on the 37th floor explains how the tower survives the not uncommon earthquakes in this part of Mexico.

➕ 210 E2
✉ Eje Central Lázaro Cárdenas and Francisco Madero ☎ 55 5518 7423
🕐 Daily 9am–10pm 💲 Inexpensive
🚇 Bellas Artes

15 Zócalo

As city center squares go, Mexico City's Plaza de la Constitucíon (known as the Zócalo) dwarfs most of its global rivals, and the national flag rippling in the middle of the plaza is equally vast. The Zócalo is at the heart of the Centro Histórico and around it are arrayed some of the city's grandest sights: the Palacio Nacional (► 46) on the east side, the Catedral Metropolitana (► 43) to the north and Templo Mayor (► 44–45) between them on the northeast corner.

The square is the setting for state functions throughout the year, such as Revolution Day in November, when it is filled with crowds and parades. Leading away from the Zócalo are major avenues lined with shops and offices. Its history dates from the Aztec period when the area to the north of the square was Tenochtitlán.

➕ 210 E2 🚇 Zócalo

16 Xochimilco

Xochimilco is an amazing network of canals and islands lying 28km (17 miles) southeast of the city center. It is a popular

The striking Torre Latinoamericana

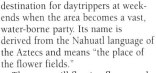

The University's central library, with its impressive Juan O'Gorman mosaic

destination for daytrippers at weekends when the area becomes a vast, water-borne party. Its name is derived from the Nahuatl language of the Aztecs and means "the place of the flower fields."

There are still floating flower and vegetable gardens, known as *chinampas*, past which visitors are punted in the painted, flat-bottomed boats called *trajineras*. When you arrive at Xochimilco you will be faced with touting from taxi drivers and boat owners. Government tour guides wear a badge. Xochimilco village itself is an enjoyable place to explore, with quaint churches and shops.

🚻 206 C3
🚇 Tasquena, then *tren ligero* (light train) to Xochimilco 🚤 Boat rental: expect to pay US$14 per hour

Brightly decorated boats cruise the canals of Xochimilco

🔟 Ciudad Universitaria

Architecture addicts should make an excursion to the Ciudad Universitaria, beyond the suburb of San Angel (➤ 48–49). This is the campus of Mexico City's university, built between 1950 and 1955, which means that it is blessed with some classic modernist buildings. Visitors can go into some of the campus buildings, such as Universum, the university's science museum.

🚻 210 B1 (off map) ✉ Coyoacán
🚇 Universidad

Where to... Stay

Prices

Expect to pay for a double room per night:
$ under US$50 $$ US$50–150 $$$ over US$150

Camino Real $$$

The Camino Real is one of the most stylish places to rest your head. Designed by Mexican maestro Ricardo Legorreta, the elegant hotel is far from the dour minimalism usually expected of hotels at this level: bright pink and canary yellow are the themed colors and murals and sculptures abound. The bedrooms are luxurious, with marble bathrooms and high-tech extras. Tennis courts, a gym, two pools and several bars are among the facilities.

⊞ 210 A2 (off map) ⊠ Mariano Escobedo 700, Polanco ☎ 55 5263 8888; www.caminoreal.com/mexico Ⓜ Chapultepec, Polanco

Four Seasons $$$

Elegant and richly decorated, the Four Seasons is one of the most desirable residences in the city. Despite the well-equipped business center and season ticket for the Bellavista Golf Club, it is also geared for tourists, with free tours of the city led by an art historian departing on weekend mornings. Decor in the bedrooms is also several levels above the usual chain hotel, with luxurious fabrics and warm colors. Many of the rooms overlook the inner courtyard. Entertainment includes a tequila bar, spa and pool. Children are also welcomed with complimentary milk and cookies; children under 18 can share their parents' room at no extra charge.

⊞ 210 B1 ⊠ Paseo de la Reforma 500, Colonia Juárez ☎ 55 5230 1818; www.fourseasons.com/mexico Ⓜ Sevilla

Habita $$$

This hip hot spot in bourgeois Polanco is notable for its contemporary design and the social scene that whirls around the roof-top bar and ground-floor restaurant, Aura. It is the leading example of a design hotel in Mexico City and treads the thin line between style and substance. Rooms are large and luxurious but glass frontage means sound can travel. Extras include a spa, a roof-top pool and the projection of films (silent) onto the wall of a neighboring building at night. Habita is better suited to visiting DJs and actors than families.

⊞ 210 A2 (off map) ⊠ Avenida Presidente Masaryk 201, Polanco ☎ 55 5282 3100; www.hotelhabita.com Ⓜ Polanco

La Casona $$$

On a wide, residential street the pink façade of La Casona hides a chic, if slightly rickety, hotel with 29 rooms. Each bedroom is individually decorated with fine furniture, which adds to the hotel's charm. Despite the old-fashioned style, there are modern features such as televisions in the bedrooms and a business center. However, service in the underused restaurant could be sharper. The location is slightly out-of-the-way, on the border of Roma and Condesa – you'll need to take a taxi (expensive if booked through the hotel) to the nearest nightlife.

⊞ 210 B1 ⊠ Durango 280, Roma ☎ 55 5286 3001; www.hotel lacasona.com.mx Ⓜ Sevilla

Sheraton Centro Histórico $$$

Within walking distance of the Alameda and the Zócalo, the Sheraton Centro Histórico's location close to the junction of Juárez and the Paseo de la Reforma is its chief selling point. The high-rise hotel is a geared toward business travelers, but with 457 rooms to fill, special rates are worth looking for. Bedrooms are a cut above the bland business fare and the corner rooms have great views. Expect a wide range of international cuisines in the hotel's restaurants.

210 D2 ⊠ Avenida Juárez 70, Colonia Centro ☎ 55 5130 5300; www.starwoodhotels.com Ⓜ Hidalgo

Sheraton Maria Isabel $$$

This businesslike hotel is a vast (755 rooms) landmark in a prime location overlooking the Paseo de la Reforma and within walking distance of the Centro Histórico. Its lofty marble lobby sets the tone and the luxurious theme is continued into the tastefully decorated bedrooms, all with a desk and wireless internet. The beds are exceptionally comfortable and there is 24-hour room service. Facilities include a fitness center, an outdoor pool and two tennis courts.

210 B2 ⊠ Paseo de la Reforma 325, Colonia Cuauhtemoc ☎ 55 5242 5555; www.starwoodhotels.com Ⓜ Insurgentes

W Mexico City $$$

The W brand offers unparalleled personal attention and designer style, and the Mexico City hotel, the chain's first in Latin America, goes all-out to impress. From the elegant, Oriental-inspired lobby bar, with its carp pool under the floor, to the funky restaurant, Solea, the public spaces are exceptionally appealing. However, the wow-factor is reserved for the wrap-around windows of the bedrooms with spectacular views of Mexico City. Bedroom decor verges on the decadent, with vermilion red walls and crisp white bedlinen. Be warned: the bathrooms are not enclosed.

210 A2 (off map) ⊠ Campos Eliseos 252, Polanco ☎ 55 9138 1800; www.whotels.com Ⓜ Auditorio

Where to...
Eat and Drink

Prices
Expect to pay per person for a meal, excluding drinks:
$ under US$10 $$ US$10–20 $$$ over US$20

Agua Luna $$-$$$

The contemporary minimalism of Agua Luna is matched by the *alta cocina* Mexican cuisine. The airy restaurant, near the Chapultepec Park, specializes in seafood dishes such as shrimp with black bean sauce. Prices are high end due to the prime location.

210 A2 (off map) ⊠ Campos Eliseos 142, Polanco ☎ 55 5250 3550 Ⓛ Mon–Sat 8–12, Sun 8–6 Ⓜ Auditorio

Bistro Mosaico $$-$$$

Be transported to a bona fide Parisian bistro at this much-loved restaurant on the north side of Parque México where Michoacán meets Avenida Insurgentes. Wine-sipping patrons populate a large, high-ceilinged room decorated with posters of French scenes. The deli counter sells quiches, cakes, sandwiches on fresh-baked bread and takeaway specialties. There's a short menu of meat, fish and pasta dishes with starters such as pâté, salads and *ceviche*. It's a very busy restaurant but the welcome is warm from the white-shirted, black-tied staff.

210 A1 (off map) ⊠ Michoacán 10, Condesa ☎ 55 5584 2932 Ⓛ Daily 9am–11pm Ⓜ Juanacatlán

Café Toscana $

Overlooking a small park with tree-lined avenues and children playing, this pleasantly hip neighborhood coffee shop serves the closest you'll get to a European-style espresso in Mexico City. The coffee is by Illy and is expertly made.

🕂 210 A1 (off map) ⊠ Corner of Michoacán and Parque España, Condesa 🕾 No phone ⓘ Daily 8–7 🔘 Chilpancingo

Cicero $$

Refined Mexican cuisine is served in a theatrical hacienda-style setting, with antiques and a cosy wood-paneled bar. This is the place to indulge to the full – try the plantains stuffed with ground beef as a starter.

🕂 210 B1 ⊠ Londres 195, Zona Rosa 🕾 55 5512 6868 ⓘ Mon–Sat 1pm–1am 🔘 Insurgentes

La Buena Tierra $$

An all-organic menu of sandwiches, paninis, salads and main meals draws Condesa's health-conscious residents to this popular cornerside eatery. All the food is freshly prepared and delicious and there's an equally long list of fruit juices and smoothies in addition to coffee, beers and wine. Service is prompt and professional. This is a great spot for a quick snack while you explore this vibrant neighborhood; for an early start you can also grab breakfast here.

🕂 210 A1 (off map) ⊠ Atlixco 94, Condesa 🕾 55 5211 4242; www.comidomi.com/labuenatierra ⓘ Daily 8–8 🔘 Patriotismo

Los Danzantes $$$

Dine in style in beguiling Coyoacán. Los Danzantes, in prime people-watching position on the main square, offers traditional Mexican food and drink with a twist. You'll be greeted by a glass of mezcal from their own distillery before being ushered to your table in the vibrantly decorated dining room. The food is modern Mexican, with traditional ingredients (including grasshoppers) used in regional specialties, but you can play safe with the menu.

🕂 206 C4 ⊠ Plaza Jardin Centenario 12, Coyoacán 🕾 55 5658 6451; www.losdanzantes.com ⓘ Mon–Wed 1:30–11pm, Thu–Fri 1:30pm–midnight, Sat–Sun 1:30pm–1am 🔘 Viveros

ⓦⓦ Los Girasoles $$-$$$

The chefs at Girasoles have raided the larder of pre-Colombian and conquistador-era Mexico for recipes Although you'll find Maguey worms fried in butter, chilli and beer, it's not a gimmick: most of the menu is comprised of hearty mains such as peppers stuffed with ground beef, pork and fruit. Starters include the Cilantro 1517 soup, a recipe from the conquistadors. The chicken Xochitl broth is also recommended – add chili to taste – and you can finish with a sweet dessert. There's a branch of Los Girasoles in the heart of the historic centre and a bustling new restaurant in a plaza on President Masaryk in Polanco (tel:55 5282 3219).

🕂 210 E3 ⊠ Plaza Manuel Tolsá, Calle Tacuba 🕾 55 5510 0630; www.restaurantelosgirasoles.com ⓘ Sun–Mon 1–9pm, Tue–Sat 1pm–midnight 🔘 Bellas Artes

Moheli $

The southern neighborhood of Coyoacán doesn't suffer from a shortage of cafes and restaurants and this funky café/delicatessen is one of the best. It's often packed with a young, lively crowd refueling on coffee, bagels and baguettes.

🕂 206 C4 ⊠ Francisco Sosa 1, Coyoacán 🕾 55 5554 6221 ⓘ Sun–Wed 8–10:30, Thu–Sat 8–11 🔘 Miguel Angel de Quevedo

ⓦⓦ Rincón Argentino $$-$$$

Beef is a Latin American obsession and this Argentinian restaurant is one of the best places in the city to savor a rare steak seared on a wood-fired grill. The dark, wood-lined interior resembles a rustic South

American lodge, but the food and wine list are far from basic. Reservations are recommended.

🚹 210 A2 (off map) ☒ Presidente Mazaryk 177, Polanco ☎ 52 54 8775; www.rinconargentino.com.mx ⓔ Daily 12–3, 7–11 Ⓜ Polanco

🍷🍷🍷 San Angel Inn $$$

Indulge yourself at this landmark restaurant occupying a one-time Carmelite monastery in San Angel. Have a margarita in the bar before heading into the formal dining room (jackets and ties are requested). Dishes range from international classics, such as lobster bisque, to Mexican dishes such as Veracruz-style sea bass, a house specialty. Steaks come in a variety of styles, while vegetarians are well catered for. There's traditional Mexican music in the evenings.

🚹 206 C4 ☒ Diego Rivera 50 and Altavista ☎ 55 5616 2222; www.sanangelinn.com ⓔ Mon–Sat 1–1, Sun 1–10 Ⓜ Miguel Angel de Quevedo, then take a taxi

Where to...
Shop

FASHION AND DESIGN

In Condesa you can browse funky womenswear by Mexican designer **Carmen Rion** (Michoacán 30, tel: 52 64 6179, www.carmenrion.com, open daily 11–7 or 8). She also has imaginative jewelry designs, accessories, and men's shirts in pastel colors. Also in this neighborhood, and offering interior design at a good price with an unerring taste, is **Artefacto** (Calle Amatlán 94, tel: 55 5286 7729, www.artefacto. com.mx, open Mon–Fri 10–8, Sat 11–8, Sun 11–6). There are several branches of the store across Mexico City, stocking household accessories, glassware, soft furnishings and gifts. Fun, designer gifts, gadgets and home accessories are

sold in the small but funky **Groben Boutique** (Nuevo León 96, tel: 55 8596 4494, open Tue–Sun 11–8).

ARTS AND CRAFTS

FONART (Avenida Juárez 89, tel: 55 5521 0171, www.fonart.gob.mx, open Mon–Sun 10–7) is the best place to buy traditional Mexican crafts in the capital – the prices are high, but the FONART foundation helps preserve and promote the work of indigenous groups across Mexico. All sorts of the items, including silver, pottery and textiles, are for sale.

Shoppers descend on Coyoacán's central square, Plaza Hidalgo, on Sundays (open 10–6) to plunder the stalls in the **craft market** offering an assortment of low-priced craft items, including clothes and ornaments. When you're feeling hungry, venture into the Tostados. **San Angel's Saturday craft market** is an open-air bazaar (Plaza San Jacinto, open Sat 10–6) with a great

selection of crafts from all over Mexico, including traditional jewelry, clothing and pottery from indigenous peoples.

The modern **Galeria Hilario Galguera** (Francisco Pimental 3, tel: 55 5546 9001, www.galeria hilariogalguera.com) sprang to fame in 2006 by hosting the first art exhibition in Mexico by British *enfant terrible* Damien Hirst. It's located in an imposing 100-year-old building just off the Paseo de la Reforma in the San Rafael district.

DEPARTMENT STORE

The capital's leading department store **El Palacio de Hierro,** (Moliere 222, Polanco, tel: 55 5283 7700, www.elpalaciodehierro. com.mx, open Mon–Sat 11–9, Sun 11–8) stocking everything from electrical items and homeware to baby clothes and perfumes, is at the corner of Moliere and Homero. You'll find global brands here as well as Mexican designers.

Where to...
Be Entertained

MUSIC AND THEATER

Sala Manuel Ponce (Avenida Hidalgo, tel: 55 29 93 20) is the city's top jazz venue, in the elegant confines of the Palacio Bellas Artes, and is the setting for a wide-ranging repertoire of acts. Classical music concerts, including operas, are staged in the **Teatro de la Ciudad** (Donceles 36, tel: 55 18 49 23), next to the Museo Nacional de Arte. The **Auditorio Nacional** (Paseo de la Reforma 50, tel: 55 52 80 92 50, www.auditorio.com.mx, box office open Mon–Sat 10–7, Sun 11–6), on the north edge of the Bosque de Chapultepec, is one of the capital's top concert halls with an eclectic calendar of rock, folk and classical performances.

BARS AND CLUBS

With the closure and refurbishment of Love nightclub, **City Hall** (Moliere 480, tel: 55 45 8655, www.cityhall.com.mx, open Fri–Sat 11pm–5am), in Polanco, has assumed the mantle of Mexico City's most cutting-edge nightspot. Electronic dance music of all types is the soundtrack for a high-energy party crowd. This where most foreign DJs and dance acts will be booked.

Diagonal (Presidente Mazaryk 169, tel: 55 2624 3250, www.tapasdiagonal.com, open Mon–Wed 2pm–midnight, Thu–Sat 1pm–1:45am) is a favorite haunt of Polanco's beautiful people. This tapas bar serves bite-size Spanish food, punchy cocktails and local and imported beer and wine. If people-watching isn't enough, you can also surf the internet wirelessly and from time to time Diagonal's iPod nights enable guests to inflict their musical tastes on other diners.

The **Whiskey** (W Mexico Hotel, Campos Eliseos 252, tel: 55 9138 1800, www.whotels.com, open daily noon–2am), also in Polanco, is an ultra-stylish lounge bar. Here you will find leather-lined alcoves, hidden background lighting, funky house music, a koi carp pool under the floor, booted and miniskirted hostesses and enough of a martini menu to keep most people happy.

Don't let the bouncers put you off at **Cinnabar** (Nuevo Leon 67, tel: 55 5286 8456, www.cinnabar.com.mx, open daily 1pm–midnight). This is where the worlds of media, fashion and film in Mexico City collide but it's a welcoming venue in Condesa serving punchy cocktails and southeast Asian cuisine.

WRESTLING AND BULLFIGHTING

Lucha Libre – the highly theatrical wrestling matches between masked wrestlers – is hugely popular in Mexico and gaining in fame around the world (▶ 22). Many of the larger-than-life characters are household names in Mexico and the Friday night spectacles at the **Arena de México** (Dr Lavista 189, tel: 55 5588 0266), south of the Paseo de Reforma, make for an entertaining night out.

Bullfighting is an integral part of Mexican life. Mexico City's bullring, **Plaza México** (Augusto Rodin 241, tel: 55 5563 3961) is the largest bullring in the world, with a capacity of more than 50,000. It is located between the San Angel neighborhood and Roma. Fights take place on Sundays throughout the year. Seats in the shade are more expensive than those in the the sun, and they get cheaper the higher up the amphitheater's tiers you sit. Cushions can also be rented.

Northern Mexico and Baja California

Getting Your Bearings

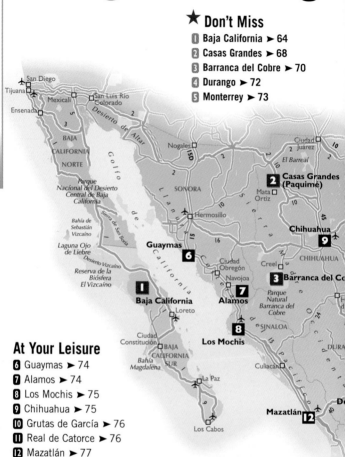

★ **Don't Miss**

At Your Leisure

Cactus-strewn landscape with the Sierra de la Giganta mountains in the background

Northern Mexico extends along the longest border in the world between a developing and a developed country. The American states of California, Arizona and Texas are separated from Mexico by barren desert and, in places, a wall. On the Mexican side, this is a harsh, dry, mountainous landscape spread across the desert states of Sonora, Chihuahua, Baja California and Coahuila. Although there are no man-made wonders on the scale of Chichén Itzá, the natural world can spring some dramatic and memorable surprises here.

Lagoons on the Baja California peninsula, a 1,610km (1,000-mile) finger of land that points into the Pacific Ocean and is separated from the Mexican mainland by one of the deepest stretches of water in the world, attract gray whales every winter. These massive mammals give birth and nurture their young within sight of the Baja shore before beginning their annual migration back up the Pacific coast to Alaska.

On the mainland, the Barranca del Cobre (Copper Canyon) system of canyons dwarfs Arizona's Grand Canyon. One of the world's most scenic railway trips crosses this region, taking a day to slowly chug from Los Mochis to the city of Chihuahua. But you don't have to be a rugged outdoors lover to enjoy northern Mexico. If you want to let your hair down, Cabo San Lucas and San José del Cabo, at the tip of Baja California, rival Cancún. Los Cabos, as they're known, make an increasingly popular and affordable choice for American Spring Break students; Cabo San Lucas attracts a raucous, hard-drinking crowd while San José del Cabo is where more mature visitors base themselves. And Monterrey, the capital of Nuevo León state to the east of Chihuahua, is perhaps the country's most sophisticated (or Americanized) city outside of Mexico City.

One word of warning: don't underestimate the distances involved in seeing the whole region. Use domestic airlines to save time traveling by road.

Page 59: Barranca del Cobre

Right: Rocky coastline between San José del Cabo and Los Arcos

**After the delights of party town Cabo San Lucas, journey
across the Sea of Cortez to catch the Chihuahua Al Pacifico
for one of the world's most amazing train rides.**

Northern Mexico and Baja California in Five Days

Day One

Start with a day of
relaxation in ❶ **Baja
California's Los Cabos**
(➤ 66), although you
could well be feeling
the effects of Cabo San
Lucas's fun-filled
nightlife the next day.
The surf at most
beaches is too rough for
bathing, however, all
the resort hotels have
swimming pools (Casa
del Mar left). Try Mi
Casa (➤ 79) for dinner.

Day Two

Take the bus up to La Paz, the capital of southern **Baja California** (➤ 65),
for the 45-minute flight across the Sea of Cortez to ❽ **Los Mochis** (➤ 75),
the starting point for the Chihuahua Al Pacífico (➤ 70), an unforgettable
train ride through the Copper Canyon highlands. Stay overnight in Los
Mochis. El Farallon (➤ 80) is a good choice for dinner.

Day Three

Catch the early morning train to Creel, seeing
the best bits of the ❸ **Barranca del Cobre**
(Copper Canyon) region (left; ➤ 70–71), from
the comfort of a first-class railway carriage.
Check into the Lodge at Creel hotel (➤ 78),
and spend the night in a luxurious log cabin.

Day Four

Explore the rugged landscape around **Creel** (➤ 70–71), the center of the indigenous Tarahumara people, who live and farm in the canyons and sell handicrafts (below) in the town. You can take daytrips into Copper Canyon itself, or simply meander past curious rock formations, such as the Valley of the Mushrooms, on foot, horseback or bicycle.

Day Five

After spending a second night in Creel – you'll be too tired after all the fresh air and exercise to consider moving on too soon – take the bus or train onward to Chihuahua. The bus is quicker. In central **9 Chihuahua** (➤ 75–76), you can shop for the best-made cowboy boots in Mexico and have lunch at La Casa de los Milagros (➤ 79), which serves good Mexican food. Non-shoppers can make plans to take the bus (3–4 hours) to **2 Casas Grandes** (➤ 68–69) and the Paquimé ruins, northern Mexico's major archaeological site.

❶Baja California

Whale-watching, big surf and all-night parties: it's no wonder that Baja California is booming. The peninsula, 1,610km (1,000 miles) long, stretches from the edgy border town of Tijuana to the sybaritic resorts of Los Cabos. In between, the deserts are populated by towering cardones cacti and the surrounding waters are rich in marine life and watersports.

Northern Baja

The focal point of northern Baja California is **Tijuana**, the lively city where Mexico reaches across the Tortilla Curtain to San Diego in southern California. Long a place to party – Hollywood's glitterati would cross the border to frequent Tijuana's bars during the Prohibition years – Tijuana has a well-deserved reputation for hedonism and even seediness.

Much of the action is centered on Avenida Revolución, a street lined with bars, hawkers and souvenir shops all intent on prying dollars from unwary hands. This is an unfair, inaccurate representation of the real Mexico, but it is one that many visitors to Tijuana experience: after all, it is very easy for foreigners, especially young Americans looking to drink before they are 21 years old, to cross the American border at San Ysidro on foot. A slightly classier night out can be had in the Zona Río, the streets around the Plaza Rio Tijuana close to the Río (River) Tijuana. Tijuana's restaurant scene will surprise and delight diners, with some well-established eateries offering excellent Mexican specialties – several are in the Zona Rio.

Aside from eating, drinking and dodging *mariachi* bands, Tijuana has a standout attraction in the unusual shape of the **Centro Cultural Tijuana**, a modern cultural center that hosts theater, dance and music. The globe-shaped **Omnimax Theater** at the center shows Mexican and English-language films.

Above: Lively downtown Ensenada

Right: The beach near La Paz

Above: Boats at rest in Loreto's marina

South of Tijuana, **Ensenada** is a popular weekend destination for Americans in search of a less tacky introduction to Mexico. The seaside town has several attractive promenades, in particular Avenida López Mateos. Much of Baja's fast-growing wine industry is based in or near Ensenada – you can taste the results at **Las Bodegas de Santo Tomás**, Mexico's premier winery, dating back to 1888. Between Tijuana and Ensenada, **Puerto Nuevo** has gained fame as the place to eat lobster (► 80).

La Paz and the Sea of Cortez

The Sea of Cortéz, named after the Spanish conquistador Hernán Cortés, might be narrow, but it is one of the deepest undersea gulfs in the world. This makes it exceptionally cold and therefore fertile – it is home to a vast spectrum of creatures, from the minuscule life forms that make up the diet of some species of whale to hordes of voracious Humboldt squid, hammerhead sharks and 7.5m-wide (25-foot) manta rays. Other residents of the sea include benign whale sharks and playful sea lions.

La Paz, the state capital and a friendly, compact seaside town, is the best place from which to explore the sea, with tour operators offering boat trips and sea kayaking expeditions. The town is the financial and industrial hub of southern Baja and evidence of the pearl fishing industry, an important source of income for the area a century ago,

The Trans-Peninsular Highway

To drive from **Baja North** to **Baja South** means taking the 1,610km (1,000-mile) Trans-Peninsula Highway. It's a **multi-day trip**, as you should avoid driving at night because of the risk of livestock on the single-lane road. Between Tijuana and La Paz there's little to see apart from the scrubby Baja **desert**, unless you're intent on hunting out remote surfing

beaches. The best option for the time-pressed traveler is to fly to La Paz, which receives flights from several Mexican cities and from Los Angeles or Los Cabos.

remains. For tourists, La Paz's appeal lies in the range of tour operators in the town, the marina with its million-dollar motorboats and sunset walks along the Malecón. Some 24km (15 miles) north of La Paz, **Playa el Tecolote** is a traditional, family beach, although there are beaches closer to the town center. The offshore islands of **Espiritu Santo** and **Isla Partida** are unspoiled, unpopulated nature reserves with a sea lion population and abundant birdlife (► 180–181).

A short drive to the north of La Paz is **Loreto**, a beguiling beachside town with none of the brash commercialism of Los Cabos. Low-key Loreto was one of the five areas highlighted by the Mexican government in the 1970s for tourist development (the others were Cabo San Lucas, Cancún, Huatulco and Ixtapa). Thankfully, insensitive development hasn't mate-

Right: The fine sandy beach at San José del Cabo

A Whale of a Time

The gray whales that migrate south from Alaska to breed in the Pacific coastal lagoons halfway down the west coast of Baja are the region's marine superstars. These giant mammals gather every **winter** (typically arriving in January and departing in April) to calve and feed their young in Laguna San Ignacio and Laguna Ojo de Liebre (also known as Scammon's Lagoon). Several operators offer whale-watching trips. The boats are not permitted to approach the whales, but the creatures sometimes come right up alongside.

Left: This sculpture of a whale's tail can be found at the entrance to La Paz

Right: The Camino Real hotel at Loreto

rialized and Loreto enjoys clean seas, pristine beaches and a spectacular setting. It was from Loreto that the Franciscan priest Father Junípero Serra embarked on his journey north to found San Diego and San Francisco. Today, Loreto is a recommended destination for escapists.

Los Cabos

Cabo San Lucas and its slightly more sedate sister, **San José del Cabo**, are collectively known as Los Cabos (or simply Cabo), an abbreviation bestowed by the government's tourism initiative. The towns, 28km (17 miles) apart, are located at the very tip of Baja California, where the Pacific Ocean churns past the point and up into the Sea of Cortéz. This means that although Los Cabos are beach resorts, few beaches are suitable for bathing: Playa Médano in Cabo San Lucas is the best bet if you want to get wet.

TAKING A BREAK

The following are good places to look for a restaurant or bar: the Zona Río south of Centro or Avenida Revolcuión in **Tijuana**; along the seafront or Avenida 5 in **La Paz**; Boulevard Cardenas in **Cabo San Lucas**; Plaza Mijares in **San José del Cabo**; and around Boulevard Costero Lopez Mateos in **Loreto**.

➕ 198/199
Baja California

Tijuana
➕ 198 B5
Tourist Information
✉ Avenida Revolución at 3rd and 4th ☎ 664 685 2210

Omnimax Theater, Centro Cultural Tijuana
✉ Paseo de los Héroes
☎ 664 687 9600;
www.cecut.gob.mx
🕐 Times vary according to events
💲 Prices vary according to events

Las Bodegas de Santo Tomás
✉ Avenida Miramar
☎ 646 174 0836;
www.santo-tomas.com
🕐 Daily 9–5 💲 Moderate

La Paz
➕ 198 B1
Tourist Information
✉ Paseo Obregon ☎ 612 124 0103

Los Cabos
➕ 198 B1
Tourist Information
✉ Plaza San José, San José del Cabo ☎ 624 146 9628

BAJA CALIFORNIA: INSIDE INFO

Top tips Gang-related **crime** is on the increase in Tijuana – exercise care in taking taxis and stay in the tourist areas of the city. Most violence is not directed at tourists but petty criminals are not uncommon in Tijuana.

• Some stretches of the coastal area and 244 islands of the Sea of Cortéz are **protected reserves** where 695 plant species, 891 fish species and 15 species of whale can be found.

• **U.S. citizens** will need their **passport** when they return to the U.S. from Mexico by air, land or sea from mid-2008.

• You can find **more information** at www.discoverbajacalifornia.com, which covers northern Baja; www.visitcabo.com, the website of the Los Cabos Tourism Board, and www.visitmexico.com.

② Casas Grandes

Casas Grandes is a dusty, unremarkable town about two hours' drive due south of the border with Texas. However, it is not the town of Casas Grandes that is the attraction, but Paquimé: a maze-like collection of ruins 8km (5 miles) from Casas Grandes. Paquimé is Northern Mexico's most important archaeological site. Now a UNESCO World Heritage Site, the town reached its apogee in the 14th century when it was a highly developed and cultured center of commerce for the southern Mesoamerican region and what is now the southwest United States and northern Mexico.

The town's inhabitants built diagonal walls to block out direct sunlight, T-shaped narrow doorways for defensive reasons and plumbing that delivered hot water from thermal springs into the homes of residents via channels. Many of the construction methods used for the multistory buildings can still be seen and the archaeological digs at Paquimé – only a fraction of the

The partially restored ruins at the archaeological site of Casas Grandes, which includes pyramids and ball courts

The area around Casas Grandes consists of rocky scrubland

site has been uncovered – have revealed that the inhabitants crafted jewelry and bred macaws, perhaps for ceremonial purposes. The site is well-maintained and most points of interest are clearly labeled and explained.

There's no escaping the fact that Paquimé is a long way from other attractions in Northern Mexico, although it's an undeniably beautiful place when the setting sun sets off the ochre-colored adobe ruins.

To make the most of your time here, take a taxi (or one of the daily buses) to **Mata Ortiz**, 30km (20 miles) south of Casas Grandes. The village is famous for its distinctive tribal pottery, which features handsome, bold black, white and red patterns and symbols on a plain background. Smooth-glazed vases, masks, plates and ornaments are sold at galleries in Mata Ortiz, although prices are high for pieces from the most sought-after potters in the village.

TAKING A BREAK

Although you can get drinks at Paquimé, it's a good idea to take some bottled water with you. In Casas Grandes itself there are plenty of inexpensive eateries around **Avenida Minerva** and **Avenida 16 de Septiembre**.

➕ 200 C4

Paquimé
➕ 200 C4
✉ 8km (5 miles) from Casas Grandes
🕐 Daily 8–5 🎫 Inexpensive 🍴 Refreshments on site

Museo de las Culturas del Norte
✉ Paquimé ☎ 636 692 4140 🕐 Tue–Sun 10–5 🎫 Inexpensive

CASAS GRANDES: INSIDE INFO

Top tips Vist Paquimé **late in the day**, in order to appreciate it at its best in the setting sun.
• If can't make the journey to **Mata Ortiz**, the onsite museum at Paquimé features examples of pottery from the village.

3 Barranca del Cobre

One of the world's natural wonders, the Barranca del Cobre (Copper Canyon) area of the Sierra Madre highlands is four times the size of the Grand Canyon in the U.S.; Copper Canyon itself is just the most accessible and visited canyon in this dramatic landscape.

Creel is the Copper Canyon's main center of sightseeing and activities. It's a rough-and-ready but charming mountain town that is now dominated by the daily arrivals from the railway. Avenida López Mateos runs parallel to the train tracks and is lined with budget hotels, restaurants, outfitters and shops. Creel is a friendly, laidback place, but its surroundings are spectacular. Half- or full-day excursions reveal a landscape of rock formations, gnarled pine forests, canyons large and small and the popular Lake Arareko, where you can rent rowing boats. The Copper Canyon is 25km (16 miles) away and can be visited by tours departing Creel.

Creel and its environs are populated by Tarahumara Indians, who have lived in the area for 500 years. They sell handicrafts in the local shops and can be seen farming small parcels of land among the rugged terrain. The Tarahumara are famous for their high-speed, endurance running: One legend tells of a Tarahumara Indian who ran 965km (600 miles) in

The Railway

The best way to appreciate the Copper Canyon is to take the train. Nicknamed CHEPE, the **Chihuahua al Pacifico Railway** connects the state capital of **Chihuahua** (► 75–76) to the coastal town of **Los Mochis** (► 75) with 921km (572 miles) of undulating track. Every day two passenger trains wheeze each way up and down the gradients, skirting precipitous drops: the lowest point of the trip is Los Mochis at 200m (656ft) above sea level, the highest is San Juanito at 2,439m (8,002 feet). Tickets for the train can be purchased from

travel agents at either starting point (or at intermediate towns) or direct from the station on the day of travel, although you won't be guaranteed a place and you will need to be at the station not long after 5am (the express train departs at 6am, the slower, second-class train departs at 7am). The full journey takes 14 hours but it is a good idea to break the journey in the highlands at the town of **Creel**.

The beautiful blue waters of Lake Arareco, 6km (4 miles) south of Creel

five days to deliver what must have been a very important message. Running races between tribal villages can cover 240km (150 miles), over rocks and through forests. It's an ability partially explained by the altitude of their territory, and was once employed to chase down wild animals.

At 2,400m (7,875 feet) Creel gets very cold in the winter and not all hotels provide adequate heating. Autumn is a good time to visit – the temperature is more comfortable than summer or winter and the autumn rains cause the trees and shrubs in the canyons to bloom. At lower levels, for example around the village of **Batopilas**, the canyon is subtropical. At 1,800m (5,900 feet) Barranca Batopilas (Batopilas Canyon) is deeper even than Barranca del Cobre (Copper Canyon), a mere 1,760m (5,775 feet) deep.

TAKING A BREAK

There is a **dining carriage** on the train with an extensive menu and waiter service.

✚ 200 C3

Chihuahua al Pacifico Railway
❓ Tickets for same-day travel are usually available from the main station in Chihuahua, Los Mochis and intervening stops, but it is best to reserve ahead at a travel agent or tel: 614 439 7212; www.chepe.com.mx

BARRANCA DEL COBRE: INSIDE INFO

Top tips For the **best views** ask for a seat on the right side of the train if you're traveling from Los Mochis to Chihuahua, or on the left side of the train if you're journeying from Chihuahua to Los Mochis.
• The most **spectacular stretch of scenery** is between El Fuerte (near Los Mochis) and Creel.

④ Durango

While Durango, south of Chihuahua, is a down-to-earth, friendly place, the dusty film sets of numerous Westerns were the scene of a many a shoot-out.

Durango was founded in 1563, but it gained fame when the timeless, unspoiled landscapes surrounding it were used as backdrops for some of Hollywood's most successful Westerns in the 1960s and 1970s, including *The Wild Bunch* (► 12–13). The area is still used as a film set these days. The best known, and one you can tour, is **Villa del Oeste** – a tongue-in-cheek Western theme park, although it won't detain you long.

Durango itself is compact enough to walk around, and the plazas, particularly Plaza de Armas, are perfect for whiling away an evening. The baroque cathedral stands on one side, while another graceful old building, the 18th-century Casa del Conde de Suchil, stands to the east of the plaza. Today it is a bank, but the original interior can still be seen. The Museo de Cine on Avenida Florida, west of Plaza de Armas, is a good place to learn more about the Western movie industry and buy souvenirs. A rather more impressive sight is the Teatro Ricardo Castro, a striking art nouveau venue, two blocks west of Plaza de Armas; poke your head around the door to see the original French interior. Also worth a look is the Palacio de Gobierno and its vivid murals by 20th-century Mexican artists such as Guillermo Bravo, located on the grand Avenida 5 de Febrero and home to state government offices.

One of the best ways to get around this region

Below left: Durango's cathedral, on the main square

Bottom: Villa del Oeste

TAKING A BREAK
There are several good restaurants on **Avenida Constitución**.

✚ 204 C5
Tourist Information
✉ Avenida Florida 1006 ☎ 618 811 1107 🕓 Daily 10–7

Villa del Oeste
✉ 12km (7.5 miles) north of Durango on the road to Parral
🕓 Sat–Sun 11–7 (hours may vary according to season)

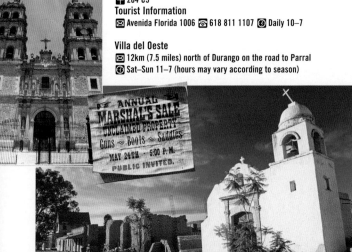

ANNUAL
MARSHAL'S SALE
UNCLAIMED PROPERTY
Guns ~ Boots ~ Saddles
MAY 24TH ~ 5:00 P.M.
PUBLIC INVITED.

⑤ Monterrey

Nuevo León's state capital is a thriving hotbed of modern architecture, stylish bars, up-to-the-minute art galleries and outstanding museums. In the surrounding area you can go climbing and caving with weekending locals.

Outside the capital, Monterrey is Mexico's most modern city. The skyscrapers hide a rich cultural scene and an increasing number of great restaurants and bars in the cobbled streets of Barrio Antiguo, the Old Town neighborhood.

The city center revolves around the massive Macro Plaza, the collective name for seven parks and plazas between the Zona Rosa and the Barrio Antiguo. Macro Plaza is heralded by the 70m (230-foot) Faro del Comercio sculpture in Plaza Zaragoza, a rust-red obelisk designed by Luis Barragán (1902–88). On the east side of the plaza, the superb **Museo de Arte Contemporáneo** displays work by Frida Kahlo and Diego Rivera, in addition to seasonal exhibitions of contemporary art. North of the museum, on the opposite side of Raymundo Jardon, Monterrey's cathedral has seen better days. For a taste of Mexico's history visit the **Museo de Historia Mexicana**, an angular, modernist marvel housing a series of exhibition spaces describing the key advances in Mexican history from the pre-Columbian period to the present day.

Monterrey's stand-out construction is its **Planetario Alfa**, resembling a metal tube offset into the ground. Located in the Alfa cultural complex, 7km (4 miles) from the city center, it has several floors of interactive exhibitions on science and astronomy. Outside, there is an observatory, a science garden, a pre-Hispanic garden and a glass building, the Pabellon, designed by Mexican artist Rufino Tamayo.

Luis Barragán's impressive Faro del Comercio shoots a green laser around the city at night

TAKING A BREAK

The best places to eat tend to be in the **Barrio Antiguo**.

🏠 202 C3

Tourist Information
✉ Antiguo Palacio Federal, Avenida Zaragoza
☎ 800 832 2200 🕐 Mon–Fri 8:30–6:30, Sat–Sun 9–5

Museo de Arte Contemporáneo
✉ Avenida Zuazua and Raymundo Jardon
☎ 81 8342 4820; www.mytol.com/marco
🕐 Tue, Thu, Sat 11–7; Wed and Sun 11–9, closed Mon 💷 Inexpensive, free on Wed

Museo de Historia Mexicana
✉ Plaza 4000 Anos ☎ 81 8345 9898;
www.museohistoriamexicana.org.mx
🕐 Tue–Fri 10–7, Sat–Sun 10–8, closed Mon
💷 Expensive, free on Tue

Planetario Alfa
✉ Avenida Roberto Garza Sada 1000
☎ 81 8303 0001; www.planetarioalfa.org.mx
🕐 Tue–Sun 10:30–8 💷 Moderate

At Your Leisure

6 Guaymas

Guaymas, in Sonora state, is renowned for two things: seafood and the annual *Día de la Marina* festival in June – both are closely linked to the town's status as one of Mexico's largest ports. The seafood is fresh from the Sea of Cortéz and you shouldn't pass up the chance to enjoy some of the super-sized shrimp served in the town's seafood restaurants. The *Día de la Marina* festival commemorates some of the naval battles that have taken place in the area: Guaymas has been at the center of several notable conflicts. The town was founded by the Spanish in 1769 and in 1847 it was attacked by US forces during the US-Mexico war. In 1866 it was France's turn to occupy Guaymas.

Today, however, Guaymas is notable for being a transit point to and from Baja California. The ferry from Santa Rosalia arrives here three times weekly (advance booking recommended). There are few reasons to linger in Guaymas, although the 17th-century Iglesia de San Fernando is worth a look. Most people continue their journey into mainland Mexico, although San Carlos, a short bus ride up the coast, is a diverting resort popular with game-fishing visitors looking to hook marlin, wahoo and tuna.

➕ 199 F2
Tourist Information
✉ Calle 19 and Avenida 6
☎ 622 226 0313 🕐 Mon–Fri 9–3
🖥 www.ferrysantarosalia.com

The delightful old fishing port of Guaymas

7 Alamos

Alamos is a fast-rising colonial town north of Los Mochis (► opposite). The town's origins lie in the veins of silver running through the Sierra Madre range, which were mined in the 17th century and exhausted in the early 20th century. Since maturing into a delightfully relaxed and attractive town, Alamos has been designated a National Historic Monument and is being considered for UNESCO status; it has already won approval from a large number of expats.
Accessible by bus from the coastal town of Navojoa (or by private

plane), Alamos is a pleasant place in which to stay for a couple of days; longer visits are best for those who come for the birdwatching, nature walks and horseback riding into the backcountry. The focal point is Plaza de Armas, around which the Museo Costumbrista de Sonora, which covers the cultural highlights of Sonora state, and the Catedral Nuestra Senora de la Concepción are oriented. Locals and visitors congregate in the beautiful square on winter evenings; temperatures and humidity are high in the summer.

➕ 200 B2
Tourist Information
✉ Avenida Juárez 6 ☎ 647 428 0450
🕙 Mon–Fri 9–6

8 Los Mochis

Los Mochis is a key hub for travel around the northwest of Mexico. The airport receives flights from La Paz in Baja California and provides onward travel to other Mexican towns. The Chihuahua al Pacifico Railway (➤ 70) terminates in Los Mochis, and the port of Topolobampo, 24km (15 miles) south of Los Mochis, receives daily ferries from La Paz.

➕ 200 B2
Tourist Information
✉ Avenida Allende and Calle Ordonez
☎ 668 815 1090 🕙 Mon–Fri 9–4

The ornate facade of Chihuahua's 18th-century cathedral

9 Chihuahua

It's "Viva la Revolution" in Chihuahua, which is closely connected to two of Mexico's most revolutionary sons. But the overwhelming reason why most people come to Chihuahua, a modern, commercial city surrounded by arid hills and scrubland, is to join or leave the Copper Canyon railway journey (➤ 70–71). While you wait for your train, several sights in Chihuahua's state capital merit a visit. One of the best ways of getting an overview of Chihuahua is to take a sightseeing bus tour from the central Plaza de Armas, departing every half hour. Before you join the tour, you are bound to spot Chihuahua's 18th-century cathedral, known locally as the Parroquia del Sagrado, on the Plaza de Armas.

Chihuahua's revolutionary history is described in the **Museo de la Revolución Mexicana** located in the house once occupied by General Pancho Villa (and also known as the Quinta Luz). Villa is celebrated as one of the leaders who overthrew the dictator Porfirio Diaz in the Mexican Revolution of the early 20th century. In 1913 Villa settled in

Chihuahua with his wife Luz Corral. The peaceful interlude didn't last long: he was assassinated in 1923 and you can see the bullet-riddled car in which he was killed at the museum.

Chihuahua's second revolutionary hero, Father Miguel Hidalgo, a leader of Mexico's independence movement, was executed by the Spanish in 1811 at the **Palacio de Gobierno**, northeast of Plaza de Armas, on Plaza Hidalgo.

Although Chihuahua is most often a staging post for trips to and from the Copper Canyon, it's also an excellent place to mingle with the boot-wearing, stetson-sporting locals and shop for your own cowboy accessories (►81).

➕ 201 D3
Museo de la Revolución Mexicana
✉ Calle Décima 3010 ☎ 614 416 2958 ⏰ Tue–Sat 9–1, 3–7, Sun 9–5

Palacio de Gobierno
✉ Aldama and Guerrero ☎ 614 429 3300 ⏰ Mon–Fri 8:30–6, Sat–Sun 10–5

🔟 Grutas de García

The Grutas (caves) de García, 45km (28 miles) from Monterrey, is arguably Mexico's most extensive cave network. The caves extend deep into the Sierra El Fraile hills and are reached by a cable car from the base of the hills; the nearest village is Villa de García and tour buses depart regularly for the caves. Tours delve into the 50-million-year-old

The Grutas de García are dramatically illuminated

caverns, visiting 16 vast caves filled with stalagmites and stalactites.

➕ 202 C3
☎ 818 347 1599 ⏰ Daily 9–5
💲 Moderate

⓫ Real de Catorce

Once a silver-mining town, until the money dried up and the town died, this ghost town is slowly coming back to life. Real de Catorce is an enchanting mountain town 2,745m (9,000 feet) up in the Sierra Madre Oriental, where visitors can wander among decaying mansions, dilapidated churches and long since abandoned warehouses. It is tourists who are breathing life back into Real de Catorce, although the current population isn't anywhere near the 40,000 residents it had at its height.

Best accessed by bus from Matehuala, the village is cut off from the rest of the world by a one-way 2.5km (1.5-mile) tunnel. Expatriates and incoming Mexicans are in the process of resurrecting some of Real de Catorce's best-looking buildings and opening galleries and cafés. The town is quiet for much of the year but the Fiesta de San

Right: Real de Catorce's parish church
Bottom: Fishing boats at Mazatlán

Francisco in October sees thousands of visitors thronging the streets.

➕ 202 C2

Tourist Information

✉ Presidencia Municipal ☎ 488 887 5071; www.realdecatorce.net

🔢 Mazatlán

The tourist capital of Sinaloa state, Mazatlán's main appeal lies in the Zona Dorada, a Pacific beach resort comparable to Puerto Vallarta and Acapulco, and the old town (Viejo Mazatlán) around Plaza Machado on Calle Carnaval, which is several miles south. Outside these areas, Mazatlán boasts Mexico's largest west coast port with its attendant trade and a tourist office keen to promote the city's annual events, which include a marathon, a triathlon and a Carnival.

While the hotels (and souvenir sellers, fast-food restaurants and hawkers) are concentrated in the Zona Dorada, the old town is more deserving of a visit, with the Catedral de Mazatlán and Plaza Revolución its hear. The cathedral was completed in the early 20th century – which might explain the concoction of styles including neoclassical and Gothic. Streets with restaurants, galleries and shops radiate from Plaza Revolución, which bustles with activity. But the highlight of the old town is the opera house, the **Teatro Angela Peralta**. Plays, concerts and dance shows are staged in this 19th-century venue.

The old town and the Zona Dorada are linked by a *malecón* (seafront) and halfway up the Acuario Mazatlán is the city's **aquarium**. Don't expect jumping killer whales; it's on the small side, but there is plenty of life in the tanks to amuse families.

➕ 204 A4

Tourist Information

✉ Carnaval and Mariano Escobedo 1317 ☎ 669 981 8883; www.sinaloa-travel.com

Teatro Angela Peralta

✉ Plaza Machado ☎ 669 982 4446; www.teatroangelaparalta.com

Aquarium

✉ Avenida Deportes 111 ☎ 669 981 7815 🕐 Daily 9:30–6
💲 Inexpensive–moderate

Where to... Stay

Prices
Expect to pay for a double room per night:
$ under US$50 $$ US$50–150 $$$ over US$150

ALAMOS

▽▽ Hacienda de los Santos $$$

This boutique hotel is less than three hours north of Copper Canyon. Thanks to its own airplane hangar, complete with a nine-seater plane, it can be accessed direct from Arizona. The Hacienda is the perfect place to switch off, with a full-service spa and a cozy home cinema. Luxuriously furnished rooms and suites are spread around the three converted colonial mansions and feature fireplaces and their own bathrooms.

➕ 200 B2 ⊠ Molina 8 ☎ 647 428 0222; www.haciendadelossantos.com

CHIHUAHUA

▽▽ Hotel Mirador $$

This large, modern motel-style hotel is a short walk from the historic centre of Chihuahua and the city's shopping streets Libertad and Juaréz. Rooms are clean and spacious if basic; noise can be a problem from the parking area. The restaurant serves breakfast, lunch and dinner, although it is worth making the trip into the city center for a special meal. Business services are very good, with computers and free internet available to guests.

➕ 201 D3 ⊠ Avenida Universidad 1309 ☎ 614 432 2200; www.bestwestern.com

café-restaurant. Activities, including kayaking, fishing, snorkeling and diving, can be organized, although neighboring Baja Outdoor Activities outfitter can help with trips.

➕ 198 B1 ⊠ Avenida Obregón ☎ 612 122 4084; www.clubelmoro.com

CREEL

▽▽ The Lodge at Creel $$

The top dog in Creels pack of hotels is the Lodge. Its competition gets the backpackers but the Best Western-affiliated Lodge is busy with Copper Canyon sightseers. The timber-clad cabins are exceptionally cosy, with blanket-laden beds and gas fireplaces. Sensitive diners at the restaurant might be put off by the animal heads and skins hung around the room. The large bar is the discerning drinker's best bet in Creel if Tío Molcas (▶ 82) is full.

➕ 200 C3 ⊠ Avenida Lopez Mateos 61 ☎ 635 456 0071; www.thelodgeatcreel.com

LA PAZ

▽▽ Club El Moro $$

El Moro is the leading hotel in central La Paz, with smart, clean suites fitted with air-conditioning and television. There's a pool and a

LORETO

▽▽ The Inn at Loreto Bay $$–$$$

This sprawling, semi-circular, modern resort is tucked between the Baja hills and the Sea of Cortéz. With eight tennis courts, a 72-par golf course and assorted watersports, it's a great location for active types but party-seekers will want to be somewhere more lively. Rooms are airy and decorated in a Mexican theme; some have balconies or terraces too. The restaurant doesn't always live up to expectations.

➕ 199 E1 ⊠ Misón de Loreto Boulevard ☎ 613 133 0010; www.innatloretobay.com

Where to...
Eat and Drink

LOS CABOS

Casa Natalia $$$

Casa Natalia is a well-established favorite of seasoned Los Cabos visitors. The 16 rooms are comfortable and charming, but one of the key attractions is the outstanding Mi Cocina restaurant. Breakfasts are also delectable. Children under 13 are not permitted which means that this is very much a laidback, adult retreat. San José del Cabo's nightlife is on your doorstep.

🚹 198 B1 ☒ Boulevard Mijares 4,
San José del Cabo ☎ 624 142 5100;
www.casanatalia.com

Las Ventanas al Paraíso $$$

This is one of the most exclusive resorts on a peninsula already crowded with luxury getaways. Guests are taken direct to their palatial rooms, sprinkled around the resort's landscaped grounds, rather than waiting in a lobby.

Dining options include a seafood grill and a tequila and ceviche bar. There's a wide range of sports and activities available, and the hotel's spa is worth the price of admission.

🚹 198 B1 ☒ Km19.5 Carretera
Trans-Peninsular ☎ 624 144 0300;
www.lasventanas.com

The Westin Resort and Spa $$$

The 243-room Westin is one of the more stylish resorts in Los Cabos, with an outline that curves along the shore and mimics the Arch of Cabo San Lucas. Rooms are very comfortably furnished and have a balcony. A spa completes the sybaritic experience although more active guests can play tennis, go fishing or play a few holes of golf. There are several bars and restaurants, although downtown Cabo San Lucas is quite a drive away (20km/12 miles).

🚹 198 B1 ☒ Km22.5 Carretera
Trans-Peninsular ☎ 624 142 9000;
www.starwood.com

Prices
Expect to pay per person for a meal, excluding drinks:
$ under US$10 $$ US$10–20 $$$ over US$20

CABO SAN LUCAS

Mi Casa $$

Lively Mi Casa is highly regarded, and a great choice to start a night on the town in Cabo San Lucas. The kitchen in this restored colonial hacienda sends out excellent, refined Mexican dishes to a bustling crowd of diners grouped around colorful, open-air tables. The mole poblana (chicken in a dark, spicy sauce) with rice, beans and warm corn tortillas is notable, as is the chiles en nogado (red pepper stuffed with creamy walnut sauce) and the pescado sarandeado (barbequed red snapper). There's often live music, which enhances the whole experience.

🚹 198 B1 ☒ Avenida Cabo San
Lucas, corner Lazaro Cardenas
☎ 624 143 1933;
www.micasarestaurant.com
🕒 Mon–Sat noon–3, 7–11,
Sun noon–3

CHIHUAHUA

La Casa de los Milagros $

On a street running parallel to the main shopping thoroughfare of Libertad, La Casa de los Milagros serves up sublime quesadillas and other Mexican snack food in a restored colonial building. Behind the heavy doors, youthful Mexicans and travelers sip coffees and enjoy light Mexican meals in the tiled inner courtyard or explore the art-filled rooms of the mansion. The café stays open late at the week-ends, when there is live music and a festive atmosphere.

➕ 201 D3 ⊠ Avenida Victoria 812, Centro Histórico ☎ 614 437 0693 ⊙ Mon–Thu 5–12, Fri–Sun 2–2

LA PAZ

5th Avenida Café $

Looking out onto the central square, 5 de Mayo, in La Paz (a couple of blocks inland from the seafront), this large but comfortable café serves coffees, frappuccinos and fresh-baked pastries. A major attraction is the wireless internet and a couple of computers available for surfing.

➕ 198 B1 ⊠ Central Plaza ☎ 612 123 5094 ⊙ Daily 7am–11pm

Les Tres Virgenes $$

Since opening in a quiet spot one block from La Paz's central zócalo in November 2006, this restaurant has jumped to the top of the town's dining hotspots. The open-air courtyard, behind the yellow-painted facade, has well-spaced tables (with maps under the glass) and a brick oven on one side. You can choose Pinots, Cabernets, Carmeneres and Chilean reds and whites from the lengthy wine list. The sea bass marinated in herbs with tomato compote and the chef's signature side dish, roast garlic and mint pureed potato, are a must. All the fish is caught locally by Baja fishermen. Starters include zingy mesquite grilled baby octopus (herb-infused and spicy). Mains include Puerto Nuevo lobster with beans and rice, and Angus beef medallions in jalapeno sauce. The open kitchen, eager-to-please service from the staff and low-key Spanish music all add to the enjoy-ment of this.

➕ 198 B1 ⊠ Madero 1145, Constitución ☎ 612 165 6265 ⊙ Daily noon–3, 8–11

LOS MOCHIS

El Farallon $$

The two best restaurants in Los Mochis – a town not noted for its dining potential – happen to be opposite each other, just a couple of blocks from the central zócalo. El Farallon (across Álvaro Obregón from the Espana restaurant) is a large, lively, colorful seafood restau-rant with a fishy themed decor. Seasonal seafood is served with an extensive choice of sauces or piquant marinades, or just steamed with ginger and vegetables. Shrimp is a specialty and there are hot or cold entrees. The atmosphere is smart but relaxed, and the staff will be happy to elaborate on any dish on the menu.

➕ 200 B2 ⊠ Avenida Álvaro Obregón 499 ☎ 668 812 1428 ⊙ Daily 12:30–3, 7–10:30

PUERTO NUEVO

La Casa de la Langosta $$

Puerto Nuevo, south of Tijuana, has become a place of pilgrimage for Southern California lobster-lovers thanks to the unique way the crus-taceans are cooked in hot oil. Up to 700,000 lobsters are served annu-ally in the town and the three-story Casa de la Langosta is one of the best places to sample them. You can have lobster burritos or lobster omelets for breakfast, steamed lobster with wine, lobster thermi-dor or even a combo plate. And there are plenty of other options if the restaurant is fully booked, such as the Ortega chain.

➕ 198 B5 ⊠ Corner of Tiguron and Azuelo ☎ 661 664 4102 ⊙ Daily 8am–late

SAN JOSÉ DEL CABO

▽▽ Damiana $$

This colorful, romantic restaurant, renovated from a mid-18th-century hacienda, offers fine patio dining in a delightful courtyard in the heart of San José. The sophisticated cuisine includes char-broiled lobster and *ranchero* shrimp in cactus sauce, plus a few vegetarian dishes. Finish your meal with the regional Damiana liqueur. It's very popular with the locals so reservations are recommended.

🚩 198 B1 ☒ Paseo Mijares 8 🕾 624 142 0499 🕙 Daily 10:30–10:30

La Panga Antigua $$

Rustic meets chic at one of San José del Cabo's hot spots. You can try several small plates of appetizers to get a taste of chef Jacobo Turquie's modern Mexican cooking or order one of the main dishes – the fresh seafood is recommended. There's an open-air courtyard, draped in foliage, plus an indoor lounge bar. The food is complemented by a decent wine list.

🚩 198 B1 ☒ Zaragoza 20 🕾 624 142 4041; www.lapanga.com 🕙 Daily 12–10:30

Where to... Shop

Shopping and souvenir-hunting opportunities in Northern Mexico are impressive. They range from designer outlets in raucous Cabo San Lucas to craft stalls in mountain villages and air-conditioned malls in Monterrey. Chihuahua is arguably the best place in the country to get decked out in cowboy clothing; the leather boots sold here are very high quality. Pottery is another good buy in Northern Mexico, with the cheap and rustic styles of the Tarahumara Indians in Creel contrasting with the elegant, refined pieces from Mata Ortiz.

GIFTS AND SOUVENIRS

Buy authentic Cuban cigars at **Amigos Smokeshop and Cigar Bar** (Hidalgo 11, tel: 624 142 1138,

open Mon–Wed 9–8, Thu–Sat 9–1) in central San Jose del Cabo. Brands include Romeo y Julieta and Cohiba. A selection of tequilas is a sideline.

Crafts, including baskets, women's belts, pots, rugs and musical instruments are sold in **Artesanias Mision** (Central Plaza, open Mon–Sat 9–1, 3–6, Sun 9:30–1), a large shop beside the main square in Creel. The quality does not differ significantly from the other souvenir shops in Creel but proceeds go to the Tarahumara Children's Hospital.

In Cabo San Lucas, all the art in the **Golden Cactus Gallery** (Guerrero and Madero, tel: 624 143 6399, www.goldencactusgallery. com, open Mon–Sat 10–6, Sun 11–3) refers in some way to Baja, although the artists come from all over Mexico and the U.S. It's a good place to pick up a memento of your trip to Cabo San Lucas, with a roster of up to 20 artists displaying their work inside.

Central de Botas (Libertad 602, Col. Centro, tel: 614 416 2578, open Mon–Sat 9:15–8, Sun 9:45–3), in Chihuahua, is one of a row of stores selling cowboy boots in a rainbow of colored leathers, as well as snakeskin and ostrichskin, but beware of boots that are made from protected species. Brands include Justin and Cuadra.

You'll find as large a selection of cowboy hats as you could wish for, plus belts, belt buckles, friendly service and country and western music at **La Rosa Amarilla** in Chihuahua (Avenida Juarez 206, Col. Centro, tel: 614 415 5335, open Mon–Sat, 9–8).

DEPARTMENT STORE

La Paz's main department store in the town center, **Dorian's** (16 de Septiembre 111, tel: 612 122 8014, open Sun–Thu 10–9, Fri–Sat 10–10), is stocked with men's and women's clothing, shoes, toiletries and other household items.

Where to...
Be Entertained

THEATER

The cultural heart of La Paz – and its architectural highlight – is the **Teatro de la Ciudad** (Avenida Navarro 700, tel: 612 125 0486). The swooping concrete structure hosts dance, music and dramatic performances in a packed seasonal schedule. Book at the theater's box office.

NIGHTLIFE

Creel's nightlife revolves around **Tío Molcas** (Avenida López Mateos 35, no phone, open daily 10am–late), a small bar at the back of the restaurant of the same name. The cosy room, with chunky wooden tables and timber ceiling, quickly fills with locals and visitors clutching bottles of Indio beer and warming themselves around the log fire.

MUSIC

Outside of Mexico City, Monterrey has perhaps Mexico's most sophisticated social scene, and many of the city's hipsters pass through the gay-friendly **Akbal Lounge** (Abasolo Ote 870, tel: 81 8340 4332, www.akballounge.com, open daily 7pm–3am). Weekend revelers dance to house music in the luxurious, baroque interior. Downstairs the casual **Casa de Maíz** restaurant serves southern Mexican street food.

THE OUTDOORS

In La Paz **Baja Outdoor Activities** (P.O. Box 792, Centro, tel: 612 125 5636, www.kayakinbaja.com) is the leading adventure outfitters in Baja California, offering a high standard of service, safety and guiding on all its trips. Kayaking tours are the mainstay of BOA (▶180), but fishing and whale-watching trips are also available. A popular combination is to spend a few days kayaking in the Sea of Cortez then the rest of the time watching for whales.

At the **Baja Adventure Company** (tel: 612 124 6629, www.bajaecotours.com), also in La Paz, Johnny Friday's guides take whale-watchers out to the lagoons of San Ignacio where gray whales give birth to their young from January to April.

In San Jose del Cabo, surfing safaris are the specialty of **Baja Wild** (Plaza Costa Azul 5, tel: 624 172 6300, www.bajawild.com), where guides take surfers to deserted breaks in boats. Land safaris are also offered, as well as kayaking, snorkelling and hiking. In season, whale and turtle watching tours are also available.

There are several fine golf courses around San Jose del Cabo but the 18-hole **Cabo Real course** (Km 19.5 Carretera Trans-Peninsular, tel: 624 144 1200, www.caboreal.com), designed by Robert Trent Jones II, is perhaps the most challenging. It has hosted PGA tournaments and is a favorite of many pro golfers, not least because of three spectacular oceanfront holes that can afford views of whales breaching for the lucky.

The **3 Amigos** (Avenida López Mateos 46, tel: 635 456 0179, www.amigos3.com) is a tour operator offering, trucks, bicycles, scooters and camping gear for rental in Creel. Equipment is in a good state of repair and the staff are happy to provide free maps and advice. Tours of Copper Canyon are also available.

Central Mexico West

Getting Your Bearings

The silver mines of Mexico's highlands yielded not only precious metals, but also a legacy of wealthy, colonial towns – such as Zacatecas and Guanajuato – each rich in historic buildings and enchanting streetscapes. Most can be explored on foot. Often clinging to hillsides or straddling gorges, the silver towns are sprinkled across the Mexican heartland of the Sierra Madre, from Zacatecas in the north to Morelia, the state capital of Michoacán, in the south. In between, San Miguel de Allende is a comfortable expat enclave, and nearby Querétaro is the dynamic, polished capital of Querétaro state.

The area covered by this region include the coastal states of Nayarit, Jalisco, Colima and Michoacán and the inland highland states of Aquascalientes, Guanajuato, Querétaro, Hidalgo and México. The landscapes here are high and dry – altitude can reach as much as 1.6km (1 mile) above sea level and the arid conditions mean that agriculture can be difficult. Guadalajara, capital of Jalisco and the birthplace of several Mexican traditions, including tequila (from Tequila), *mariachi* music and the Mexican hat dance, is 1,540m (5,050 feet) above sea level. The Central West region of Mexico extends to the Pacific coast, occupying the middle chunk of wave-pounded coastline. Several purpose-built resorts, that include well-established Puerto Vallarta attract visitors from all over the world, but it isn't to escape to an uncrowded beach with a surfboard and suntan lotion.

Left: Statue of Pancho Villa, Zacatecas

★ Don't Miss

Dining out in Guanajuato

Page 83: The
Church of
Guadalupe,
Morelia

At Your Leisure

Right: Laguna
Avandaro, Valle
de Bravo

The towns and cities of the central highlands – San Miguel de Allende, Guanajuato and Guadalajara – are a cultured introduction to colonial Mexico, before you dip your toes into the Pacific at the resort of Puerto Vallarta.

Central Mexico West in Five Days

Day One

4 San Miguel de Allende (below; ➤ 95) is an easy-going introduction to Mexico and easily reached via the Norte (North) bus station of Mexico City, with several services daily from at least two operators. It's a five-hour journey so take an early bus. After checking into your hotel you can

explore the old town's historic heart, dipping into the many art galleries and admiring the carefully preserved colonial buildings. Eat at one of the new wave of upscale eateries such as Nirvana (➤ 104).

Day Two

Spend the morning in San Miguel, then take the afternoon bus for the 90-minute journey to **3 Guanajuato** (➤ 92–94), perhaps the most outstanding colonial town in this area. Book a room at a central hotel, then explore the Centro Histórico. The Alhóndiga de Granaditas museum provides an introduction to the city and its history. In the evening take in a performance at the Teatro Juárez (➤ 106).

Day Three

After breakfast, take a tour of Guanajuato's churches. There's a superb bird's-eye view of the city from the cable car to the top of El Pípila, a hilltop monument to a Mexican revolutionary (above). Have lunch in one of the cafés in the center; try Truco 7 on El Truco. In the afternoon, visit the Museo Casa Diego Rivera, dedicated to the artist Diego Rivera, who was born in the city. If you missed out on the Teatro Juárez, catch a performance tonight, or have dinner at El Gallo Pitagórico (➤ 103).

Day Four

Take the morning bus for the four-hour journey to **2 Guadalajara** (right; ➤ 90–91), arriving in time for a late lunch. Highlights in Mexico's second-largest city include the buildings around the Plaza de Armas and the city's shops. In the evening, take a taxi to the Zona Rosa, where many of Guadalajara's best Mexican restaurants are located, such as El Sacromonte on Pedro Moreno.

Day Five

It's less than six hours to **9 Puerto Vallarta** (➤ 100) by bus from Guadalajara, but to save time a direct flight (with Aeromexico) takes 45 minutes, although the fare will be ten times the price of a bus ticket. Get into the swing of things at this Pacific resort with a *mojito* at La Bodeguita del Medio. Watch the sun go down, then steel yourself for one of the liveliest dining towns in the country. Most of the best restaurants are south of the River Cuale.

❶ Zacatecas

Zacatecas wows visitors with a show-stopper of a cathedral, several good museums and the same colonial charm as Guanajuato, but without so many visitors.

Zacatecas, capital of the state of the same name, repays the extra effort required to reach it many times over. Few tourists make the trip, so you won't have to share the ancient streets with the hordes, but there are still excellent restaurants and hotels. Zacatecas made its fortune in the silver-mining boom of the 16th and 17th centuries; by the 18th century 20 percent of Mexico's silver was being extracted from the mines of Zacatecas. Wealthy residents constructed gorgeous, pink-hued limestone mansions and official buildings, such as the Palacio de Mala Noche and the Palacio del Gobierno, now municipal offices. The Palacio de Mala Noche (Palace of the Bad Night), on Avenida Hidalgo, takes its name from a mine of the same name, owned by a Basque called Manuel de Rétegui, who gave away as much money as he made from the mine. Avenida Hidalgo is one of two main thoroughfares in the city (the other is Avenida Juárez) and the city can easily be covered on foot. Enter the Palacio del Gobierno, on the Plaza de Armas, to see a mural by Antonio Pintor Rodríguez detailing the history of Zacatecas.

Top: View over the city

Above: Mural by Antonio Rodriguez in the Palacio de Gobierno

The star attraction of this UNESCO World Heritage Site is its fabulous 18th-century cathedral backing onto the Plaza de Armas. Even from the summit of the Cerro de la Bufa, the hilltop to the northeast of the city reached by cable car, the twin towers of the magnificent cathedral loudly proclaim their presence. The exterior of the cathedral grabs the attention with an over-the-top display of baroque stonework (known as Churrigueresque in Mexico) that took 23 years to complete. The building glows pink in the light of the rising and setting sun.

Brothers Rafael and Pedro Coronel collected a surprising variety of art, from Mexican folk art to European and modernist pieces by the likes of Goya, Miró and Picasso. The **Museo Pedro Coronel**, west of the cathedral, houses their art collection, while traditional Mexican folk masks are exhibited in the **Museo Rafael Coronel**, located in what remains of the Ex-Convento de San Francisco on the corner of Abasolo and Matamoros to the north.

Commencing from Cerro del Grillo, Zacatecas's *teleférico* crosses the city to end at the top of the Cerro de la Bufa. It operates daily from 10 to 6, saving the walk up Cerro de la Bufa and providing superb views over the city during the 10-minute trip. Cerro de la Bufa's place in Mexico's revolutionary history is commemorated by the statue of rebel Pancho Villa on its slopes: the revolutionary leader defeated President Huerta's army here in 1914. The Museo Toma de Zacatecas tells the story.

To grasp the importance of silver mining to Zacatecas, venture down the musty, twisting tunnels and across the rope bridges of La Mina Eden, a once lucrative silver mine to the west of the city center. Today, it is a more upbeat place, complete with an underground disco, La Malacate.

TAKING A BREAK

Most of the interesting restaurants are on Hidalgo and Juárez. For coffee, try the **San Patrizio Caffe** on Hidalgo.

205 D4
Tourist Information
Avenida Hidalgo 403, Colonia Centro
492 924 0393
Mon–Sat 9–8, Sun 10–7

Museo Rafael Coronel
Abasolo and Matamoros
492 922 8116
Thu–Tue 10–4:30
Inexpensive

Museo Pedro Coronel
Plaza de Santo Domingo
492 922 8021
Fri–Wed 10–4:30
Inexpensive

Right: The domed church of Santo Domingo

ZACATECAS: INSIDE INFO

Top tip To reach Zacatecas you can **take a bus direct from Mexico City** (up to 8 hours), Guadalajara (4 hours) or Querétaro (6 hours) but there are no direct routes from San Miguel de Allende. However it's a safe, easy route to **drive yourself** from San Miguel to Zacatecas. Aeromexico and Mexicana both **fly from Mexico City** to Zacatecas's airport, some distance north of the city.

② Guadalajara

Easygoing and accessible, Mexico's second-largest city is full of surprises. Shoppers for crafts will be spoiled for choice, while sightseers will lose themselves in the historic center of the City of Roses.

Until recently, Guadalajara was an unassuming state capital. Suddenly the city boomed, swallowing its surrounding suburbs and sprawling across the high mountain plateau of the Sierra Madre. But this expansion means that although there are bleak industrial sectors, the city's Centro Historico is largely untroubled by development. Treats here include, in the Plaza de Armas, the cathedral, a mammoth construction that has survived more than one earthquake. Facing the cathedral, the Palacio del Gobierno offers a more unified and austere aspect. Inside, there is a mural by José Clemente Orozco (1883–1949) of Miguel Hidalgo looming over a stairway. Hidalgo was one of the key leaders of Mexico's war of independence from Spain; after his execution for treason in 1811 his head was displayed in Guanajuato for a decade.

The cathedral of La Asunción, with its twin yellow towers

The Plaza de Armas itself is one of the social hotspots of Guadalajara, with roving musicians and live music (the birthplace of *mariachi* music is said to be the Plaza de los Mariachis, to the east of downtown). East of the Plaza de Armas, the Plaza de la Liberación is overlooked by the **Museo Regional de Guadalajara** in a beautiful former seminary. Children will love the natural history exhibits on the ground floor, while the upper floor's galleries cover the history of this part of Mexico, including a fine collection of colonial art.

Guadalajara's strengths also include some of the region's best shopping. The Plaza Tapatía, further east, boasts the city's best department stores; use the footbridge to reach the Mercado Libertad (also known as San Juan de Dios), one of Mexico's largest covered markets. Then visit the neoclassical **Instituto Cultural Cabanas** on the east side of Plaza Tapatía and admire its collection of Orozco sketches and murals.

More shopping opportunities exist in the suburbs (once villages) of Tonalá and Tlaquepaque, to the south of Guadalajara. **Tonalá** is known for its Sunday and Thursday markets and the workshops and stores selling pottery and other crafts. **Tlaquepaque** majors in more sophisticated art and crafts, with boutiques displaying one-off items; it's a pleasant place to while away an afternoon.

Top: Mercado Libertad

Above: A *mariachi* band in Plaza de los Mariachis

TAKING A BREAK

Although there are plenty of cafés and restaurants in the Centro Histórico near the principal attractions, to sample the best food head for the **Zona Rosa**.

Below: Village rodeo near Guadalajara

➕ 204 C3
Tourist Information
✉ Morelos 102 ☎ 33 3668 1600
🕐 Mon–Fri 9–8, Sat–Sun 10–2

Museo Regional
✉ Liceo 60 ☎ 33 3614 5257
🕐 Tue–Sat 9–5:30, Sun 9–5
💲 Inexpensive

Instituto Cultural Cabanas
✉ Cabanas 8 ☎ 33 3818 2800
🕐 Tue–Sat 10–6, Sun 10–2:45
💲 Inexpensive

GUADALAJARA: INSIDE INFO

Top tip A **free tour** of the city departs from the City Hall daily during holiday periods (Christmas, Easter, summer) at 10am. Contact the city tourist office for precise times.

③ Guanajuato

Guanajuato is a beguiling, beautiful city, resting on the folds and contours of the Sierra Madre. Founded on silver mining, its wealth supported numerous colonial mansions, plazas and churches, all carefully preserved today. Spend at least a day wandering the maze of alleys.

**Opposite
Top: The neo-classical
Teatro Juárez**

**Middle:
Callejón del
Beso (Alley of
the Kiss)**

**Bottom: Jardín
de la Union**

Of all the silver cities in the Mexican heartland, Guanajuato is the one to visit if you're short on time. Prettier than Guadalajara and less gentrified than San Miguel de Allende, it's a gem that local and international conservation experts have been at pains to preserve (it was made a UNESCO World Heritage site in 1988). You'll find that the city center is largely free from garish signs and unnecessary traffic signals. Avenida Juárez, which becomes Obregón after the Plaza de la Paz, is the main thoroughfare. Unlike ordered Morelia, Guanajuato has a haphazard layout, so let curiosity get the better of you and follow the narrow, cobbled alleys (known as *callejones*) that splinter off from Juárez; the Centro Histórico is compact and easily navigated on foot. Unusually, the central *zócalo* (square) is an unassuming, triangular garden, the Jardín de la Unión. It is faced by the 17th-century Iglesia de San Diego, with its eyecatching rococo facade, and the imposing Teatro Juárez (► 106). The theater, designed in a neoclassical style in the late 19th-century, complete with Doric columns and a well-preserved art nouveau interior and a steel roof, is the showpiece venue for the Festival Internacional Cervantino (► 94).

Continue west along Obregón to the Basilica de Nuestra Señora de Guanajuato on Plaza de la Paz; admire the gold-leafed interior, the chandeliers and the soaring ceiling. Guanajuato's historic wealth is evident in the solid-silver pedestal of the wood statue of the Virgin Mary in this church; the statue itself is believed to date from the 8th century and was given to the city by King Philip I of Spain in gratitude for the treasure that was flowing to Spain from Guanajuato.

If you take the fork in the road north here you will reach the domed Iglesia de la Compania de Jesus and its Churrigueresque

**Above: The
Templo de San
Diego, with its
ornate carvings**

facade. The church's neighboring seminary buildings are now occupied by the university. If you follow the road, which becomes Pocitos, westward, one of the red-painted houses on the right is the birthplace of the muralist Diego Rivera. It is now a museum, the **Museo Casa Diego Rivera**, containing some of his personal effects and examples of his work,

including preparatory sketches for some of his best known works. Also on Pocitos is the Museo del Pueblo, with its art collection. Farther west still, at Panteon Municipal, the Museo de las Momias is a somewhat macabre (and decaying) collection of mummified bodies exhumed from the local cemetery.

Guanajuato's most important museum is the **Alhóndiga de Granaditas**, on Avenida Juárez. The granary was a fortress during the early part of the wars of independence and was the site of a massacre of Spanish soldiers and prisoners who were holed up in the building. Later episodes saw the heads of executed rebels, including Father Miguel Hidalgo, posted at the corners of the Alhóndiga. They're not there now: instead the museum has a detailed assortment of exhibits from the pre-Columbian and colonial periods.

For a good view over the city, hike up to the monument of El Pípila, the Mexican fighter who set the doors of the Alhóndiga ablaze and precipitated the first victory for the independence forces. It is on a hill called Hormiguero, to the south of the city and can also be reached by a cable car from Plaza Constancia, behind the Teatro Juárez.

TAKING A BREAK

Make your way to **Plazuela San Mernando**, at the northwestern end of the Centro Histórico.

Top: View over the rooftops

Above: The bearded face of Don Quixote on the unusual Cervantes Monument

✚ 205 E3
Tourist Information
✉ Plaza de la Paz 14, Col. Centro
☎ 473 732 1982
🕐 Mon–Sat 10–2, 4–7:30, Sun 10–2

Basilica de Nuestra Señora de Guanajuato
☎ Plaza de la Paz
🕐 Daily 9–8
💵 Inexpensive

Museo Casa Diego Rivera
✉ Calle Pocitos 47
☎ 473 732 1197
🕐 Tue–Sat 10–6, Sun 10–2
💵 Inexpensive

Alhóndiga de Granaditas
✉ 28 de Septiembre
☎ 473 732 1112
🕐 Tue–Sat 10–2, 4–6; Sun 10–3
💵 Inexpensive

GUANAJUATO: INSIDE INFO

Top tip The annual **Festival Internacional Cervantino** brings day-to-day life to a standstill in Guanajuato. It's a two-week celebration of music, drama and dance scheduled for October. Ostensibly inspired by Miguel Cervantes, the 16th century poet, playwright and novelist (*Don Quixote* is his best-known work), it embraces a wildy entertaining variety of arts today (www.festival cervantino.gob.mx). Reserve accommodations in advance.

4 San Miguel de Allende

San Miguel is Mexico seen through the prism of a magazine shoot: it's almost too perfect. A sizeable expatriate community has packed the old town with brightly painted property, art galleries and chic restaurants and bars.

San Miguel de Allende (➤ 182–184) is Mexico-lite, a useful decompression chamber for newcomers to the country arriving from Mexico City, just four hours away by bus. The mountain town has an undeniably spectacular setting, although only the tiny old town is worthy of attention. San Miguel's cobbled streets, sometimes crawling with traffic, are thick with art galleries and boutiques and other small businesses. None of this, however, detracts from San Miguel's genuine pleasures: a dramatic, Gothic church in the sedate central *zócalo*, and technicolor views down quaint streets.

Above: The Church of San Miguel Arcángel

Hard on the heels of its well-heeled visitors is a horde of upmarket hotels, most with spas. San Miguel is also one of Mexico's top destinations for eating out.

TAKING A BREAK

Wander along **Mesones**, one block north of the Jardín, till you find a place that catches your eye.

➕ 205 E3
Tourist Information
✉ Jardín Principal ☎ 415 152 6565 🕐 Mon–Fri 10–5, Sat 10–2

Below: Eating outside Meson de San José

5 Querétaro

Modern, yet full of history, Querétaro has some fine examples of baroque and Moorish architecture in its compact cobbled center. It's a pleasant place to explore, where you can follow the final days of Emperor Maximilian.

This modest but wealthy city was made a UNESCO World Heritage Site in 1996, because it is "an exceptional example of a colonial town whose layout symbolizes its multiethnic population." UNESCO's reference is to the Indian groups, the Tarasco, Otomi and Chichimeca who lived alongside the Spanish in Querétaro. This peaceful coexistence led to the construction and preservation of a large number of 17th- and 18th-century civic buildings. One illustration of the city's prosperity is the fact that it could to afford to build its own aqueduct, visible from behind the 16th-century Convento de la Santa Cruz.

The historic core of the city is the Jardín Zénea. Both the Iglesia de San Francisco and the Museo Regional adjoin the Jardín, which becomes a stage for elaborate nativity scenes over the Christmas period. The museum occupies the monastery next to the church and it covers the war for independence from Spain, in which ill-fated Emperor Maximilian's final role was to await execution in Querétaro's yellow-painted Convento de la Santa Cruz. He was shot in 1867 on the Cerro de las Campanas (Hill of Bells), west of Querétaro. Maximilian, an Austrian, had held the Mexican crown for just three years.

TAKING A BREAK

Head to **Plaza de Armas** or **Plaza de la Corregidora** and take your pick from the outdoor eating areas surrounding these two popular squares.

➕ 206 B4
Tourist Information
✉ Luis Pasteur 4 Norte, Centro Histórico
☎ 442 238 5072;
www.queretaro.gob.mx
🕐 Daily 9–8

Above: The Church of Santa Rosa de Viterbo

Left: Delightful pedestrian-only area of the city

⑥ Morelia

Step back in time in Michoacán's state capital, one of the country's finest examples of a colonial city with glorious churches, handsome plazas and four centuries of history. Millions of migrating Monarch butterflies can't be wrong.

View across the Mil Cumbres, in the Michoacán highlands near Morelia

Morelia was founded in a high valley during the middle of the 16th century, when it was named Valladolid. It was renamed in 1828 to honor José Maria Morelos, who led the fight for independence from Spain. The birthplace of Morelos, the Museo Casa Natal de Morelos on Corregidora, is now a public library and museum.

From the outset, Morelia was planned as a grand and harmonious city: its avenues and boulevards were broad and straight, its plazas large and its civic buildings palatial. The cathedral is truly awe-inspiring. Completed in 1744, it is one of the tallest in Mexico and arguably the most dramatic, with a beautiful baroque facade. The plazas on either side of the cathedral, the Plaza de Armas and the Plaza Melchor Ocampo, are adorned with trees, fountains and secluded archways, drawing locals and visitors in the evenings.

Like most colonial cities in the heartland, Morelia can be comfortably explored on foot. Opposite the cathedral is the Palacio del Gobierno: the murals above the flights of stairs are by Alfredo Zalce (1908–2003) and depict often violent scenes from Mexico's history in vivid color. For a fuller picture of Michoacán's state history head for the **Museo Regional Michoacán**, on the corner of the Plaza de Armas. The 18th-century palace is now one of Mexico's oldest museums, having spent more than a century amassing a collection stretching from pre-Columbian times to the 20th century.

Morelia's UNESCO World Heritage status is in part due to its spectacular aqueduct, another sign of the city's wealth. It starts from the Fuente de las Tarascas (Fountain of Tarascas) and runs for up to 2km (1.2 miles) across the city. Don't worry if you miss it during the day; it is illuminated at night.

And the monarch butterflies (► 16)? They fly south from Canada every year to the old mining town of Angangueo (a four-hour drive from Morelia), arriving between October and March. You can walk among them as they cling to the fir trees of El Rosario Butterfly Sanctuary, just outside Angangueo.

Left: Morelia's baroque cathedral

Below: Inside the dome of the Church of Guadalupe

TAKING A BREAK

Head for the restaurants in the streets north of the zócalo, such as **Café Europa** or **Super Cocina La Rosa** on Tapia and Prieto.

➕ 205 E2
Tourist Information
✉ Palacio Clavijero, Calle Nigromante 79
☎ 443 312 8081
🕐 Mon–Fri 9–8, Sat 9–7, Sun 9–3

Museo Regional Michoacán
✉ Allende 305
☎ 443 312 0407
🕐 Tue–Sat 9–7, Sun 9–4
🎟 Inexpensive

MORELIA: INSIDE INFO

Top tips Morelia sweets are little bits of heaven. The city is famous for its *dulces morelianos*, which come in all shapes and flavors. They're not just boiled sugar – many are made with dried fruit, nuts and milk, and they are mouth-wateringly delicious. Where can you get your fix? There's a whole market dedicated to sweets – the Mercado de Dulces – to the west of the Palacio Clavijero, or seek out the delightful shop, Dulces Morelianos, on Calle Real, Avenida Madero Oriente 440, where the quality is much better.

At Your Leisure

7 Aguascalientes

As its name suggest, Aguascalientes sprang up around hot springs. Despite its industrial foundations,

Mural, Aguascalientes' Palacio de Gobierno

the historic core has some excellent places of interest for art lovers, including the Museo José Guadalupe Posada in the Jardín El Encino, dedicated to Mexico's modern art movement. Posada was an influential artist and many of his works are exhibited here. Work by the Mexican artist Saturnino Herrán is shown at the Museo de Aguascalientes (Zaragoza 507), and more contemporary art can be seen at the Museo de Arte Contemporáneo, on the corner of Morelos and Primo Verdad.

➕ 205 D3
Tourist Information
✉ Palacio de Gobierno, Plaza de la Patria ☎ 449 915 9504;
www.aguascalientes.gob.mx
🕐 Tue–Sun 10–5

8 Tequila

Tequila is produced from the spiky blue agave plants that surround the town. The pulped plants can be brewed into the peasant staple, *pulque*, the only slightly more palatable *mezcal* or a surprising variety of tequilas. The area's first tequila distillery, Jose Cuervo's 200-year-old La Rojena distillery at the end of Sixto Gorjon, is still in busines today and you can take factory tours of the visitor center, **Mundo Cuervo**.

On Tequila's main plaza, the Museo Nacional de Tequila is dedicated to the drink. Also in the town center, the Tequila Sauza visitor center is housed in a converted hacienda. Tequila itself can only be produced within certain strictly regulated areas around the town; if it is not brewed here, it has to be labeled *mezcal*. Another insight into Tequila is provided by the Tequila Express (www.tequilaexpress.com.mx), a train service that departs weekends from Guadalajara and stops at the town of Amatitán for a tour of the Herradura tequila distillery.

Field of blue agave for making tequila

➕ 204 C3
Mundo Cuervo
✉ La Rojena, Jose Cuervo 75
☎ 374 742 2170; www.mundocuervo.com
🕐 Tours Mon–Sat 10–4, Sun 11–1

Playa Mismaloya, south of Puerto Vallarta

9 Puerto Vallarta

Puerto Vallarta is a stylish, up-and-coming beach resort, offering a mix of sophisticated revelry and modern amenities, but without the downmarket trappings of Acapulco. If it's authentic, gritty Mexico you seek, don't look here – this is a world of international hotel chains and fast-food outlets. There is an air of romance here still; this is where Richard Burton and Elizabeth Taylor set tongues wagging in the 1960s after filming *Night of the Iguana*.

The main resort is based around the Bahía de Banderas, a gently curving, beach-lined bay that is home to a variety of marine life, including whales, dolphins and huge manta rays. There are few historic sites, although the Zona Centro does have a couple of places of interest: the Templo de Guadalupe and Los Arcos, a row of arches.

However, people don't visit Puerto Vallarta for history, they come for the huge range of activities, including horseback-riding and mountain biking in the hills around the resort, and the watersports along the coast. It is also an especially gay-friendly resort. Playa Los Muertos is one of the best beaches in town. When swimming, watch out for the undertow, more prevalent at some beaches than others. To really escape the crowds, head south to the secluded beaches of Conchos Chinas, close to Playa los Muertos.

➕ 204 B3
Tourist Information
✉ Zona Comercial, Hotel Canto del Sol
☎ 322 224 1175 🕐 Mon–Fri 9–2, 4–7, Sat 9–1

10 Manzanillo and the Costa de Oro

One of Mexico's largest ports, Manzanillo can't compete with the Pacific resorts to the south for sheer sun-lazing fun, but it does have several attractions, especially if you enjoy game fishing. The self-styled "Sailfish Capital of the World" has an annual fishing tournament in November, and visitors who want to get out on the water will find it easy to reserve a boat. Manzanillo's white sand beaches, the Costa de Oro, extend several kilometers south of the town, punctuated by large-scale resorts and golf courses.

➕ 204 C2
Tourist Information
✉ Boulevard Miguel de la Madrid
☎ 314 333 2264 🕐 Mon–Thu 9–3, 5–7, Fri 9–3, Sat 10–2

11 Chapala

The pleasant resort town of Chapala is located on the shores of Mexico's largest lake and is a favorite spot for expatriates to settle, thanks to its warm climate. The town has plenty of hotels, restaurants and recreational facilities catering to the foreign influx. You can take boat tours of the lake from the pier at the end of Madero, the town's main street. British writer D. H. Lawrence, who said that Mexico changed him forever, passed through Chapala while writing *Mornings in Mexico* (1927).

➕ 205 D2
Tourist Information
✉ Madero 407 ☎ 376 765 3141
🕐 Mon–Fri 9–7, Sat–Sun 9–1

12 Tequisquiapan

A charming colonial retreat in Querétaro state, Tequisquiapan's claim to fame was its hot springs. Now limited by industrial use of the water, there are still several cooler thermal ponds and some well-watered gardens in the town. Tequisquiapan itself is a pleasant place to explore for a day, with a colonial central plaza surrounded by arched arcades.

➕ 206 B4
Tourist Information
✉ Plaza Principal ☎ 414 273 0295
🕐 Mon–Fri 9–7, Sat–Sun 9–1

The Church of Santa María, Tequisquiapan

🔟 Toluca
Toluca is the highest city in Mexico at 2,680m (8,793 feet). It retains a large number of the colonial buildings constructed by the Spanish in the 17th century, but it has also developed into an industrial powerhouse. Stick to the historic part, around the Plaza de los Mártires, which is overlooked by the Palacio Nacional and the cathedral. Toluca has a better-than-average range of shops, with many sheltering under the Portales, 19th-century arcades running along Avenida Hidalgo.

➕ 206 B3
Tourist Information
✉ Corner of Urawa and Paseo Tollocan
☎ 722 212 5998
🕐 Mon–Fri 9–7, Sat 9–1

🔟 Valle de Bravo
West of Toluca (on Highway 134) is Valle de Bravo, a weekend getaway for many Mexico City residents. The old town is set around a new lake, created by a hydroelectric dam project. Like Chapala, boating, fishing and other watersports are the

main appeal, but the colonial town has several appealing restaurants and shops on Callejón El Arco.

➕ 206 B3

🔟 Malinalco
Make a trip south of Mexico City to Malinalco to see some of the best-preserved Aztec temples in the area. You'll need to climb the 400 or so steps through the jungle to the top of Cerro de los Ídolos, but the views from here are excellent. The temple is well signposted from the town center. It was carved directly into the rock, with an intimidating entrance in the form of a snake. Once inside, you will see seats, representing an eagle and a jaguar, and a hole in the center of the temple's floor for blood offerings to the Aztec gods. In the center of the town, an Augustinian temple and convent, with elaborate frescoes, is an interesting counterpoint to the Aztec temple.

➕ 206 B3
🕐 Tue–Sun 9–6 💲 Inexpensive

Valle de Bravo's main plaza

Where to... Stay

Prices
Expect to pay for a double room per night:
$ under US$50 $$ US$50–150 $$$ over US$150

GUANAJUATO

⬥⬥⬥ Quinta las Acacias $$$

In a European-style colonial mansion overlooking the city, built by Albert Malo in 1890, the Quinta las Acacias welcomes guests to one of Guanajuato's prettiest neighborhoods. There are 17 rooms, some with whirlpools and each with good views of Acacia Park or the surrounding mountains; the themes of the suites range from European sophistication to Mexican exuberance. Guests enjoy the delicious breakfasts of fruit and filling Mexican dishes. With intoxicating Guanajuato beckoning outside the front door, there should be little time left over to use the open-air Jacuzzi, games room and library.

➕ 205 E3 ✉ Paseo de la Presa 168 ☎ 473 731 1517; www.quintalasacacias.com

MORELIA

⬥⬥ Hotel de la Soledad $$

This small-scale hotel, in a beautiful converted monastery, lies just north of the cathedral. The comfortable rooms are decorated with carved wood furniture and surround a peaceful central courtyard with a fountain.

➕ 205 E2 ✉ Zaragoza 90 y Melchor Oca ☎ 443 312 1888; www.hsoledad.com

NAYARIT

⬥⬥⬥ Casa Las Brisas $$$

La Casas Las Brisas, with just seven rooms, is a sybarite's hideaway, north of Puerto Vallarta, offering superb accommodation in suites with private balconies, patios and ocean views. The suites are in a plain but pretty style with whitewashed walls and tiled floors. There's a pool for lazing around when you don't want to go the short distance down to the sea. The restaurant is also a paragon of excellence, with a daily changing menu. The experience of living in your own private beach house doesn't come cheap.

➕ 204 B3 ✉ Playa Careyeros, Punta Mita ☎ 329 298 4114; www.casalasbrisas.com

⬥⬥⬥ Four Seasons Resort Punta Mita $$$

The Four Seasons Punta Mita, 42km (26 miles) north of Puerto Vallarta, is an outstanding luxury resort, not least thanks to its Jack Nicklaus-designed golf course and its unrivaled spa facilities. The 30 suites are located in Mexican-style *casitas*, with beachfront terraces, shutters and teak furniture. There are an additional 165 airy rooms. Facilities include four restaurants, three bars, tennis courts, pools and the golf course.

➕ 204 B3 ✉ Bahía de Banderas, Nayarit ☎ 329 291 6000; www.fourseasons.com/puntamita

QUERÉTARO

⬥⬥⬥ La Casa de la Marquesa $$$

If you are in Querétaro, consider staying in this beautiful 18th-century architectural treasure. The house was built by the town's marquis as a gift to his wife and contains some interesting Moorish features. Today, the Casa de la Marquesa is an extraordinary, family-owned luxury hotel in the converted mansion with 25 opulent rooms furnished with Mexican

Where to...
Eat and Drink

Prices
Expect to pay per person for a meal, excluding drinks:
$ under US$10 $$ US$10–20 $$$ over US$20

GUANAJUATO

El Gallo Pitagórico $$

Burn off some calories on the climb up to this great Italian restaurant – look for the blue house behind the Iglesia de San Diego and the Teatro Juárez – and enjoy the stunning view over central Guanajuato. Lasagna is the specialty here, but there is also a full menu to choose from, including a variety of pasta dishes, and there's a top-floor bar in which you can enjoy an aperitif with your view.

➕ 205 E3 🖂 Constancia 10 ☎ 473 732 6758 🕒 Tue–Sun 12:30–3, 7–11

MORELIA

Fonda Las Mercedes $$

Dine inside or out at this stylish but traditional restaurant in a converted mansion in Morelia. The international menu sticks to tried and trusted favorites, such as generous steaks and crêpes filled with squashes and cheese, but it is the elegant colonial surroundings that really add luster to this local gem. Try a soup for a starter – there are plenty to choose from.

➕ 205 E2 🖂 León Guzman 47 ☎ 443 312 6113 🕒 Mon–Sat 1–1, Sun 1–7

---

antiques. It's on the same street as the cathedral and the Palacio del Gobierno. Suites have gorgeous period features, as well as modern facilities, including air-conditioning. A restaurant, bar and café provide food and drink throughout the day, and there is spa treatments.

➕ 206 B4 🖂 Avenida Madero 41 ☎ 442 212 0092; www.lacasadelamarquesa.com

SAN MIGUEL DE ALLENDE

La Puertecita Boutique Hotel $$$

Quiet, private and exclusive, this haven of tranquility is a 20-minute walk uphill from the center of San Miguel (the hotel offers shuttles to the town at all times). This mid-sized boutique hotel occupies the side of a gorge, with steps leading up and down to the separate units. Each is individually decorated, surrounded by landscaped gardens and offers charming views. There is a small heated swimming pool, cold pool, Jacuzzi and a spa center. Meals are served at the excellent restaurant which hosts a popular barbeque buffet on Sundays plus barbeque and seafood nights during the week. There's no better retreat in San Miguel, although you'll need to take a taxi back after a night out in the town center.

➕ 205 E3 🖂 Santo Domingo 75 ☎ 415 152 5011; www.lapuertecita.com

ZACATECAS

Quinta Real Zacatecas $$$

This luxurious hotel stands in the shadow of the colonial aqueduct and incorporates part of the old Palza de Toros (the city's bullring until 1976). The dining room looks out over the arena. The rooms are stunning, with huge beds and superb bathrooms.

➕ 205 D4 🖂 Avenida Ignacio Rayon 434 ☎ 492 922 9104; www.quintareal.com

PUERTO VALLARTA

▼▼▼ Café des Artistes $$$

Puerto Vallarta's most garlanded restaurant is chef Thierry Blouet's Café des Artistes, which encompasses the Cocina de Autor dining room for culinary fireworks, the more modestly priced (just) Café des Artistes bistro and the Constantini wine bar. The bistro, in a stunning, whitewashed room with crystals hanging from the high ceiling, serves Mexican and French specialties (sometimes on the same plate); no reservations. Blouet's ambitious signature restaurant raises the temperature, with an open kitchen and three- to six-course tasting menus. He also offers ad hoc cookery classes with courses ranging from beginners to advanced. See the website for details.

🛉 204 B3 ☒ Guadalupe Sanchez 740, Colina Centro ☎ 322 222 3228; www.cafedesartistes.com ⏱ Bistro: 6pm–11pm. Restaurant: 6pm–11pm, closed Sep. no children under 13

De Santos $$–$$$

One of the swankiest venues in town, De Santos is a restaurant where both food and music are taken to heart; one of the owners is a member of a hit Latin band. The food side of things is represented by a Mediterranean menu that makes the most of local seafood. Musically, expect to be accompanied by jazz, flamenco and lounge music during your meal. As the hour gets later people migrate to the dance floor and De Santos becomes a nightclub at the stroke of midnight. If that's too lively, head up to the open-air Skybar on the top floor, an elegant, moodily lit space filled with soft chairs and cushions.

🛉 204 B3 ☒ Morelos 771, Colonia Centro ☎ www.desantos.com.mx ⏱ Daily 5pm–late

QUERÉTARO

La Mariposa $

The Mariposa (butterfly) has been serving cakes, coffees and snacks in Querétaro since 1940. The simple, family-run café has an adjoining bakery and the aroma alone is enough to attract passers-by. A restaurant serves more substantial Mexican meals and provides sandwiches to take out. It's a good, cheap spot in which to refuel.

🛉 206 B4 ☒ Angela Peralta 7 ☎ 442 212 1166 ⏱ Daily 8–10pm

▼▼▼ Los Espejos $$

Enjoy the finest haute cuisine in a romantic courtyard setting in the stunning 300-year-old mansion-style Meson de Santa Rosa hotel. Not to be missed, if only for a drink. Excellent, friendly service and a relaxed atmosphere.

🛉 206 B4 ☒ Pasteur Sur 17 ☎ 442 242 2623 ⏱ Lunch and dinner

SAN MIGUEL DE ALLENDE

▼▼▼ La Capilla $$–$$$

Perhaps San Miguel's most refined restaurant, La Capilla, in the Centro Histórico, has a menu that bridges European and Mexican cuisines, using the freshest ingredients. Dishes range from the standard (lamb chops in a mustard, mint and honey glaze) to the exotic (chicken breast with a caramelized mango and garlic sauce and fried plantains). The terrace has views of the Parroquia, with its neo-Gothic facade, which is especially beautiful at sundown. Upstairs, the bar and chocolaterie offer further temptation, with tapas served between drinks. However, be prepared for the stiffest prices in San Miguel.

🛉 205 E3 ☒ Cuna de Allende 10 ☎ 415 152 0698; www.la-capilla.com

▼▼▼ Nirvana $$

Take a break from Mexican food at Nirvana. The chef gets full marks for effort for the modern fusion cooking with the menu boasting such dishes as Peking duck with blackberry sauce. Not all his ideas succeed, however, but the combination of the entertaining venue (the interior design has water features

Where to... Shop

The colonial cities of this part of Mexico are packed with gift shops and other outlets aimed at visitors. Beyond the general souvenir shops, several cities specialize in particular products and crafts. Pátzcuaro is famed for its folk art, much of it produced in Michoacán state itself – ceramics, often with a distinctive green glaze, are a specialty, as is copperwork. San Miguel's galleries deal in more polished, contemporary artworks from local and foreign artists. Guadalajara is also a good hunting ground for traditional arts and crafts. Silver items make their way to Guanajuato from Taxco, and jewelry also finds its way into Puerto Vallarta's shops.

In Guadalajara craft salespeople from all over the region sell their wares – everything from cowboy hats to pots and pans – at **Mercado Libertad** (south of Plaza Tapatía, open daily 10–6), a huge market also known as San Juan de Dios. Note: don't try the street food unless you're sure it has been hygienically prepared.

A wide selection of folk art and crafts is available at the **Mercado Tonalá** (Tonalá, 15km/9 miles southwest of Guadalajara, open Thu and Sun). Look particularly for the pottery, glass and ceramics.

West of Guanajuato's city center, the **Mercado Hidalgo** (Avenida Juárez, Col. Centro, main entrance opposite Calle Mendizabal, open daily 7–9) sells local specialties such as embroidered dresses, basketware and *charamusca* – a confection of melted, twisted brown or white sugar.

The in-house shop at **Casa de las Artesanías** in Morelia (Fr. Juan de San Miguel 129, tel: 443 312 1248, open Mon–Sat 10–8, Sun 9–5), a state-run museum, stocks some high quality crafts, including

pottery, copperware, musical instruments, lacquered ornaments and figurines, all made in Michoacán state. You can watch artists making items and see how traditional techniques have been maintained.

In Pátzcuaro **Casa de los Once Patios** (between Calle Lerin and Calle Coss, open daily 10–7, shops keep their own hours), a series of courtyards is crowded with shops selling good quality Michoacán crafts – lacquerware, pottery, religious art and musical instruments.

San Miguel de Allende is a town over-run by art galleries – there were more than 40 at the last count – but **Galería Izamal** (Mesones 80, tel: 415 154 5409, www.artistsof sanmiguel.com, open daily 11–3, 4–8) can claim to be one of the originals. It is an artist's cooperative, meaning that you buy direct from the artists, who staff the gallery, and discounts may be negotiated. The seven members produce work in a variety of styles, from line drawings to flamboyant paintings.

with fire displays and lots of foliage) and superior service makes up for any shortcomings. Note: For snacks, the busiest eatery in San Miguel is the tapas and fondue joint on San Francisco.

🚹 205 E3 ⊠ Mesones 101 ☎ 415 150 0067 ⏰ Wed–Mon 8am–10:30pm

ZACATECAS

Café Nevería Acrópolis $

The venerable Acrópolis has been serving breakfasts, lunches and evening meals to locals since 1943 and is a Zacatecan legend. The no-frills food, such as tasty *chilaquiles* (tortilla strips) and *huevos rancheros* (eggs, salsa and corn tortillas), is plain but filling. The café can't be beat as a breakfast spot, and the strong coffee will get the day going with a bang. The Acrópolis is in the González Ortega market.

🚹 205 D4 ⊠ Avenida Hidalgo, next to the cathedral ☎ 492 922 1284 ⏰ Daily 8–10pm

Where to...
Be Entertained

The mountain towns of central Mexico are not renowned for their all-night nightclubs; for those you will have to head to beach resorts such as Puerto Vallarta. However, even the smallest towns will have a lively bar-restaurant scene, often revolving around the *zócalo*. Guadalajara has its own symphony orchestra, which performs at the historic Teatro Degollado, while Guanajuato is noted for its outstanding theaters and hosts an arts festival in October. Morelia has a flourishing folk-music scene with bars and clubs putting on live acts regularly. Puerto Vallarta has all the bars and clubs you would expect of a leading Mexican resort, from chic little martini bars to vast techno-playing dance clubs.

NIGHTLIFE

In Guanajuato, **La Copa** (Sopena, Col. Centro, tel: 473 732 2566, open Tue–Sat 10–late), a salsa bar across from Teatro Juárez, offers drinks, lessons and loud music – mostly salsa and merengue.

Zacatecas' unusual bar-nightclub, **La Malacate** (La Mina El Edén, Calle Antonio Dovalí, tel: 492 922 3002, open Thu–Sun 10am–2am) uses a space hewn straight from the rock in La Mina El Edén, hundreds of feet below the surface. It's popular so book in advance.

THEATER

In Guadalajara, the base for the university's famous Ballet Folklorico and the Guadalajara Philharmonic, the **Teatro Degollado** (Calle Degollado, tel: 33 3614 4773) is a working theater with regular music and drama productions. There's a ballet show at 10am most Sundays.

The stately **Teatro Juárez** (Sopena, Col. Centro, tel: 473 732 0183) is the principal host for Guanajuato's annual Cervantes Festival, one of Mexico's leading arts festivals, which takes place in October. Outside this time it hosts dance, theater and musical productions. You can book at the ticket office in the foyer and it's worth seeing a show just to enjoy the red velvet-trimmed seating and the painting of Constantinople over the stage.

Smaller than the Teatro Juárez, the **Teatro Cervantes** plays a major role in Guanajuato's annual Cervantes festival (you can see a statue of the Spanish writer's creations, Don Quixote and Sancho Panza, outside) while also putting on seasonal shows during the remainder of the year (Plaza Allende, tel: 473 732 1169).

THE OUTDOORS

Fly by the seat of your pants through the jungle treetops with the Puerto Vallarta outfitter **Canopy Tours** (tel: 322 223 0504, www.canopytours-vallarta.com). They use zip lines, strung from tree to tree, to swing visitors through parts of the jungle that normally birds only reach.

The Canopy Los Veranos eco-reserve is also a good place to go bird-watching and wildlife-spotting with the same operator.

Puerto Vallarta, surrounded by hills, jungle and beaches but not too far from civilization, is a great place to go mountain biking. **Ecoride** (Miramar 382, tel: 322 222 7991, www.ecoridemex.com) takes guests (mountain bikes can be provided) on one of several routes of varying difficulty and distance.

Central Mexico East

Getting Your Bearings

Combine the relaxed Caribbean pace of life with the forward-looking cities of Puebla and Xalapa, then add some awe-inspiring ancient ruins and charming mountain towns, and you get some idea how diverse this region of Mexico can be. Although its individual attractions stand up to others elsewhere in the country, it can seem like the east side of central Mexico has slipped off the radar.

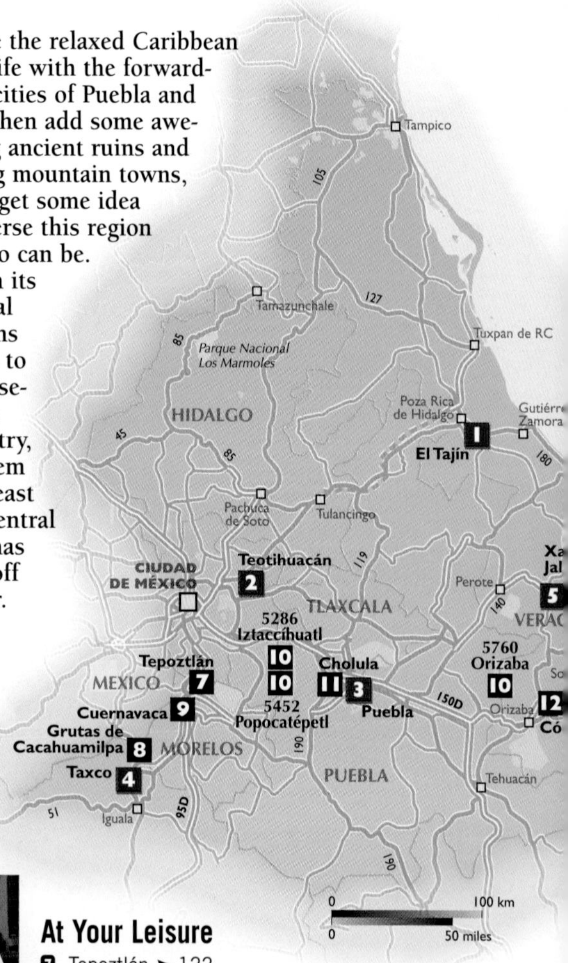

Getting ready to play

Tampico

Tamazunchale 127

Parque Nacional Los Marmoles

HIDALGO

Poza Rica de Hidalgo

Tuxpan de RC

Gutiérre Zamora

El Tajín **1**

Pachuca de Soto

Tulancingo

CIUDAD DE MÉXICO

Teotihuacán **2**

TLAXCALA

Perote

Xa Jal **5**

VERAC

5286 Iztaccíhuatl

Tepoztlán **7**

Cholula **11**

10
10

5760 Orizaba **10**

So

MEXICO

Cuernavaca **9**

5452 Popocatépetl

Puebla

Orizaba

12

Grutas de Cacahuamilpa **8**

MORELOS

Có

Taxco **4**

PUEBLA

Tehuacán

Iguala

0   100 km
0   50 miles

At Your Leisure

★ Don't Miss

**Popocatépetl
is off limits
while seismic
activity
continues**

El Tajín, to the north, is a mysterious, enchanting Totonac
ruin whose jungle-surrounded temples contrast with the wide
open expanses of Teotihuacán, a similarly unexplained ruin
close to Mexico City. The two most dynamic cities in the
region are the university city of Xalapa (Jalapa) and the
colonial gem of Puebla. Xalapa lies close to the Caribbean
coast and if you continue south you'll reach the tropical port
of Veracruz, a lively, music-filled city. South of here, Veracruz
state becomes enveloped in steamy, lowland jungles.

Returning inland, the terrain rises up to the central Sierra
Madre Oriental mountain range and site of an important
Mexican triumph over colonial forces at Puebla. Although
this historic city is surrounded by modern, industrial
suburbs, its colonial heart satisfies most senses, with
gorgeous sights and delicious local specialty dishes.

To the southwest of Mexico City, in the far west of
the region, Taxco is the quintessential colonial
mountain town, with an enticing tradition
of silver-smithing for those interested
in buying jewelry.

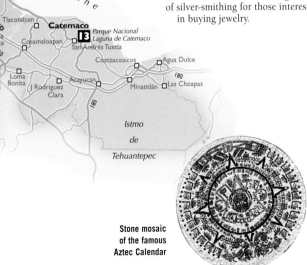

**Stone mosaic
of the famous
Aztec Calendar**

Tropical ports, historic cities and ancient ruins; in five days you can get a taste of eastern central Mexico and its distinctive culinary and cultural background. And if you have time, stop at the volcanoes of Orizaba for a glimpse of the fiery geology of the region.

Central Mexico East in Five Days

Day One

Set off as early as possible from Mexico City for a day trip to **2 Teotihuacán** (► 114–115; detail of painted wall above), a pre-Hispanic capital of Mexico. There's a café at the Aztec site with cold drinks, coffee and snacks, or bring a packed lunch from your hotel. A tour of the site should take up to half a day, allowing you to return to Mexico City for an early night (► 55–57 for restaurants in the capital).

Day Two

It's an early start: take a flight to **5 Xalapa** (► 119) from Mexico City (Aeroméxico flies direct). A day in Xalapa (Jalapa) will give you enough time to savor the university town's excellent museums (Olmec figure left) and sophisticated social scene. There is a wide range of cafés and restaurants to choose from; one of the best is La Casona del Beaterio on Zaragoza (► 127). Overnight in Xalapa.

Day Three

Head south by bus or rent car to **6 Veracruz** (➤ 120–121), the tropical port with a distinctly Caribbean attitude to life. Have a light lunch and a pick-me-up at the Gran Café del Portal (➤ 127) and dinner at the grand Hotel Mocambo (➤ 127). Stay overnight in the town.

Day Four

Start the journey back to Mexico City via the coffee-producing town of **12 Córdoba** (➤ 124), the volcanic national park of **10 Orizaba** (➤ 123) and the majestic colonial city of **8 Puebla** (➤ 116–117). There's a smooth, four-hour bus service direct to Puebla from Veracruz on toll roads if you want to head straight for the historic city. If you take the bus straight to Puebla, you will be able to buy snacks at the intermediate bus stops. If you stop at Córdoba, try one of the restaurants on Avenida 1 in the town center.

Day Five

Spend the day in Puebla exploring the beautiful colonial heart of this historically important city; it's a photographer's paradise with its fabulous Talavera-tiled buildings (above). Puebla is famous for its food, with several regional specialties and many excellent restaurants, one of the most famous being the Fonda de Santa Clara on Calle 3 (right; ➤ 126). You can return to Mexico City from Puebla; alternatively the modern city is a useful transportation hub for flights elsewhere in Mexico.

El Tajín

The most elaborate ruins on the Gulf coast, El Tajín was the center of the Totonacs' world. Like the Mayan sites to the south, the ruins display a knowledge of astronomy and an interest in human sacrifice.

Although the peak of Totonac civilization at El Tajín came at about AD 600, the pre-Columbian site is thought to date from 500 years earlier. It lay undiscovered in jungle until 1785, although the first archaeologists didn't arrive until the 1940s. El Tajín remains only partially recovered from the jungle, but that just adds to the mystique surrounding the place.

There are several pyramids around the clearing (the entire settlement would have covered 1,050ha/2,595 acres), the most interesting of which is the 18m-high (60-foot) **Pirámide de los Niches**. The 365 niches on the exterior correspond to the number of days in a year – but the reason why is still unknown. Perhaps an offering may have been placed in a different niche every day. At the top of the pyramid engraved panels on a temple show a cacao plant, an important crop for the Totonacs.

As well as cocoa beans, the Totonacs also liked sport: alongside the Pirámide de los Niches is one of the largest of the 17 ball courts on the site, **Juega de Pelote Sur** (Southern Ball Court). Engraved panels around the edge of the court give an exciting insight into the rules and rituals of the game.

The Voladores (Flying Men of Papantla) demonstrate an ancient Totonac ritual

One image of a decapitated player standing next to Mictlantecuhtli, the god of death, suggests that human sacrifice formed part of the post-match commiserations for the losing team. You can see a statue of Tajín, the god of thunder, on the east side of the ball court.

While the Southern Ball Court and the Pirámide de los Niches appear to be the ceremonial and spiritual heart of the city, the administrative area of the city, **El Tajín Chico**, lies to the north. It is thought that this is where the city's ruling elite lived in their palaces. Even further from the Pirámide de los Niches, the **Plaza de las Columnas** is a restricted-access area of delicately carved columns. South of the Pirámide de los Niches the **Plaza del Arroyo** is one of the oldest parts of El Tajín and consists of four crumbling pyramids around a grassy square.

El Tajín is also famous for its flying dancers, the *Voladores*. These acrobats swirl, upside down, around a pole in a re-creation of a Totonac ritual. There are daily shows by the entrance of El Tajín, and you can also seem them in flight at the Bosque de Chapultepec (► 38–39) in Mexico City.

Top: The Pyramid of the Niches

When visiting El Tajín try to base yourself in the traditional town of **Papantla**, a short drive to the south. There are regular buses and tours to El Tajín from Papantla.

Above: Detail of a Totonac carving

TAKING A BREAK

There's a restaurant in the visitor center and museum at the entrance, but you can also buy snacks and bottled water from **vendors** in the **parking lot**.

➕ 207 D4
✉ Off Highway 180 🕐 Daily 8–6 💰 Inexpensive

EL TAJÍN: INSIDE INFO

Top tips Take some **change** for the **Voladores performance** – US$2 (MEX$20) will be enough.
• **Arrive at 8am**, when the gates open, to make the most of the cooler temperatures. There is very **little shade on the site**.

One to miss Avoid staying in the closest town, Poza Rica. **Papantla** is a much **better place** to spend the night.

2 Teotihuacán

The colossal ruins of Teotihuacán are perhaps the most breathtaking in all of Mexico. The capital of the pre-Hispanic Mexican empire, the city was peopled by a mysterious culture that had vanished by AD 800, leaving behind this marvel.

The scale of the ruins at Teotihuacán is staggering – the tallest structure on the site, the Pyramid of the Sun, is the third largest pyramid in the world, at 65m (213 feet) high. It was named Teotihuacán, meaning "the place where men become gods," by the Aztecs. The site is based around the broad 4km (2.5-mile) **Avenida de los Muertos** (Avenue of the Dead) and the whole layout is carefully aligned to the points of the compass, again perhaps for ceremonial reasons.

Right: View across the site from the Pyramid of the Moon

At the northern end of this avenue is the **Pirámide de la Luna** (Pyramid of the Moon), which is smaller and easier to climb. Several mass burial sites and tunnels have been excavated in the heart of the pyramid, which are thought to be the result of human sacrifice. Close to the Pyramid of the Moon, on the west side of the Plaza de la Luna, is the **Palacio**

de Quetzalpapálotl (Palace of the Precious Butterfly) where the priests who may have perfomed these sacrifices lived. The palace's columns are decorated with carvings of the quetzal bird, and there are detailed murals depicting animals in the adjoining **Palacio de los Jaguares** (Palace of the Jaguars). Continue through this palace to a temple decorated with carvings of parrots, flowers and shells. The onsite **Museo de la Pintura Mural Teotihuacana**, behind Gate 3, provides background on the murals, carvings and paintings discovered here.

Midway down the Avenida de los Muertos is the **Pirámide del Sol** (Pyramid of the Sun). Its base measures 215m by 215m (705 feet by 705 feet) and it was designed in four stepped platforms in AD 200, pre-dating the great Mayan pyramids of the Yucatán. Where Mayan pyramids used stone, the Pyramid of the Sun is built from adobe blocks and earth, then covered with a painted stucco. If you cross the peripheral path behind the Pyramid of the Sun you will find the reconstructed **Palacio de Tepantitla**. The brilliantly restored frescoes inside give a fascinating insight into life in Teotihuacán, depicting priests in headdresses, ball games and animals.

Top right and above: Wall markings and carving on the Palace of the Precious Butterfly

Back on the Avenida de los Muertos, the south end of the avenue brings you to La Ciudadela, a vast square plaza dominated by the **Templo de Quetzalcóatl** on its eastern flank. It

is thought that Teotihuacán's ruler resided in this citadel. There are represen-
tations of the rain god Tlaloc and the plumed serpent Quetzalcóatl inside
the temple. La Ciudadela is adjacent to Gate 1, while Gate 2 is opposite the
Pyramid of the Sun and Gate 3 enters the site at the north end of the avenue.

TAKING A BREAK

There's a **café** on site with snacks and bottled drinks.

+ 206 C4
⊠ 30 miles (50km) northeast of Mexico City **🕐** Daily 7–6 **👋** Inexpensive; moderate with
camera permit. Onsite museum: free

TEOTIHUACÁN: INSIDE INFO

Top tip Most people visit the site as a **day trip** from Mexico City (a bus journey
from Mexico City's Terminal Norte takes one hour direct to Los Pirámides).

Hidden gem Ask to be **guided to the palaces** that lie beyond the perimeter
fence. These include the **Palace of Tepantitla**, which is filled with murals, and
the **palaces of Tetitla and Atetelco**, both also displaying wonderful Aztec art.

3 Puebla

Puebla has a superb historic core that sparkles with the city's signature Talavera tiles. After exploring its many churches, try some of the fantastic regional cooking in the city's restaurants.

The colonial city of Puebla has always been an important trading stop. Its colonial heart is decorated in the cobalt blue and sunny yellow Talavera tiles for which the city is famous. They're used on exteriors, such as the domes of the city's countless churches, and in interior designs. Puebla is also renowned for its culinary inventions, in particular *chiles en nogada* and the *mole poblano* sauce (➤ 126), variations of which are served by almost every restaurant in the city.

Don't be put off by the modern outskirts; any exploration of the Centro Histórico will be steeped in the city's Spanish heritage, beginning with the grand *zócalo*. Brooding over the paved plaza, Puebla's huge cathedral doesn't inspire from the outside, but its interior, with marble floors and gold-leaf altar, is much more exciting. Bishop Juan de Palafox y Mendoza, who contributed his own money towards the cathedral's construction, which began in 1575, also founded the library next door. In the Casa de la Cultura, which incorporates the Biblioteca Palafoxiana (Tue–Sun 10–4:30), you can catch concerts and art exhibitions.

The **Museo Amparo**, two blocks south of the *zócalo*, boasts one of Mexico's finest collections of pre-Hispanic art, distributed across two colonial buildings. The first portion of the collection offers a taste of the Mesoamerican cultures that thrived before the arrival of the Spanish: Olmecs, Mayans and Totonacs. The second half of the museum is the counterpoint: it draws together colonial art and furniture from after the Spanish conquest of Mexico.

Above:
Decorated pots and plates for sale

Left: The inside of the Rosary Chapel (Capilla del Rosario) is a riot of gilded and carved stucco

Left: Balcony showing Puebla's famous Talavera tiles

Other notable museums include the Museo José Luis Bello on Zetina Gonzalez, with its collection of 16th- to 18th-century Talavera tiles. The Museo de Santa Monica on Avenida 18 is housed in a former 17th-century convent where nuns were hidden after the Reform law of 1857 outlawed them.

Many of the city's 60 or more churches are decorated with Talavera tiles. Two of the finest are the church of San Cristóbal on Calle 4 Norte and Calle 6 Oriente, which has a Churrigueresque (baroque) exterior, and the 18th-century church of San José on Calle 2 Norte and Calle 18 Oriente, which has a beautifully tiled exterior and extravgant altar-pieces inside. On Calle 5 de Mayo, the church of Santo Domigo is noted for its outstanding Capilla del Rosario (Rosary Chapel). The inside of the chapel's dome is a breath-taking display of gold leaf, painting and sculpture.

TAKING A BREAK

Take a break with some of the strong coffees from the cafés and restaurants around the *zócalo*; try **La Princesa**.

✚ 206 C3
Tourist Information
✉ 5 Oriente 3 ☎ 222 777 1519 🕐 Mon–Sat 10–7, Sun 10–1

Below: The Rosary Chapel of the Church of Santo Domingo

Museo Amparo
✉ Calle 2 Sur, 708 ☎ 222 229 3850; www.museoamparo.com
🕐 Wed–Mon 10–6 💲 Inexpensive

PUEBLA: INSIDE INFO

Top tips The **State Tourist Office** offers private tours of the historic center.
• Foodies can also take **lessons in cooking** the perfect *mole poblano* at Mesón Sacristía de la Compañía hotel (6 Sur 304, tel: 222 232 4513).

4 Taxco

Take a day to explore Taxco, one of Mexico's most appealing colonial towns. Built on the profits of silver mining, it is an excellent place in which to buy silver jewelry.

Southwest of Mexico City, on the road to Acapulco, Taxco has been largely unaffected by its increasing popularity. It has a charming colonial center, with whitewashed houses and cobbled streets, and a glorious church, the Iglesia de Santa Prisca. And the silver tradition is still strong here, with numerous shops selling jewelry in traditional designs. But most of all, it's an enjoyable place to explore on foot for a day.

It was Frenchman José de la Borda who put Taxco on the map after discovering a fabulously rich vein of silver in the 18th century. He funded the construction of Taxco's church, the Iglesia de Santa Prisca, on the town's central *zócalo*, from the local pinkish stone. The 18th-cenutry church's facade is a Churrigueresque (baroque) masterpiece, with carved figures around its two towers and a large, tiled dome. On the north side of the *zócalo*, named Plaza Borda, the whitewashed Casa Borda was also built by the French family and hosts art exhibitions by local artists. Behind the church, on Delgado, the Museo Guillermo Spratling is a large museum holding a personal collection of pre-Hispanic objects assembled by the American architect William Spratling. He nurtured the town's silver traditions back to life in the early 20th century by opening a jewelry workshop. Adjacent to his museum, the Museo del Arte Virreinal concentrates on religious art.

Taxco's rose-colored Iglesia de Santa Prisca, with its two towers, stands out in the town

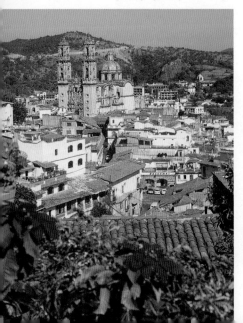

Continue east to the cable car station. Taxco is spread over several hilltops in the Sierra Madre, and the *teleférico* over town gives a bird's-eye view of Taxco as it ascends to the Hotel Monte Taxco from Los Arcos.

TAKING A BREAK

Join other travelers at **Café Sasha**, a friendly place in the center of town (► 126–127).

✚ 206 B3
Tourist Information
✉ Avenida de los Plateros 126
☎ 762 622 6616;
www.guerrero.gob.mx
🕐 Mon–Fri 8–3, Sat 9–11am

⑤ Xalapa

The state capital of Veracruz is a smart, dynamic city but it retains a charming atmosphere. Its leading attraction is the superb Museo de Antropología.

Xalapa (Jalapa) lies in a mountainous but temperate area of inland Veracruz, between the coast and the Parque Nacional Cofre de Perote, a national park based around the 4,282m (14,049-foot) peak of the same name. But Xalapa isn't overwhelmed by its imposing natural surroundings – far from it. The city, built on a hillside, is dominated by the University of Veracruz, which has ensured that Xalapa has museums, cultural attractions and a social life that lives up to anywhere else in Mexico. There's a thriving student culture amid the colonial courtyards and fragrant gardens watered by the high annual rainfall – watch out for late afternoon downpours. Parque Juárez takes prime position in the heart of the city and has an arts center, El Agora, and a museum, Pinacoteca Diego Rivera, with a siginificant collection of the artist's work. You can enjoy more art in the Palacio de Gobierno to the east of the park. However, for the unmissable Museo de Antropologia you will need to travel north on the road out of town.

Housed in a modern building, the **Museo de Antropología** has exhibits on Veracruz's history, from the Totonac founders of the city to the Aztec warlords of the 15th century via the Olmecs. The items from the Olmec period form the backbone of the museum. They include some remarkable stone heads, carved from basalt and standing almost 3m (10 feet) high and 1.5m (5 feet) wide. There is also some beautiful jewelry, statues and decorated pottery. Look for El Senor de las Limas, the statue of a priest holding a lifeless child.

Xalapa is a cultural hotbed of activity, with a well-regarded modern art gallery, Galeria de Arte Contemporáneo on Xalapenos Illustres, but it's also a good base for trying some of the adventure activities of the region, such as whitewater rafting on the surging rivers of Veracruz (► 128).

TAKING A BREAK

The museum has a **café**, but you might like to bring a packed lunch to eat in the surrounding parkland.

Above: Two of the giant Olmec heads in the Museo de Antropología

✚ 207 D4
Tourist Information
✉ Boulevard Cristóbal Colon 5
☎ 228 812 8500
🕙 Mon–Sat 9–5, Sun 10–2

Museo de Antropología
✉ Avenida Xalapa
☎ 228 815 0920; www.uv.mx/max/
🕙 Tue–Sun 9–5 💷 Inexpensive

⑥ Veracruz

Steamy, swinging Veracruz has a zest for life that is simply intoxicating. This lively port is where Caribbean marimba meets Mexican *mariachi* and the whole town bounces to the rhythms.

In Veracruz, February means only one thing: Carnaval. The port is where Catholic Mexico is infused with extrovert Caribbean culture and during the annual Carnaval costumed dancers invade the streets to celebrate their good fortune. However, Veracruz hasn't always had such good fortune. The town, looking out into the scalloped Gulf of Mexico, was close to where Hernán Cortés first set foot on Mexico, some 25km (16 miles) to the north at La Antigua. After the Spanish had established themselves here, Veracruz was the site for centuries of occupations, battles and pirate raids.

Today, the city is much more relaxed. The action is centered on the Plaza de Armas, the city's vibrant, colonnaded *zócalo* in the old town to the north of the main city. Scattered with palm trees and iron lampposts and benches, it's where Veracruz's *jarochos* (locals) watch the world go by. The Palacio Municipal and 18th-century cathedral face each other across the plaza's corner.

Another place to see and be seen, especially in the evening, is the Paseo del Malecón (seafront), reached by walking from the *zócalo* down Zamora. Although the city's beaches are not worth much attention, you can take boat tours of the harbor from the *malecón*. A couple of blocks in from the seafront, the **Museo Histórico Naval** chronicles Veracruz's varied fortunes over the centuries. Just around the corner on Zaragoza, the

Right: Playing outside a bar in the Plaza de Armas

Bottom left: The Cathedral, on Plaza de Armas

Bottom right: The *Marigalante*, a replica of Christopher Columbus's flagship, the *Santa María*

Museo de la Ciudad offers a more rounded view of the city's history. The principal historical attraction is what remains of the city's fortifications, the fort of San Juan de Ulúa, north of the city center on a promontory across the harbor. You can take a guided tour of the dungeons, moat and ramparts and see where the Spanish made their final stand in Mexico in 1825.

Veracruz's second stand-out sight is the **Acuario de Veracruz**, the city's aquarium, probably the best in Latin America. As well as thousands of species of fish, the creatures on view include sea turtles and manatees. There are interactive exhibits where children can touch the fish.

TAKING A BREAK

The seafood restaurants on the road south to Boca del Rio are worth the trip; **La Fragata** restaurant at the Hotel Mocambo is especially good (➤ 127).

✚ 207 E3
Tourist Information
✉ Palacio Municipal, Plaza de Armas
☎ 229 989 8817;
www.veracruz-puerto.gob.mx/turismo/
🕐 Mon–Fri 8–8, Sat–Sun 10–6

Museo Histórico Naval
✉ Arista 418
☎ 229 931 4078 🕐 Tue–Sun 9–5 💲 Free

Museo de la Ciudad
✉ Avenida Zaragoza 39
☎ 229 931 8410
🕐 Tue–Sun 10–6 💲 Inexpensive

Acuario de Veracruz
✉ Boulevard Manuel Avilá Camacho
☎ 229 932 7984;
www.acuariodeveracruz.com 🕐 Mon–Thu 10–7,
Fri–Sun 10–7:30 💲 Moderate

VERACRUZ: INSIDE INFO

Top tip Don't bother dipping your toes in the sea at the city's beaches – they're relatively dirty. The further south you go, however, **the cleaner the beaches get.**

At Your Leisure

7 Tepoztlán

A short bus ride from Mexico City, Tepoztlán is taking over from nearby Cuernavaca as a peaceful, scenic retreat from the capital. The upwardly mobile town, with new shops and restaurants opening all the time, is the sacred birthplace of the Aztec serpent god Quetzalcóatl and many of the traditions and rituals associated with the Aztecs have been retained, despite an increasingly New Age presence in the town. The town's craft market, in the *zócalo*, is generally very good. The small Tepozteco pyramid perches high up on a hilltop overlooking the town and takes a moderate effort to reach on foot. Tepoztlán is surrounded by the rugged crags and cliffs of the Parque Nacional El Tepozteco and the views from the pyramid are superb.

➕ 206 C3
www.tepoz.com.mx

Tepoztlán craft market

8 Grutas de Cacahuamilpa

These caverns are some of the most spectacular in Mexico. They can be reached on a day trip from Taxco's Futura bus terminal and a guide is required to tour the caves; there's an illuminated 2km (1.2-mile) circuit, although only a fraction of the network is open to the public. The highest chambers soar 70m (230 feet) above visitors, and the stalactmites and stalagmites are up to 75 million years old. It makes an interesting day out for the family.

➕ 206 B3
✉ 30km (19 miles) northeast of Taxco
🕐 Daily 10–5 💰 Inexpensive

9 Cuernavaca

Sunny Cuernavaca is where Mexico City's residents come when they need to get away from their city's high-pressured life. South of the capital, the city is rich in history, as it was also used as a relaxing retreat by the Aztec rulers. The arrival of the Spanish in 1521 turned the city into a regional trading center, but first Cortés demolished the city's Aztec pyramid and built the Palacio de Cortés on the east side of the pretty *zócalo*. The palace houses several murals by Diego Rivera and a museum detailing the history of the area. More work by Rivera and other leading Mexican artists can be viewed at the **Museo Robert Brady**. Next to the museum, Cuernavaca's cathedral resembles a fortress rather than a place of worship. It was built in the 1520s shortly

Dining out in Córdoba

Tunnels totalling some 8km (5 miles) in length have been excavated from inside the pyramid, which has a vast base 450m by 450m (1,475 feet by 1,475 feet). It is thought to have been dedicated to the god Quetzalcóatl. Modern Cholula has a large *zócalo*, with the imposing Franciscan convent of San Gabriel on one side and plenty of restaurants and cafés to try.

✚ 206 C3
Tourist Information
✉ Calle 12 Oriente and Avenida 4 Norte
☎ 222 261 2393; www.puebla.com.mx
🕐 Mon–Fri 9–7, Sat–Sun 9–2
🚌 Frequent buses from Puebla (30 mins)

12 Córdoba

The colonial city of Córdoba lies on the main highway (150) between

Veracruz and Puebla and is a good stopping point if you are driving. Although the city has morphed into a modern Mexican town, a flavor of its colonial past can still be had at the Plaza de Armas in the old town. Try some of the rich coffee at one of the square's cafés, brewed from beans grown in the local highlands. On the north side of the plaza, the Portal de Zevello is where the last Spanish viceroy, Don Juan O'Donojú, signed the Treaty of Córdoba with General Iturbide in 1821, recognizing Mexican independence.

✚ 207 D3
✉ Palacio Municipal ☎ 271 717 1700; www.cordoba.com.mx
🕐 Mon–Fri 8–7, Sat–Sun 10–2

13 Catemaco

Blessed with an idyllic lake, Catemaco relies on fishing and tourism for income, although it has a quirky sideline in witchcraft and spiritualism if the first two fail. The town's lake is the main reason for making the 4-hour bus journey from Veracruz – you can take boat trips on the lake, spotting macaque monkeys (imported from Thailand) and a variety of colorful birdlife in the lush forest on the lake shore. Catemaco is also a place of pilgrimage for Mexico's *brujos* (shamans), many of whom live and work in the area.

✚ 207 E3
✉ North side of the *zócalo* ☎ 294 943 0016; www.catemaco.com.mx
🕐 Mon–Fri 9–3, 6–9

Tourist boats tied up along the shores of Lake Catemaco

Where to... Stay

Prices
Expect to pay for a double room per night:
$ under US$50 | $$ US$50–150 | $$$ over US$150

CUERNAVACA

Las Mañanitas $$–$$$

This colonial-style inn lies in immaculately landscaped grounds with luxuriant tropical gardens, ponds and a waterfall, and is an excellent place to get away from it all. The airy suites have antique furnishings and paintings by some of Mexico's finest artists, and some also have fireplaces and large terraces. The restaurant has won awards for its innovative regional cuisine, featuring *sopa de tortilla* and chicken in *mole verde*.

📍 206 C3 🖂 Ricardo Linares 107, Col. Centro ☎ 777 314 1466; www.lasmananitas.com.mx

PUEBLA

Camino Real Puebla $$$

The Camino Real Puebla occupies the 16th-century former convent of La Concepción, which has been carefully and beautifully restored, and lies just one block from the *zócalo*. The hotel's 84 rooms are individually decorated and retain some of the building's original features, enhanced by the understated style of furnishing. Facilities include office services and an elegant restaurant, El Convento, which is noted for its excellent brunch buffet, as well as its fine international and Mexican dishes.

📍 206 C3 🖂 7 Poniente 105, Histórico Centro ☎ 222 229 0909; www.caminoreal.com/puebla/

Hotel del Portal $$

The beautiful, colonial-style Hotel del Portal is situated right on the central *zócalo* in the historic heart of Puebla, and is popular with both vacationers and businesspeople. All the rooms are tastefully furnished and decorated, and the hotel's restaurant/bar, La Taberna, offers snacks and fast-food throughout the day. Children under the age of 12 can stay in the room with their parents free.

📍 206 C3 🖂 Juan de Palafox y Mendoza 205 ☎ 222 246 0211

TEPOZTLÁN

Posada del Tepozteco $$

One of the loveliest places to stay in Morelos state, the Posada del Tepozteco is in a beautifully renovated colonial hacienda, one block from downtown, west of the main plaza, with lush gardens, terraces and superb views over the nearby Tepozteco National Park. Many of the large, comfortable rooms have a private terrace and Jacuzzi, and the restaurant is great for alfresco dining.

📍 206 C3 🖂 Paraíso 3, Barrio San Miguel ☎ 739 395 0010; www.posadadeltepozteco.com.mx

VERACRUZ

Hotel Veracruz Calinda $$

The Veracruz Calinda lies in the historic heart of the city, across the main square from the cathedral. It offers a blend of elegant accommodations and modern facilities, with a restaurant and a rooftop swimming pool, and is within walking distance of many of the city's restaurants, boutiques and nightclubs.

📍 207 E3 🖂 Avenida Independencia s/n, Esquina Miguel Lerdo ☎ 229 989 3800

Where to...
Eat and Drink

Prices

Expect to pay per person for a meal, excluding drinks:
$ under US$10 **$$** US$10–20 **$$$** over US$20

On the coast of Veracruz there is a distinctive Caribbean edge to the dishes, with spicy specialties such as *huachinango a la veracruzana* (red snapper in hot tomato sauce) and *ceviche* (fish marinated in lime). Venture inland to Puebla and the flavors become heavier and richer, with the *chiles en nogada*, large but mild *poblano chiles* stuffed with a fruity meat mix, and the city's famous *mole poblano* sauce, flavored with garlic, chili and chocolate and served with meat and dishes such as enchiladas. You'll find that most restaurants serve some sort of *mole poblano*. Other towns have their own particular quirks: Xalapa, surrounded by coffee-growing hillsides, is the place to sample some fine coffee, while Taxco's local delicacy is *jumiles*, a small beetle seasoned with garlic and chilli and rolled in tortillas.

CUERNEVACA

Gaia $$

Once home of the famous comic actor Mario Moreno (otherwise known as "Cantinflas"), the colonial house has been stripped and recast as a Nuevo Mexican restaurant. The surroundings couldn't be more stylish, from the minimalist, white-washed, candlelit dining room to the swimming pool in the garden, illuminated so that Diego Rivera's mosaic of the Greek goddess Gaia on the bottom tempts you to dive in.

➕ 206 C3 ⊠ Juárez 102 ☎ 777 312 3656 ⊙ Mon–Sat 1pm–late, Sun 1–8pm

PUEBLA

Fonda de Santa Clara $$

Try some of the local dishes at this famous Pueblan taverna-style restaurant. This branch, in the Centro Historico, has a bright interior with pretty arches and wood furniture. House specialties include various themes on the *mole* sauce, including *mole poblano* with chicken, but also introduces *tinga poblano*, a local recipe of shredded pork. The Fonda de Santa Clare is a family-friendly place and there are snacks, soups and salads for those with smaller appetites.

➕ 206 C3 ⊠ Calle 3 Poniente 307 ☎ 222 242 2659; www.fondadesantaclara.com ⊙ Daily 8am–10pm

TAXCO

Café Sasha $

This funky little café, on the first floor of a colonial building opposite the Hotel Los Arcos, was started by travelers Sasha and Javier in 1999 and has earned its place at the heart of Taxco's social scene. It's a great place to meet locals and visitors as you enjoy a light meal (pasta, pizza, salads, vegetarian dishes and Mexican snacks are served) or an espresso among the artworks and potted plants. The service is informal but attentive, and the breakfast is excellent.

Where to...
Shop

The shopping highlight of this region is clearly Taxco and its countless silver shops. The town, where silver nuggets remain a viable currency, was the birthplace of Mexico's Silver Renaissance, but the era of individual, skilled artisans crafting handmade pieces is coming to an end. Instead, it's a case of buyer beware if you are hunting for a unique work of art because many of the shops in Taxco now stock identical, mass-produced pieces of jewelry. Yes, the prices are favorable, but for a truly special piece of silver-smithing you should expect to pay more. Fortunately there are a few names intent on preserving Taxco's silversmithing tradition: Antonio Pineda, Emilia Castillo and the

dine out in the sprawling tropical gardens surrounded by native palms. The views of the Tepozteco mountains are superb.

➕ 206 B3 ✉ Calle Juan Ruiz de Alarcón 1 ☎ 762 628 5150; www.cafesasha.com 🅖 Daily 8am–midnight

TEOTIHUACÁN

🍷🍷 Restaurant La Gruta $$

La Gruta (The Cave) occupies an immense cave right next to the pyramids. Sunlight filters in through the roof adding to the magical atmosphere. In this unique setting you can dine on traditional Mexican food, prepared using the freshest regional ingredients.

➕ 206 C4 ✉ Zona Arqueologica de Teotihuacan s/n, outside Gate 5 ☎ 594 956 0104; www.lagruta.com.mx 🅖 Daily 11–7

TEPOZTLÁN

🍷🍷 Axitla $$

Axitla has an excellent reputation for its food and setting. Choose from the menu of Mexican gourmet delicacies and American dishes and

place from which to survey the action on the *zócalo*. Sometimes the action will find you, in the form of *mariachi* players. Good food, ranging from sweet pastries and snacks to Veracruz specialties, and excellent coffee make this a popular lunch spot with the white-jacketed waiters flurrying to serve people.

➕ 206 C3 ✉ Avenida del Tepozteco ☎ 739 395 0519 🅖 Wed–Sun 10–7

VERACRUZ

La Fragata $$

Veracruz is famed for its Caribbean-flavored food and nowhere does it better than La Fragata in the grand Hotel Mocambo, an 8km (5-mile) drive south on the coast road. There's a seafaring theme at work in the dining room, appropriately enough as the chef specializes in seafood. There are also international dishes on the menu.

➕ 207 E3 ✉ Hotel Mocambo, Boulevard Ruiz Cortines 4000 ☎ 229 992 0200; www.hotelmocambo.com.mx 🅖 Daily 1–3, 7–10

Gran Café del Portal $

In a prime position opposite the cathedral, the Gran Café is the best

XALAPA

La Casona del Beaterio $$

La Casona's locally inspired dishes are among the best in town, with breakfast, lunch and dinner offering good value. There are also pasta and pancakes, if you're not ready for the chili-infused fish stew. If it's just a coffee you're after, you'll be spoiled for choice ny the wide selection of varieties.

➕ 207 D4 ✉ Zaragoza 20 ☎ 228 818 2119 🅖 Daily 8am–11pm

descendents of William Spratling, the American who rekindled Taxco's silver trade in the 1930s. Designs range from the delicate to the chunky and many pieces have semi-precious stones set in them; there should be something in Taxco for every taste. It's just a question of sorting the special from the humdrum. It helps to recognize the three varieties of silver sold in Taxco: sterling (the finest, stamped with 0.925, representing its purity), plate and nickel (or alpaca).

SILVERWARE

In Taxco, the daughter of famed silversmith Antonio Castillo maintains the family tradition of producing fine, handcrafted silver jewelry, which is available from her shop, **Emilia Castillo** (Hotel Emilia Castillo, Juan Ruiz de Alarcón 7, tel: 762 622 3471/1396, www.hotelemiliacastillo.com).

Antonia Pineda, one of the most highly regarded jewelry designers of his generation, is nurturing young silversmiths at his studio, **Pineda's** (Munoz 1, tel: 762 622 3233), in the Patio de las Artesanias in central Taxco on Plaza Borda. In the same complex, there is a museum of silversmithing where you can see some of William Spratling's original pieces and the Aztec jewelry that still inspires many of Taxco's designers.

Silver may catch the eye, but the Talavera tradition of ceramics also produces some exceptionally beautiful examples of pottery. Get a taste for them at the **El Parián market** in Puebla at Calle 2 Oriente and Calle 6 Norte. There are good and bad pieces here so you'll quickly learn to tell the difference. Or visit the **Uriarte factory** in central Puebla, west of the zócalo, to see every stage of the pottery's production and buy from the excellent selection in the factory's outlet.

Where to...
Be Entertained

NIGHTLIFE AND THEATER

Many of central **Veracruz's** bars have a slightly seedy reputation – a legacy of its days as a Caribbean port – so use your discretion. You can let your hair down in the laid-back zócalo when the city's marimba musicians come out to perform in the evening. Nightclubs are also found along the coast road as far as Playa Mocambo. **Xalapa's** nightlife quarter is around the junction of Gutiérrez Zamora and Primo Verdad.

Teatro del Estado (Avenida M. Avila Camacho, Calle Ignacio de la Llave, tel: 228 818 0834), a large, modern venue in **Xalapa** with a capacity of 1,200, stages the region's best classical concerts (from, among

others, the Xalapa Symphony Orchestra) and drama.

Puebla's gorgeous, mustard-yellow Teatro Principal (Calle 6 Norte and Calle 8 Oriente, tel: 222 232 6085) is the oldest working theater on the continent and still stages ballet, drama, concerts and musicals. Turn up when there isn't a performance on (usually 10–5) to have a look around.

THE OUTDOORS

Veraventuras (Santos Degollado 81, Int. 8, Xalapa; tel: 228 818 9779/9579, www.veraventuras.com.mx), an experienced tour operator, takes first-time white-water rafters down some of **Xalapa's** raging rivers.

Southern Mexico

Getting Your Bearings

The farther south you go, the looser Mexico City's hold gets on the local government and the more independent towns and villages become, until you get to Chiapas, where a low-level guerrilla campaign has been waged since 1994. The Zapatistas, who began their uprising in San Cristóbal de las Casas, have been fighting for greater distribution of the region's wealth but, although armed, have preferred non-violent means of achieving their aims.

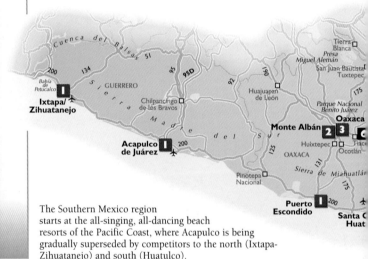

The Southern Mexico region starts at the all-singing, all-dancing beach resorts of the Pacific Coast, where Acapulco is being gradually superseded by competitors to the north (Ixtapa-Zihuatanejo) and south (Huatulco).

Behind the coastal paradise of sandy beaches, palm trees and reliable surf, the Sierra Madre de Sur rises up to the highlands. Oaxaca, surrounded by mountains, is an intoxicating UNESCO-protected state capital with colonial architecture, a fertile arts scene and excellent shopping.

Toward Guatemala are the states of Chiapas and Tabasco. The towns and villages here are home to some of Mexico's strongest indigenous Indian groups, who are keen to protect their identities. This is what makes mountain towns like San Cristóbal de las Casas such enthralling places. You could easily spend a week or longer here, exploring the villages and absorbing the local cultures. Palenque, the most magical of all the Mayan sites, lies deep in the jungle between San Cristóbal and the Yucatán.

The Mayan sites in Southern Mexico are less frequented than those of the Yucatán, but are no less interesting. Some of the attractions here are among the most remote in the country. Anticipate the extra time it will take to get around, expect an increased number of military checkpoints and plan in advance when visiting sites such as Yaxchilán, a Mayan site accessed by river. But give this region the time it deserves and you can find everything you need for a varied and relaxing trip.

Page 129: La Quebrada, Acapulco

Right: The beach at Huatulco

Left: Acapulco Bay
Below: Temple of the Foliated Cross, Palenque

Southern Mexico is a large, wild space characterized by
fewer roads than in the more developed north, so you are
more likely to fly between attractions than take the bus. This
has the advantage of avoiding some of the more risky roads,
such as Highway 199 between San Cristóbal de las Casas and
Palenque. It is also wise to travel during daylight hours.

Southern Mexico in Five Days

Day 1

Start from **7** **Villahermosa** (➤ 144),
the efficient if unattractive capital
of Tabasco state. **4** **Palenque** (right;
➤ 140–141), one of the
most thrilling Mayan sites, is just
two hours away by bus. Spend the
day exploring the jungle-covered
ruins of Palenque and stay
overnight in Palenque. Try Maya
(➤ 149) for dinner.

Day 2

Return to Villahermosa by bus and take a flight (scheduled daily)
to Oaxaca. **3** **Oaxaca** (➤ 138–139) is a fascinating city with a vibrant restaurant scene and
outlying villages, such as Tlacolula and
Santa Ana del Valle, that produce some of
Mexico's finest handicrafts. Stroll around
the center of Oaxaca, visit the Museo de
las Culturas (exhibit left) and spend
the evening sampling some of the
city's distinctive dishes. Stay
overnight in a city center hotel
(➤ 147).

Day 3

Rent a car and explore the surrounding area, with its craft markets,
rugged landscape and ancient ruins. Return to Oaxaca and spend another

night in the city. There are plenty of restaurants to choose from in and around the *zócalo* and on Avenida Alcalá.

Day 4

The flight from Oaxaca to the surfing hotspot of Puerto Escondido on the ❚ **Pacific Coast** (➤ 134–135), is one of the most dramatic in Mexico. In a small plane you will cross the mountainous Sierra Madre del Sur; try to get a window seat because the views are amazing.

Check into your hotel and spend the evening relaxing at one of the restaurants and bars towards the west end of the town's beach.

Day 5

❚ **Puerto Escondido** (above; ➤ 135) is renowned for its surf breaks and is a good place to try the sport for the first time. You can rent boards at several outfitters and take lessons if required. Although the waves at Playa Zicatela will challenge experienced surfers, quieter, sheltered spots can be found. After all the exercise, you'll want to try another of Puerto Escondido's restaurants; the town has a large Italian population, many of whom run eateries serving filling Italian food. From Puerto Escondido it is easy to return by air to Mexico City.

Acapulco and the Pacific Coast

A neon-lit beacon for hedonists since the 1950s, Acapulco can still set the pulse racing with its cliff-diving displays and frenetic nightlife. But the resort is facing competition from newer resorts on the surf-pounded Pacific coast.

Nighttime hides much of Acapulco's aging, pock-marked complexion and under the lights it is easier to imagine you are sauntering around the city of the 1950s and 1960s heyday, when the likes of Frank Sinatra, Cary Grant and Elizabeth Taylor sipped cocktails in the elegant bars. The city's bay has been welcoming holidaymakers since the 1920s, when the main road from Mexico City was opened, though it had always had an important role to play as the closest Pacific port to the capital. But the bay was clearly cut out for sun-worshippers in mind; its broad sweep is rimmed with golden sand and there are superb views from the balconies of Acapulco's high-rise hotels.

The famous cliff divers at La Quebrada, Acapulco

Beach life is centered on Hornos, Hornitos, Condesa and, on the eastern flank of the bay, Icacos. Here, a waterpark, nicknamed CiCi (Mon–Sun 10–6), has performing dolphins and sea lions. However, the most famous aquatic performances in Acapulco are delivered by the **cliff divers of La Quebrada**, a rocky promontory close to Playa Angosta, a small cove on the west side of the peninsula. The divers jump

Ixtapa's beautiful Playa del Palmar

off the cliffs during five shows plummeting around 40m (130 feet) through the air.

In recent years, some of Acapulco's luster has worn off. There have been problems with gangs in some of the urban areas (the main tourist areas are safe) and many visitors prefer to go to other Pacific beach resorts (see below) or to Cancún. That said, the dining scene in Acapulco remains strong and there are plenty of activities for families.

Ixtapa-Zihuatanejo

Ixtapa is a modern, efficient resort with amenities that you'll find at any upscale resort in the world. It backs a 2-mile (3km) strip of sand called Playa del Palmar on which the seafront hotels manage their own little sections. It's not the best beach for swimming, due to some strong currents – bathers should try Playa Cuachalalate on Isla Ixtapa to the north of Playa del Palmar, accessed by boat from Playa Linda.

For many visitors Ixtapa's contrasting companion Zihuatanejo is the better destination. This charming, laidback fishing village is 7km (4 miles) south of Ixtapa. The negative effects of tourism have yet to affect Zihuatanejo and it's a delightful place to while away a day or two, watching the fishermen bringing in their daily catches, and lazing among the palm trees on the broad, gently shelving beach.

Above: Boating in Puerto Escondido

Puerto Escondido

South of Acapulco, the "Hidden Port" has been a long-time favorite among Oaxaca's beaches with surfers and those seeking laidback beach bliss. The world-class surf spot has had more attention since the construction of the paved road from Acapulco, but it's still remains more of a backpacker haunt than mainstream resort. Playa Marinero is the town's principal beach but surfers will want to hit the waves of Playa Zicatela, to the west, which is served by numerous beach-side cafés. Fishing trips, surfing lessons and other activities are organized by a number of experienced local operators.

Left: Carlos 'n' Charlie's, Acapulco

TAKING A BREAK

The **Costera district**, behind Playa Condesa, is a hotspot for beachside dining, and the **Old Town** on the north side of the bay has some excellent local restaurants.

Huatulco

Farther south still from Puerto Escondido is the resort of Huatulco. The bay of **Tangolunda** is the centerpiece development; it's a slick operation with upscale restaurants, shops and nightlife. Beyond the urban core, golf courses and international resort hotels account for much of the leisure options available here. West of Tangolunda, Santa Cruz is a low-key reminder of the area's history – it was a port in the 16th century, although the only boats arriving these days are luxury motor yachts to the marina.

Bahía de Tangolunda, one of Huatulco's nine bays

🚹 206 B2
Tourist Information (Acapulco)
✉ Costera Miguel Alemán 38, Acapulco
☎ 744 484 8555;
www.visitacapulco.com.mx
🕐 Daily 8am–11pm

La Quebrada
💵 Inexpensive
❓ Dives take place daily (1pm, 7:15pm, 8:15pm, 9:15pm and 10:15pm)

🚹 207 D1
Tourist Information (Puerto Escondido)
✉ Benito Juárez, Puerto Escondido
☎ 954 582 0175
🕐 Mon–Fri 9–2, 4–6, Sat 9–2

🚹 207 E1
Tourist Information (Huatulco)
✉ Benito Juárez, Bahia de Tangolunda
☎ 958 581 0176;
www.baysofhuatulco.com.mx
🕐 Mon–Fri 9–5, Sat 9–1

ACAPULCO AND THE PACIFIC COAST: INSIDE INFO

Top tip If you're feeling inspired by Acapulco's famous cliff divers, think again. They make it look easy, but the 40m (130-foot) dives are a feat of timing as much as daring. Instead, thrill-seekers should have a go at the **bungee-jump on the beachfront** at Playa Condesa in the tourist zone (contact Hacket Bungy Paradise, tel: 744 484 7529).

2 Monte Albán

One of the earliest cities in Mesoamerica is also one of its most intriguing and spectacular; Monte Albán's ruined temples and buildings are an insight into the Zapotec empire, but they ask more questions than they answer.

The Zapotecs constructed vast, complex cities and ruled their territory until about AD 800. Monte Albán, west of Oaxaca, represents the pinnacle of their city-building skills. It's still impressive today, covering the mountain-top plateau with pyramids, buildings, temples and tombs. The highlight of the site is the Gran Plaza, which may have been used for ceremonies or military functions – the Zapotecs were ruthless warriors. The plaza has a palace, temple and ball court – as with the Mayans, it is thought that losing teams were sacrificed to the gods. Also on the Gran Plaza are 14 small structures that possibly correspond to 14 regional or ethnic groups, brought together at Monte Albán.

One of the most intriguing buildings is the Edificio de los Danzantes, the Building of the Dancers. It is decorated with carved images of dancing figures but the purpose of the building has not yet been understood.

After the decline of the Zapotecs, a process that began in AD 600, the site was used by the subsequent Mixtec empire for burial tombs. The museum and visitor center contain many items recovered from the site, including gold burial masks. There are more than 200 tombs, but Tomb 7 is the most eye-opening, containing a marvelous hoard of gold, jewelry and battle items, now in Oaxaca's Museo de las Culturas (➤ 139). Other tombs also yielded incredible collections, including a figure of the Zapotec rain god from Tomb 104.

TAKING A BREAK

The **café** in the museum complex serves snacks and lunches.

✚ 207 D2	🚌 Monte Albán is a 20-minute bus	The Zapotec
✉ 10km (6 miles) west of Oaxaca	or taxi journey from Oaxaca. The last	site of Monte
☎ 951 516 1215;	bus back leaves Monte Albán at 6pm	Albán, east
www.oaxaca.gob.mx	– you're not permitted to stay at the	of Oaxaca
🕐 Daily 8–6	site any later	

③ Oaxaca

With delicious local food, handicraft shops and delightful colonial plazas, Oaxaca is one of the most appealing state capitals in Mexico. It gives a warm welcome to visitors, who may find themselves reluctant to leave.

Oaxaca had a turbulent time in 2006. The city was taken over by protestors complaining about the state governor. They barricaded themselves into the center's plazas and university after confrontations with riot police. Tourists were never targeted by them, but most people gave Oaxaca a wide berth.

Oaxaca was an Aztec settlement until, under the Spanish, it evolved into the southern capital of Mexico. Two earthquakes (in 1854 and 1931) destroyed the city but it has returned to its colonial glory. It sits at an altitude of 1,550m (5,000 feet), giving it a temperate climate throughout the year, and its compact historic center is readily explored on foot. A rich arts tradition means that your visit may well coincide with a fiesta or arts festival, even if you don't plan in advance.

Start your tour of the city at the *zócalo*, the leafy square around which the rest of city revolves. It is surrounded by cafés and restaurants among the arches of the arcades. On the south side, the Palacio del Gobierno was the focus for the demonstrators' ire in 2006. On the opposite side, the 17th-century cathedral boasts an elaborate baroque facade. However, Oaxaca's finest

Left and below: Iglesia de Santo Domingo, the jewel of Oaxaca

religious building is the 16th-century **Iglesia de Santo Domingo**, four blocks north. The Franciscan church is one of the most admired examples of baroque architecture in the world; renovations in the 1950s revealed many of the church's most beautiful features, such as a bas relief illustrating the family of Santo Domingo, the monk who founded the church. Next to the church is its former monastery, now the **Museo de las Culturas**, an excellent museum detailing Oaxaca's history and where many of the items retrieved from Monte Albán (► 137) are exhibited. Part of the same complex, the Jardín Etnobotánico informs visitors about many of Mexico's indigenous plants. The orchids are a highlight.

To the west, the Basílica de la Soledad on Avenida Independencia is an imposing 17th-century structure, which contrasts with the delicacy of the interior where you can see a sculpture of the Virgin de la Soledad. The Virgin's crown was once composed of 600 diamonds, until they were stolen in the 1980s. Note the angels supporting the basilica's chandeliers.

Churches aside, perhaps the greatest pleasure is exploring the colonial gardens and squares of Oaxaca, browsing craft stalls in the marketplaces (many of the items are locally made in outlying villages) and absorbing Oaxaca through all your senses, not least taste: the city is famous for its *moles*, the rich, spicy sauces that come in a variety of flavors including chocolate.

Above: Jade and gold necklace from Monte Albán's Tomb 7 in the Museo de las Culturas

Left: Benito Juárez market is filled with Oaxacan crafts and food

TAKING A BREAK

There are several good restaurants and cafés around the central *zócalo* and **Avenida Alcalá**, to the north.

🚹 207 D2
Tourist Information
✉ Sedetur, Independencia 607
☎ 951 516 0717;
www.oaxaca.gob.mx 🕐 Daily 8–8

Iglesia de Santo Domingo
✉ Plaza Santo Domingo

☎ Macedonia Alcalá and Gurríon
🕐 Daily 7–1, 4–7:30

Museo de las Culturas
✉ Plaza Santo Domingo, Macedonia Alcalá and Gurríon
☎ 951 516 2991
🕐 Tue–Sun 10–6 💷 Inexpensive

OAXACA: INSIDE INFO

In more depth One of Mexico's most colorful and authentic festivals, the **Guelaguetza**, takes place in Oaxaca annually on two consecutive Mondays at the end of July. It dates from the Zapotec era and showcases music, dance and costumes from indigenous communities all around the city.

❹ Palenque

The most notable Mayan ruin outside the Yucatán, Palenque has fewer visitors, but packs just as powerful a punch in a tangled jungle as the better-known Mayan sites.

Perhaps it's the lower visitor numbers or the semi-wild state of the ruins, but many of Palenque's visitors report a sense of peace and tranquility as they explore the well-preserved site. It's vast, and in just one day you will have to consider carefully what to see. The most obvious highlights are around the Palacio, at the heart of the site, but Palenque covered 130sq km (50sq miles) in its height from AD 600 to AD 700, until it was abandoned in the 10th century. It was the regional capital of what it is now Chiapas and Tabasco.

The story of Palenque's rise to power is thought to be told in the thousands of glyphs scattered throughout the site. However, only a fraction of the cryptic carvings have been deciphered, although it is fairly clear that two rulers, Pakal the Great and his son Chan Bahlum, led the city upwards.

El Palacio, a complex and impressive building, was enlarged by Chan Bahlum's son, who built the Palacio's distinctive four-story tower. Astronomers would plot the movements of the planets from the tower's windows. Hundreds of years later, in the 1840s, American archaeologist John Lloyd Stephens and British architect Frederick Catherwood lived in the palace.

At the corner of the Palacio, the **Templo de las Inscripciones** has helped experts to understand Palenque, thanks to the carvings all over the pyramid. Some of the glyphs tell that Pakal was born in AD 603 and died in AD 684; he is buried in a chamber under the pyramid, itself an unusual feature. The burial chamber, discovered by Alberto Ruz Lhuillier in 1952, is decorated with several figures from Mayan mythology, while Pakal's bones had jade ornamentation. Three stone tablets contain details of Pakal's forebears, astronomical events and even predictions as far ahead as AD 4772. Pakal's burial chamber is reached by the temple at the apex of the pyramid's steps, but to enter the Templo de las Inscripciones you will need a permit from the museum on the way into the site from Palenque town.

A passageway from the Templo de las Inscripciones leads to Templo XIII, where a woman was found buried in a stone coffin. This is called the Tomb of the Red Queen because of the coloring of the sarcophagus. Southeast of here, across a stream, the **Grupo de la Cruz** includes three temples: the most interesting is the **Temple of the Sun**, which has a very well-preserved example of the roof combs that feature on other buildings around Palenque. More glyphs describe the handover of power from Pakal to his son Chan Bahlum; the temples in this group are dedicated to the gods closely associated with Pakal's ruling dynasty. The carvings weave allegory and myth into real-life events, creating a living mythology around Palenque's rulers that must have had some political purpose. Palenque's **museum** explains in greater detail in English and Spanish.

Top: View over Palenque

Above: The Templo de las Inscripciones

Left: El Palacio

TAKING A BREAK

There is a **café** on site, but if you're staying at one of the hotels close by, you can bring a **packed lunch**.

🔵 208 C2
Tourist Information
✉ Avenida Juárez, corner Abásalo,
Palenque town ☎ 916 345 0356
🕐 Mon–Sat 9–9, Sun 9–1

Palenque Museum
✉ Km7 Carretera Palenque-Ruinas
☎ 916 348 9331
🕐 Tue–Sun 10–5 🎟 Free
❓ Site open daily 8–5

PALENQUE: INSIDE INFO

Top tips It helps to arrive on the first mini-vans of the day, to take advantage of the **cooler temperature**.
• Bring **insect repellent** – mosquitoes breed in the waterways.
• Stay at one of the hotels near the ruins to **maximize your time** – Palenque deserves a whole day.

5 San Cristóbal de las Casas

If you give it half a chance, this bewitching mountain village will get under your skin. Its rich indigenous culture, white-washed colonial architecture and idyllic highland location are just some of the things visitors fall in love with.

Close to the Guatamalan border, San Cristóbal de las Casas is the best base from which to explore the Chiapas region of southern Mexico. While Chiapas hasn't had a completely peaceful history, San Cristóbal is an increasingly popular and welcoming haven for sightseers and backpackers. The town is surrounded by fragrant pine forests and rugged hills which are home to several indigenous Indian groups, such as the Tzotzil and Tzeltal.

The focal point of the town is the *zócalo*, Plaza 31 de Marzo. Calle Real de Guadalupe, heading east from the plaza, is one of the town's main thorough-fares although there is also a shopping arcade on the pedestrianized 20 de Noviembre. The key buildings on the *zócalo* are the Palacio Municipal, which dates from 1885, and the 16th-century Catedral de San Cristóbal, which shows its age with an appealing patina of layered paint. Inside, there is a gold-leafed pulpit and several gorgeous paintings. Heading north on 20 de Noviembre is the **Templo de Santo Domingo**, San Cristóbal's most impressive church. The group of buildings includes a former monastery and museum, the

Museo de Los Altos. The church's exterior is a riot of carved angels and saints, while the interior is no less interesting, with paneled walls of cedar (harvested locally). Inside the former monastery, the museum details some of the history of San Cristóbal.

The history and traditions of the indigenous groups are described in the fascinating museum and cultural center **Na Bolom**. The museum was founded in 1951 by the Danish archaeologist Frans Blom and his wife, Swiss photographer Gertrudis Duby – together they are credited with preserving indigenous Indian groups such as the Lancandón.

The main thoroughfare in San Cristóbal de las Casas

Another delight is to simply walk the streets: on Avenida 16 de Septiembre you'll find a museum of jade and in the Plaza de las Merced there is a museum of amber. Farther afield, the Centro de Desarrollo de la Medecina Maya is a small but informative collection of medicinal plants – you'll need to take a taxi here. But most visitors to San Cristóbal simply enjoy soaking in the wonderful atmosphere of this mountain gem, visiting the street markets to buy locally made blankets, jewelry and pottery.

TAKING A BREAK

There's much more than Mexican food on offer in the **Real de Guadalupe area** of San Cristóbal – choose from French, Italian and Middle Eastern cuisine.

✚ 208 B2
Tourist Information
✉ Delegacion Regional de Turismo, Hidalgo 1-B
☎ 967 678 6570; www.turismochiapas.gob.mx
🕐 Mon–Sat 8–8, Sun 9–2

Na Bolom
✉ Avenida Vicente Guerrero 33 ☎ 967 678 1418;
www.nabolom.org (in Spanish)
🕐 Mon–Sat 9:30–2, 4–7 💲 Moderate

Above: The Templo de Santo Domingo

Left: Selling crafts in the market

SAN CRISTÓBAL DE LA CASAS: INSIDE INFO

Top tips The **Templo de Santo Domingo** is used by indigenous groups who should **not be photographed**.
• Buy **crafts** from the **Indian cooperative** in the Ex-Convento de Santo Domingo next door for a memento.
• The **volunteer staff and guides** in the **Na Bolom** museum are very knowledge-able, so feel free to ask them any questions about the area and its people.

At Your Leisure

6 Yagul

The ancient site of Yagul (above), spread across a hilltop south of Oaxaca, has the second-largest ball court in Mexico and beautiful views over the Oaxaca valley. The site began life as a Zapotec settlement before being adopted by the Mixtec civilization. The Palacio de los Seis Patios (Palace of the Six Patios) is the largest building still standing on the site.

➕ 207 E2
✉ 36km (22 miles) south of Oaxaca
☎ 951 516 0123 🕐 Daily 8–5
💲 Inexpensive 🚌 Bus service from Mitla to Oaxaca stops at Yagul

7 Villahermosa

Villahermosa has two important museums worth visiting if you want to learn more about the Mayan and Olmec civilizations. The **Parque Museo de La Venta**, set in parkland to the west of the city, displays huge stone heads found at the La Venta archaeological site in Tabasco. The heads, and other exhibits, are from the Olmec period. There is also a zoo, a sculpture trail around the park and a sound-and-light show; the Museo de Historia Natural gives more background to Tabasco's natural history, but the big cats in the zoo (including jaguars and ocelots) are the stars here. The Museo Regional de Antropología Carlos Pellicer, set on the riverside south of the city, has exhibits about regional history and culture, including the Mayan and Olmec periods. Beyond these two museums, Villahermosa is a modern but otherwise undistinguished city.

➕ 208 B3
Tourist Information
✉ Calle 13, Avenida de los Rios
☎ 993 316 3633; www.tabasco.gob.mx
🕐 Mon–Fri 8–5, Sat 8–1

Parque Museo de La Venta
✉ Ruíz Cortines ☎ 993 314 1652
🕐 Daily 8–5 💲 Inexpensive

8 Agua Azul and Misol-Há waterfalls

The soundtrack to the broad cascades of Agua Azul is that of water rushing over the rocks and falling into the deep plunge pools beneath. This series of waterfalls, surrounded by jungle south of Palenque, is a mesmerizing sight. You can swim in designated areas, but signs in English warn where not to swim. The water is clearer during the dry season (November to March). Misol-Há isn't as visually arresting, but you can walk behind the single,

40m (130-foot) cascade. There are restaurants and other amenities at both sites.

➕ 208 B2
Agua Azul
✉ 35km (21 miles) south of Palenque

Misol-Há
✉ 22km (14 miles) from Palenque
❓ Tour operators in Palenque offer day trips to sites

9 Cañon del Sumidero

Cañon del Sumidero is a national park based around a canyon east of the capital of Chiapas, **Tuxtla Gutiérrez**. The canyon is 1,000m (3,280 feet) deep and you can explore it on hiking trails that meander through the tropical jungle, which you'll share with exotic plants, butterflies, birds and monkeys. There are various activities, including kayaking and cycling, that can be organized in the park. It's an invigorating place, unlike Tuxtla Gutiérrez, which is useful only as a transit point. The closest town to the park is Chiapa de Corzo, which is 12km (7.5 miles) west of the capital and accessed by bus and minivan.

➕ 208 B2
Tourist Information
✉ Boulevard Belisario Domínguez 950, Tuxtla Gutierrez ☎ 961 602 5127; www.turismochiapas.gob.mx
🕐 Mon–Fri 8–8, Sat–Sun 9–3

Parque Ecoturistico Cañon del Sumidero
☎ 961 104 8054

Office: Chiapa de Corzo
✉ Avenida Independencia
☎ 961 600 6712; www.sumidero.com
🕐 Daily 10–4

10 Yaxchilán

To reach Yaxchilán, a Mayan site deep in the jungle, requires a bus journey from Palenque then a boat trip down the River Usumacinta. However, the effort is rewarded with a large and mysterious Mayan site in an extraordinary riverside setting straight out of an Indiana Jones movie. Jungle still shrouds much of the site, but what you can see of these giant ruins is a playground for spider and howler monkeys. Yaxchilán ("green stones" in Mayan)

Top: Agua Azul's waterfalls
Below: Cañon del Sumidero

is a Late Classic Mayan site which had links with Tikal in Guatemala. It is notable for the quality of its carvings and sculptures (a headless figure of the god Yaxachtun stands at the door of one temple), but most visitors will be awed simply by the setting.

➕ 208 C2

✉ 130km (80 miles) southeast of Palenque 🕐 Daily 8–4 💰 Inexpensive

🚌 Bus from Palenque to Frontera Corozal for 9am boat to Yaxchilán. Boat trip takes 1 hour (expensive)

🈁 Bonampak

This small Mayan site consists of a plaza with several ruined temples, one of which, the Templo de las Pinturas, contains some rare and well-preserved murals covering the walls of its three rooms. The murals, preserved by a chemical reaction in the building material, are among the finest examples of Late Classic Mayan painting. They tell the story of a battle and its unsurprisingly violent aftermath. Further paintings explain the correct protocols to follow when people were presented to the ruler's court.

As a result of the construction of a good road between Bonampak and

Ruins of Structure 41, Yaxchilán

Palenque, reaching the site has become much easier; however, it is still a 3-hour bus journey and the last leg of the trip is a 3km (2-mile) hike through jungle, so bring drinking water with you.

➕ 208 C2

✉ 176km (108 miles) east of Palenque

🕐 Tue–Sun 10–5 💰 Inexpensive

🚌 Bus from Palenque

🈁 Lagunas de Montebello

This lake district of Chiapas is a peaceful, pretty region punctuated by caves and vividly colored lakes (due to their mineral content). Agua Tinta and Bosque Azul, which are served by bus, are the most popular lakes, but you will have to put on your hiking boots to find the rest of them. The closest town is Comitán de Dominguez, on the road to Guatemala, and the lakes are almost on the border with Guatemala. Local guides may be available to show you around and even spot some of the wildlife.

➕ 208 C2

✉ 60km (37 miles) southeast of Comitán de Dominguez 🚌 Bus or *combi* from Comitán

Where to... Stay

Prices

Expect to pay for a double room per night:

$ under US$50 $$ US$50–150 $$$ over US$150

ACAPULCO

▽▽▽ Las Brisas Acapulco $$$

Las Brisas is the grande dame of Acapulco hotels. While the city offers all-night party action and an increasingly tatty appearance, the hotel provides seclusion and a taste of the faded glamor of the 1950s. Aside from the price, there are a couple of distinctive features of Las Brisas: most of the 200-plus casitas (suites) have a plunge pool and breathtaking views over the bay. Food from the restaurants is of a very high standard.

✚ 206 B2 ⊠ Carretera Escénica 5255, Fraccionamiento Las Brisas ☎ 744 469 6900: www.brisas.com.mx

HUATULCO

▽▽▽ Crown Pacific Huatulco $$$

Beyond Puerto Escondido and south of Oaxaca, Huatulco is a remote but fast-growing beach resort on the Pacific coast. However, it does have its own airport and a newly surfaced road to Oaxaca. Rather than the all-night revelry of Cancún or Acapulco, expect a smarter and more sedate resort. The lavish Crown Pacific Huatulco has been built on a terrace with spectacular views overlooking Tangolunda Bay. It has lots of steps and some rooms are reached by funicular. The large, attractive suites have a flamboyant design and some have a Jacuzzi.

✚ 207 E1 ⊠ Boulevard Benito Juárez 8, Bahía de Tangolunda ☎ 958 851 0044; www.crownpacifichuatulco.com

IXTAPA/ZIHUATANEJO

▽▽▽ Villa Del Sol $$$

This hideaway, looking onto the pristine white sands of Playa la Ropa, is a small but luxurious resort with attractive rooms and suites (35 of each) and a range of beach activities. Popular with honeymooning couples, the hotel discourages young children. In the evening you can enjoy a beachside dinner or cocktails with your toes in the sand at the Cantina restaurant, which serves Mexican and Mediterranean dishes. There is a small fitness center offering beauty treatments.

✚ 205 E1 ⊠ Playa la Ropa, Zihuatanejo ☎ 755 555 5500; www.hotelvilladelsol.com

OAXACA

▽▽▽ Camino Real Oaxaca $$$

Set around a swimming pool and 16th-century colonial courtyard, this stunning former convent has 91 suites, each decorated in a simple but luxurious style and retaining original features such as wood beams and tiled floors. The rooms are airy, with high ceilings and bright decor, and have modern amenities such as satellite television. The business center has internet access. The hotel, in the heart of the city, is renowned for the regional Oaxacan cuisine at its restaurant, and there is an equally lively cultural calendar of traditional shows and performances.

✚ 207 D2 ⊠ Calle 5 de Mayo 300 ☎ 951 501 6100; www.caminoreal.com/oaxaca

▽▽▽ Casa Oaxaca $$$

The superbly restored colonial Casa Oaxaca is just four blocks from the

Where to...
Eat and Drink

Prices
Expect to pay per person for a meal, excluding drinks:
$ under US$10 **$$** US$10–20 **$$$** over US$20

ACAPULCO

▼▼▼ Baikal $$$

Baikal is where Acapulco's hip young things hang out. When you tire of the stunning view over the bay from the cliff-top terrace, you can people-watch until your meal arrives. The menu is a blend of French cuisine, Mediterranean and Asian ingredients – making for some interesting combinations, such as shrimp au gratin with green curry.

✚ 206 B2 ⊠ Avenida Escénica 22
☎ 744 446 6845 ⏰ Tue–Sun 7–12

OAXACA

▼▼▼ El Naranjo $$

Oaxacan recipes are cooked to perfection in this well established restaurant in a beautiful colonial building. Specialties include a variety of stuffed chili peppers, the hottest being *chile de agua relleno de picadillo Oaxaqueno*. Oaxaca's famous *mole* sauces are also served, with a different sauce daily, though *mole negro* is available every day. Reservations recommended.

✚ 207 D2 ⊠ Valerio Trujano 203
☎ 951 514 1878 ⏰ Mon–Sat 1–10pm

---

central *zócalo* and is very popular with the city's artistic community. The rooms and public spaces display a blend of minimalist furnishings and artful design. It may lack some of the facilities you may expect at this price, but the atmosphere is intimate, and there is a sauna.

✚ 207 D2 ⊠ Calle García Vigil 407
☎ 951 514 4173; www.casa-oaxaca.com

PALENQUE

▼▼ Chan-Kah Resort Village $$–$$$

This resort village, with its beautiful *casitas* (bungalows) set within 20ha (50 acres) of lush jungle grounds, makes a good base for visting the ruins of Palenque, and is just a few kilometers from Palenque Town. There are two restaurant/bars, a main pool with three different levels and a river that flows through the resort. You can hear the howler monkeys and see many species of

tropical birds. It's an ideal choice for families with children.

✚ 208 C2 ⊠ Km3. Carretera a las ruinas (1.8km/1 mile north of the ruins) ☎ 916 345 1100;
www.chan-kah.com.mx

SAN CRISTÓBAL DE LAS CASAS

Casa Mexicana

This hotel, in the beautiful mountain town of San Cristóbal de las Casas, is full of life and character, thanks to the efforts of the artistic owner Kiki Suárez. The interior courtyards are bursting with plants and there are sculptures and artworks throughout. Rooms have televisions and large bathrooms. A bar and restaurant cater to guests, although you should also explore the town's eateries. You can also stay at the Na Bolom cultural center in San Cristóbal de las Casas (▶ 142)

✚ 208 B2 ⊠ 28 de Agosto 1
☎ 967 678 0698;
www.hotelcasamexicana.com

PALENQUE

Maya $-$$

The menu here consists of a wide choice of spicy local Chiapan dishes, as well as some concessions to international tastes, such as pasta with a variety of sauces. The restaurant's location, on the main *zócalo*, is superb and you can sit outside with a coffee to watch the world go by.

✚ 208 C2 ⊠ Corner of Hidalgo and Independencia ☎ 916 345 0042 ⓦ Daily 8am–10pm

PUERTO ESCONDIDO

La Galería $$

This welcoming Italian restaurant has a sister establishment behind Playa Zicatela, but this branch is just as attractive, with stone floors and local art on the walls. The menu is dominated by pasta and pizza, all expertly cooked.

✚ 207 D1 ⊠ Corner of Pérez Gasga ☎ 954 582 2039 ⓦ Daily 8–12 (late)

SAN CRISTÓBAL DE LAS CASAS

La Selva Café $

Owned by a cooperative of coffee producers, La Selva is a great place to enjoy a coffee and a snack (salads and baguettes). It's a cosy place with a several eating areas and a gallery of work by local artists. There's a choice of 30 varieties of coffee, all organic.

✚ 208 B2 ⊠ Avenida Crescencio Rosas and Cuauhtémoc ☎ 967 678 7244 ⓦ Daily 8–8

ZIHUATANEJO

Coconuts $$

Coconuts has an international menu ranging from steak to sashimi. The lunch menu offers soups, salads and wraps with a more elaborate dinner menu served from 6pm. The house specialty is a vegetable tart with goat cheese.

✚ 205 E1 ⊠ Pasaje Agustín Ramírez 1, Centro ☎ 755 554 2518 ⓦ Daily 11:30–4, 6–11

Where to... Shop

Shopping in Southern Mexico ranges from the expensive designer boutiques of Acapulco to the craft markets of highland towns such as San Cristóbal de las Casas and Oaxaca. The amber jewelry of Chiapas and the black pottery of Oaxaca make excellent souvenirs. Traditional textiles are another specialty, particularly *huipiles* (sleeveless blouses) and woven blankets or rugs. Following are some of the best outlets.

Sna Jolobil (Calzada Lázaro Cárdenas, San Cristóbal de las Casas, tel 967 678 2646, open Mon–Sat 9–2, 4–6), a worker's cooperative, is an excellent place to buy *huipiles* and other textiles.

Browse around the **Mercado Municipal** (Avenida Benito Juárez, Zihuatenejo, open daily 7am–noon)

for arts and crafts while feasting on fresh food.

La Casa del Jade in the Museo Mesoamericano de Jade (Avenida 16 de Septiembre 16, San Cristóbal de las Casas, tel: 967 678 2557, open Mon–Sat 12–8) sells some fine examples of jade jewelry and decorative pieces replicating ancient Olmec, Zapotec and Toltec designs.

Amate Books (Calle Macedonia Alcalá 307, Oaxaca, tel: 951 516 6960, www.amatebooks.com, open Mon–Sat 10–9, Sun 2–7) is the best stocked bookshop around, including 7,000 titles on Latin America.

Mercado de Artesanías (corner of JP García and Zaragoza, Oaxaca, open daily 7–5), is a cavernous indoor market and the place to find Oaxaca's less expensive crafts.

La Mano Mágica (Alcalá 203, Oaxaca, tel: 951 516 4275, www.lamanomagica.com, open Mon–Sat 10–3, 4–8) sells well-made original artworks and crafts, folk art, carvings, pottery and textiles, as well as paintings by local artists.

Where to...
Be Entertained

Southern Mexico is split between the 24-hour hedonism of the Pacific coast resorts and the enchanting highland towns of Chiapas, where a late night out might mean meandering back to your hotel under the starlight after a three-hour-long meal. Generally, if it's laser lightshows and deafening dance music you're after, Acapulco has to be at the top of your itinerary.

As you make your way down the Pacific coast, the resorts get smaller and the activities get more exciting. Surfing is the big pull at Puerto Escondido (the season runs from April to October typically), but other watersports are available all along the coast. When you reach the highlands of Oaxaca and

San Cristóbal de las Casas, expect more hands-on entertainment – this is where you'll find cookery schools, craft workshops and other such experiences.

Learn how some of Oaxaca's most distinctive dishes are cooked at Susana Trilling's **Seasons of My Heart Cookery School** (Rancho Aurora, Oaxaca, tel: 951 508 0469; www.seasonsofmyheart.com), just outside the city. She offers tuition from one-day introductions to week-long courses. You can also opt for one of the culinary tours of the region, which includes bed-and-breakfast.

Sol y Luna (Calle Reforma 502, tel: 951 514 8069, open Mon–Sat 6:30pm–1:30am) is one of the top spots in Oaxaca for jazz and Latin

music. The food is good, too. Reservations recommended.

High in the hills above Acapulco's bay, **Syboney** (Carretera Escénica, Las Brisas, tel: 744 446 5711, www.acapulcomandara.com, open Mon–Sat 10–late) is a classy piano bar and part of the Mandara nightclub complex. The minimalist bar is frequented by a mature crowd of forty-somethings who appreciate the talented singers and musicians booked each night. When the bar closes you can go upstairs to the after-hours club, **El Privado**, where the party may continue until past noon the next day. Mandara itself is a large disco where DJs play dance music – loudly. You can make reservations for tables at El Privado and Syboney.

A highlight of **Palladium** (Carretera Escénica, Las Brisas, tel: 744 446 5490, www.acapulcopalladium.com, open Thu–Sun 10–late) is its 49m-wide (160-foot) panoramic window overlooking the bay of Acapulco. But to

appreciate the stunning view you'll have to squeeze your way past throngs of clubbers dancing to the latest techno and house music. Some of the world's most famous DJs have played here – check the website for upcoming events.

Learn to dive with the PADI-accredited instructors of **Carlo Scuba** (Zihuatanejo Pier, tel: 755 554 6003, www.carloscuba.com), which has operated in Zihuatanejo's bay since 1962. Experienced scuba divers can go out on the boats for diving trips in the Pacific, spotting a wide variety of fish large and small, such as puffers, grouper, butterfly fish, parrotfish and triggerfish, and sometimes even sea turtles, eagle rays or manta rays.

A short taxi drive to the west of San Cristóbal de las Casas is the charming **Teatro Hermanos Domínguez** (Diagonal Hermanos Paniagua, tel: 967 678 3637), which stages traditional dances and music. Check locally for the upcoming performance schedule.

The Yucatán

Getting Your Bearings

The Yucatán peninsula, bulging out of southeast Mexico into the Caribbean, could be a different country. Where Mexico is mainly mountainous, the Yucatán is flat, with mangroves and salt beds at the edges. Where Mexico is often arid, the Yucatán is a watery wonderland, with *cenotes* (natural sink-holes) and caves submerged in crystal clear water.

Left: Water sports are a very popular pastime

Page 151: The spectacular clifftop site of Tulum

Top right: The rocky coastline of Isla Mujeres

The Yucatán is easy to travel around, with good quality roads and manageable distances between attractions, so renting a car in Cancún, the main point of entry, will enable you to see most of the region. The eastern section of the Caribbean coastline, the Mayan Riviera, is the area with the highest concentration of development. Its position means it can be hit by hurricanes in the fall (autumn), the last major storm being Hurricane Wilma in October 2005.

Cancún lies at the top of the Mayan Riviera, which descends via Playa del Carmen to Tulum. Inland from Tulúm, Cobá is a chance to experience a Mayan ruin that hasn't been restored. South towards Tulum there are several privately owned eco-parks designed for family entertainment rather than environmentalism. Two islands off the coast, Isla Mujeres and Cozumel, offer relaxing escapes from the raucous nightlife and high-rise hotels of Cancún. Scuba diving is a major sport here and accomplished divers can dive *cenotes*, vast submerged caves that riddle the limestone landscape.

Inland, Chichén Itzá, the most famous Mayan site, lies between Cancún and the appealing, whitewashed capital of the Yucatán, Mérida. South of Mérida is an enthralling collection of Mayan ruins from the Puuc dynasty; Uxmal is the most extensive of these. On the western coast of the peninsula Campeche and Celestún are two little-visited towns. The Yucatán has such a diverse appeal – beach-lovers will enjoy the Caribbean sands, history buffs will be amazed by the Mayan ruins and city slickers can compare Mérida and Cancún – that for many visitors there is little cause to travel onward elsewhere in Mexico.

★ Don't Miss

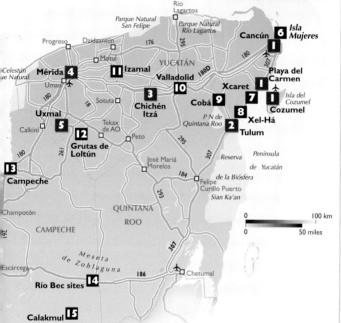

At Your Leisure

Entrance to the National
Bank of Mexico, Mérida

Five days in the Yucatán can take you from Mexico's largest
beach resort to the colonial capital of the region.
On the way you'll travel along the Caribbean coast to
spectacular Mayan ruins and try some of Mexico's
most distinctive cuisine.

The Yucatán in Five Days

Day One

Most people arrive in the Yucatán via **①Cancún** (➤ 156–157). To avoid
the excesses of Cancún, and get your holiday off to a gentle start, head
south straight for **①Playa del Carmen** (above) for the night; you can relax
on the beach as you acclimatize to the weather.

Day Two

From Playa del Carmen, continue south to **②Tulum** (➤ 158–159). It's not
the most interesting of the Mayan ruins, but it has a breathtaking setting
on cliffs overlooking the aquamarine Caribbean sea. Half a day is enough
to see Tulum, unless you get tempted to stay longer on the beaches. Drive
south and stay overnight at the Biosfera Sian Ka'an.

Day Three

Get an early start for the **Biosfera Sian Ka'an** (➤ 159), a UNESCO-
protected nature reserve which you can tour by boat. Afterward, head
north toward **⑩Valladolid** (➤ 167), a small city that makes a good base
for visiting Chichén Itzá.

Day Four

It's another early start as you beat the crowds to **3 Chichén Itzá** (➤ 160–161), the Yucatán's most well-known Mayan site. Currently you can't climb El Castillo, but the site is still an exciting place to tour. Continue onward to Mérida, the capital of the Yucatán.

Day Five

After overnighting in a city center hotel, you can get a dose of culture in the art-loving city of **4 Mérida** (➤ 162–163). Be sure to try some local Yucatecan cooking – it's one of the most distinctive Mexican cuisines. If your appetite for all things Maya has been whetted by Chichén Itzá you could also spend the day touring the Puuc region of ruins (Sayil below) south of Mérida, the stand-out attraction being **5 Uxmal** (➤ 164–165).

❶ Cancún, Cozumel and Playa del Carmen

Sun, sea, sand, shopping, beautiful beaches, good restaurants and nightlife that just won't quit: Cancún is an extremely popular holiday hotspot. Playa de Carmen offers similar pleasures on a more laid-back scale, while the island of Cozumel has some of the best scuba diving in the world.

Cancún is the party capital of the Mayan Riviera, the 130km (80-mile) stretch of sun-drenched Caribbean coast along the east side of the Yucatán peninsula. This narrow strip of mainland Mexico reaches into the sea toward Cuba, 480km (300 miles) to the northeast. Hurricane Wilma, a category 4 storm, battered the resort in the fall of 2005. Cancún made a remarkable comeback, however, and by mid-2006 practically all of its hotels, restaurants and shops had reopened—in the case of some hotels, bigger and better than ever. Even the world-famous beaches were restored; Wilma's winds and pounding waves washed away their silky-soft sand, but it was replaced by sand dredged from the seafloor.

The resort section of Cancún is located on Cancún Island, a skinny, 27km (17-mile) sandbar. The main drag (practically the only street) on the island is Boulevard Kukulcán. This four-lane road is lined on the ocean side with resort hotels from modest to luxurious, and on the lagoon side with waterfront restau-

rants and shopping malls. You can get good out-of-season deals at the international chain properties, but during high season (late December to April) they are usually full. Beaches toward the southern end of Cancún Island, like Playa Delfines, tend to have bigger surf, while those at the northern end, like Playa Tortugas, have calmer water and are more family oriented. The beaches in between that

front the major hotels are busy with sun worshippers and holiday-makers.

Playa del Carmen, 64km (40 miles) south of Cancún, is the largest community on the Riviera Maya coast. Just a small Mexican town at heart, Playa has pretty beaches and a laid-back tourist scene that centers along 10 blocks of seaside Avenida 5. It is also the departure point for ferries to Cozumel.

Left: The beach at Playa del Carmen

Top: Cancún's busy downtown at night

Above: Divers at Chankanaab, Cozumel

The beautiful, tropical island of Cozumel, as popular with cruise ship passengers as with scuba divers, also suffered at the hands of Wilma. Hotels and businesses were damaged, but thankfully the coral reefs that are the main draw for legions of divers were not extensively affected. Reefs in shallow water have some dead coral, but regrowth has begun.

TAKING A BREAK

Most of the Mexican restaurants preferred by locals in **Cancún** are in El Centro, while the international ones tend to be in the Zona Hotelera. Try Avenida 5 in **Playa del Carmen**.

🚹 209 F5
Tourist Information
✉ Centro de Convenciones Cancún, Boulevard Kukulcán, Cancún ☎ 998 884 6531; www.cancun.info 🕐 Mon–Fri 9–2, 4–7 ✉ Avenida Juárez and Avenida 15, Playa del Carmen ☎ 984 873 2804 🕐 Mon–Sat 9–9, Sun 9–5

CANCÚN, COZUMEL AND PLAYA DEL CARMEN: INSIDE INFO

Top tips High season begins in Christmas week; you may be able to find **discounted holidays** before this time, but few deals are offered after Christmas.

- Renting a car is the most convenient travel option if you intend to explore the Riviera Maya coast.

2 Tulum

Overlooking the ultramarine Caribbean, this compact 12th-century Mayan site has a stunning location and is convenient for day trippers from Cancún and Playa del Carmen.

When the Spanish arrived in Tulum early in the 16th century, it was one of the few Mayan cities still functioning, an important trading port that would have looked like a foreboding clifftop settlement from the sea. The Spanish never quite subdued Tulum, although the city died with a whimper not a bang, decades after the Spanish choked it of trade.

The site today is one of the most popular Mayan ruins in the Yucatán. It is close to the attractions of the Mayan Riviera (▶ 185–188) and the resorts of Playa del Carmen and Cancún (▶ 156–157). The backpacker shacks that line the track from the main north–south highway to the ruins remain, but with more upscale accommodations among them.

Fortified walls enclose palaces and temples at Tulum

Tulum's small size and its unexceptional post-Classic architecture doesn't compare with Mayan sites such as Uxmal, but it will occupy most visitors for half a day – more if you get distracted by the beach (be warned: the wind and currents can be strong for bathers here).

The standout structure is **El Castillo**, a temple dedicated to the god Kukulcán – look for the serpent imagery on the columns. Next to El Castillo, the **Templo del Dios Descendente** is a small temple featuring the image of a god over the doorway, thought to be associated with the setting sun or a carving of the Bee God called Ah Mucen Cab, a locally popular deity. The **Temple of the Wind** stands on a rocky promontory to the north of El Castillo and makes a great vantage point for taking pictures of El Castillo. Beyond that the **House of the Cenote**, as its name suggests, stands over a cenote. Inland, the **Templo de las Pinturas** (Temple of

Tulum looks out over the Caribbean from its clifftop location

the Paintings) has some Mayan murals and frescoes inside which are in the process of being restored. Continue south on Highway 307 to enter the town of Tulum.

TAKING A BREAK

Italian restaurants seem to dominate Tulum's **main street**. **Cabañas Copal** (Carretera Tulum Ruinas Km 5), serves tasty, health-conscious vegetarian dishes.

✛ 209 E4
✉ Highway 307, Km 130 🕐 Daily 7–5 💲 Inexpensive

TULUM: INSIDE INFO

In more depth The **Biosfera Sian Ka'an** is the largest nature reserve on the Caribbean coast of Mexico and has UNESCO World Heritage status. It is a short drive south of Tulum and has 23 archaeological sites within its boundaries, in addition to 100 mammal species and 336 bird species.
• The **Centro Ecologico Sian Ka'an** (www.cesiak.org) is an environmental group and ecotourism center that provides tours of the Biosfera in boats or kayaks, spotting birds as you glide through the mangroves. There's a 20-peso fee to enter the reserve via the coast road. Accommodations in sustainably designed cabins are also available.

② Chichén Itzá

War, sacrifice, pyramids and basketball – Chichén Itzá grabs your attention and refuses to let go. The most popular Mayan archaeological site is dominated by El Castillo, a gigantic pyramid entwined with myths, legends and stone snakes.

Nowhere in the Yucatán illustrates the grandeur and power of the Maya like Chichén Itzá. At the heart of the city was **El Castillo**, a 30m-high (98-foot) pyramid with interior passageways and chambers used in ceremonies. It was dedicated to Kukulcán, a powerful Mayan god represented by a feathered serpent known elsewhere in Mexico as Quetzalcoatl, and is not only a feat of engineering, but also a mathematical marvel. The stepped construction represents the Mayan calendar: each of the four stairways to the top has 91 steps, making 365 steps in total. Around the exterior of the pyramid are 52 stone panels, representing 52 weeks and the 18 terraces correspond to the 18 months in a Mayan year. A stone snakehead was added to the base of the steps at the north side of the pyramid. At the spring and autumn equinoxes the shadow created by the sun against the steps looks like a snake climbing then descending the pyramid, a reminder of the importance of the changing of the seasons in an agricultural society.

Above: Chichén Itzá's famous reclining *chacmool* in front of El Castillo

Right: Carved jaguar heads on the Temple of the Jaguar

Next to El Castillo, the **Temple of the Warriors** is an L-shaped array of free-standing columns. At the front of the temple, dedicated to the rain god Chac, stands a *chacmool*, a reclining figure on which sacrifices to the god were placed. A short walk north of El Castillo is **Cenote Sagrado**, also dedicated to the Chac, whose satisfaction the Mayans believed was essential to the success of their crops. Women, children, animals and valued objects such as jade, copper and gold were thrown into this 60m-wide (197-foot) well of water to placate Chac. Back in the main site, the **Juego de Pelota** is the largest ball court in Mexico. The ancient Mayan game involved teams of players trying to get a ball through the stone hoops high on the walls. Carvings around the edge of the court show players being decapitated. Were they winners or losers, who knows?

South of the principal sights, an older part of Chichén Itzá has a nunnery and an observatory, which illustrates the Mayan's interest in astronomy. The observatory's windows look out at the four points of the compass and the Mayans are believed to have predicted solar eclipses centuries in advance. Note too the intricate carvings on the upper layer of the nunnery.

TAKING A BREAK

There's a **café** at the complex entrance, but many small restaurants have sprung up on the main street of the closest village, **Pisté**.

➕ 209 E5
✉ Highway 180
☎ 985 851 0137; www.inah.gob.mx
🕐 Daily 8–6
💲 Moderate

CHICHÉN ITZÁ: INSIDE INFO

Top tips There's **very little shade** at Chichén Itzá and if you arrive at the site any later than early morning, you're in for a hot and hectic day. Take a sunhat and some water. It helps if you stay at a nearby hotel, so you can get to the site by 8am.

• The **best times to view and photograph** the ruins are early morning and late afternoon.

• The **steps of El Castillo** are deceptively steep: after several fatal accidents and rapid erosion, the authorities no longer permit people to climb the pyramid, although this decision may be reversed at a later date.

• **Tours** of the entire site with **English-speaking guides** are available from the visitor center at the front gate and the guides will shed light on Chichén Itzá's mysteries.

❸ Mérida

Take a break from the beach and enjoy a cultural diversion to Mérida, the sophisticated state capital of the Yucatán. It's a good base from which to explore the central Mayan region.

With a world-class reputation for the performing arts and a packed cultural calendar, the state capital has all-year appeal. The city is the gateway for central Mayan sites such as Uxmal (▶ 164–165) and what is known as the Puuc Zone (Puuc refers to both the Puuc hills to the south and the region's distinctively decorated Mayan architecture).

Mérida is a busy, dynamic city. Its restaurant scene is the most interesting in the Yucatán, with an emphasis on the healthy, hot, fruity flavors of Yucatecan dishes – cookery schools have opened to help spread the word (▶ 174). But it's Mérida's art scene, and a lively series of festivals and events throughout the year, that are the main draw for visitors. Many of the events are staged at the **Centro Cultural de Mérida Olimpo** on the main *zócalo*. The Olimpo was built in 1999, but blends into the colonial architecture of the Centro Historico with its arches and first-floor balcony. A planetarium, bookshop and internet café are also located in the center.

Mérida's **Plaza Principal**, surrounded by the Palacio del Gobierno, Palacio Municipal, Museo de Arte Contemporaneo, Olimpo, Casa de Montejo and Catedral San Ildefonso, is the focal point for sightseers. Inside the cathedral, the oldest on the continent, there is a statue, the Cristo de las Ampollas, carved from a tree that burned all night after being hit by lightning, but without showing any damage. The Palacio del Gobierno, on the left side of the cathedral, houses spectacular murals by Fernando Castro Pacheco.

On the opposite side of the *zócalo* is the **Case de Montejo**, built in the 16th century by the founder of Mérida, Francisco de Montejo – he spared no expense and the result remains

Below: The Arco de San Juan, one of the remaining city gates

Left: The best way to see the city is by *calesa* (horse-drawn carriage)

Impressive art-works in the neoclassical Palacio de Gobierno

one of the finest examples of colonial architecture in the Yucatán. Today it is a bank, but you can still enter and admire the interior. Also bordering the *zócalo* is the **Museo de Arte Contemporáneo**, with its changing selection of work by Yucatecan artists. Calle 60, which runs in front of the gallery, is where many of Mérida's other places of interest are located, including two small parks, Hidalgo and Santa Lucia, a church, the Iglesia de Jesús, and the ornate Teatro Peón Contreras. Beyond the Parque Santa Lucia and one block east, the **Museo de Antropología e Historia**, on Paseo de Montejo, offers an insight into the local Mayan culture with exhibits that range from beautiful jewelry to skulls with sharpened teeth.

TAKING A BREAK

Los Almendros (➤ 173) is Mérida's best-known Yucatecan restaurant.

🕂 209 D5
Tourist Information
✉ Teatro Peón Contreras, corner Calle 60 and 57 ☎ 999 924 9290; www.merida.gob.mx 🕐 Mon–Fri 8am–9pm, Sat–Sun 8–8

MÉRIDA: INSIDE INFO

Top tips Most streets in Mérida have **numbers rather than names**. Streets running north to south have even numbers, streets lying east to west have odd numbers. Address are typically described as intersections or corners between odd and even streets, making it easy to navigate around the city.
• Explore the **Centro Historico** by **horse-drawn carriage** from the Paseo de Montejo.

④ Uxmal

Uxmal is a mesmerizing collection of jungle-clad ruins that represent the high point of Mayan architecture. You'll need a day here to take it all in.

Uxmal can be reached on a tour from Mérida. It's a trip worth making because the site is the highlight of the Puuc region (► 169, Río Bec). The city dates back to the Preclassic period although many of the remaining structures were finished in the late Classic period (AD 700–900), after which the city was abandoned. The buildings are distinguished by their complex and ornate decorations – often featuring the masks of Chac, the god of rain. Chac's hooked nose juts out from walls and corners of the Palacio del Gobernador (the Governor's Palace) and the Casa de las Monjas (the Nunnery).

The first stop for many will be the **Casa del Adivino** (Magician's Pyramid), a steep-sided pyramid, 38m (125 feet) tall. The single stairway to the top is currently closed to sightseers. The two temples at the top are dedicated to

Above: detail of stone carvings at Kabah

Chac, with his mouth framing one of the doorways. Human sacrifices to him were performed here, with the bodies, minus their hearts, being tumbled down the steps.

The **Casa de las Monjas** at the foot of the pyramid is a large quadrangle that may have been used as Uxmal's army base. It is a distillation of the distinct Puuc style of design with interlocking panels of golden stone carefully carved into images of faces and snakes. As the sun moves, so the carvings seem to move. Look for Chac masks on the four corners of the exterior and the carving of the feathered serpent god Kukulcán along the top of the west side. If you follow the path out of the south side of the Nunnery into the heart of the site you will reach the squat, rectangular **Casa de las Tortugas** (House of the Turtles), which takes its name from the carved turtles circling the cornice.

Below: View over Uxmal from the Grand Pyramid

Just behind the House of the Turtles, the **Palacio del Gobernador** is arguably the most dazzling Mayan building still standing. More than 20,000 stones are used in the facade and a frieze runs the length of the building. Most of the structure is actually flattened, but steps and a jaguar-shaped throne remain, suggesting that the palace was at the administrative core of the community.

Left: Sayil's Great Palace

TAKING A BREAK

There's a small onsite **cafeteria** selling cold drinks and snacks.

🚩 209 D4 ✉ Highway 261 🕐 Daily 8–5 💰 Moderate

UXMAL: INSIDE INFO

Top tips Stay until **sunset** to get the best views and photographs.
• The price of the **sound-and-light show** is included in the ticket, but you can pay separately (inexpensive) if you just want to see the show. It starts at 7pm (8pm in summer).
• The archaeological sites of **Kabah**, **Sayil**, **Xlapak** and **Labná**, examples of the Puuc style of architecture, can be found to the southeast of Uxmal, along what is called the Puuc Route.

At Your Leisure

The ferry to Isla Mujeres

6 Isla Mujeres
Isla Mujeres is a small island lying just a 30-minute ferry ride to the north of Cancún (▶ 156–157), but time slows down as soon as you arrive. It's a quieter, less neon-lit place, famous for the fabulous scuba diving thanks to its turquoise waters and extensive reefs. Several dive operators ply their trade from the island, offering PADI training courses as well as excursions for experienced divers. Even if you're not a scuba diver, it's a tranquil escape from the mainland and there are beautiful beaches to explore, including Playa Norte, close to the main concentration of hotels on the northern tip and the beaches on the west coast of the 8km-long (5-mile) island.

➕ 209 F5
Tourist Information
✉ Rueda Medina 130
☎ 998 877 0307
🕐 Mon–Fri 8–8, Sat–Sun 9–2

7 Xcaret
One of several eco-themed parks south of Tulum, Xcaret is based around a man-made lagoon offering a wide range of activities. Don't be fooled by the "eco" label;

the emphasis is very much on fun here as demonstrated by the day trippers who make the journey south from Playa del Carmen and Cancún. Aside from the watersports and replica Mayan relics, wildlife exhibits include a saltwater pool with dolphins and two islands with big cats (such as pumas); this may turn off some visitors.

➕ 209 F5 ✉ Highway 307, 7km (4 miles) south of Playa del Carmen
☎ 998 883 3143; www.xcaret.net
🕐 Daily 8:30am–10pm 💲 Expensive

Above: Snorkeling at Xel-Há
Below: Stone carving at Cobá

8 Xel-Há
Xel-Há is managed by the same company that operates Xcaret and offers a similar range of activities, although Xel-Há is described as a one-of-a-kind water park. You can snorkel, swim in cenotes and swim with dolphins.

➕ 209 F4
✉ Chetumal-Puerto Juarez, km240
☎ 998 8883 3293; www.xel-ha.com
🕐 Daily 9am–late
💲 Expensive

9 Cobá
Turn inland from Tulum and drive for 48km (30 miles) and you'll reach

Cobá, an interesting opportunity to explore Mayan ruins that have not yet been restored and swamped with sightseers, making it much easier to imagine being back in the Mayan world. Not only that, but Cobá is one of the largest Mayan sites on the peninsula. The straight white roads, paved with limestone, that criss-cross the region are known as *sacbeob* and 40 of them pass through Cobá. Experts believe that they may have some astrological or ceremonial significance. The jungle is still draped over many of the buildings and structures at Cobá and part of the fun is wandering around the site without getting lost; remember to bring plenty of drinking water. Handily, the main group of structures, the Cobá Group, is close to the entrance and include a ball court and a pyramid. The highest structure at Cobá and among all the Mayan ruins is Nohuch Mul, a gigantic pyramid with superb views from the top.

✚ 209 E5 🕐 Daily 7–6
💵 Inexpensive

Valladolid's Franciscan cathedral

🔟 Valladolid

Don't overlook Valladolid, halfway between Cancún and Mérida. The Yucatán's third largest city is an attractive and sedate base for touring the central Yucatán, including Chichén Itzá (▶ 160–161). The town was a Mayan settlement, called Zaci, that was eventually taken by the Spanish who built Valladolid's Franciscan cathedral. The Palacio Municipal on the colonial plaza and the Iglesia de San Bernardino de Siena and its neighboring convent are a short walk southwest of the *zócalo*. Valladolid's natural attractions are just as notable: the city is close

to three *cenotes* (deep, subterranean lakes) in which you can swim. The best-looking is the Cenote Dzitnup, 7km (4 miles) west of the *zócalo*. It can be reached by taxi. The well is artificially lit although note that the steps leading down to it are quite steep. Cenote Samulá can also be accessed by taxi from Valladolid.

✚ 209 E5
Tourist Information
✉ East side of the *zócalo*
☎ 985 856 1865
🕐 Mon–Sat 9–8, Sun 9–1

🔟 Izamal

The "Yellow City," named after the canary-yellow color of its key buildings is a pleasant town dominated by the Franciscan Convento de San Antonio de Padua at its

Stained-glass window in Izamal's Convento de San Antonio de Padua

center. The Spanish probably built such an imposing religious building – it has the second largest atrium in the world – in response to Izamal's status as a key religious site for the Maya, who believed the town was founded by the god Itzamná. There are several Mayan sites around the town (many on Calle 20) but the convent, to which the Pope paid a visit in 1993, merits the most attention. Outside the convent, horse-drawn carriages line up around the *zócalo* to take visitors on sightseeing tours of Izamal. You can't fail to miss Izamal's 36m-high (118-foot) Pirámide Kinich Kakmó, the fifth highest in Mexico.

✚ 209 D5
✉ Between Mérida and Valladolid with bus services from either

12 Grutas de Loltún

Delve deep underground in the magical caves of Loltún, the largest cave network in the Yucatán. Many of the subterranean chambers are like natural, inverted cathedrals with spiky stalactites and stalagmites protruding from the floors and ceilings. The caves lie on the local road between Labna and Oxcutzcab, in the Puuc region south of Mérida. You must take a guided tour (departing six times daily) to enter the caves, but once inside you can explore the breathtaking rock formations at your own pace. The caves were inhabited by humans several thousand years ago, who left now-faded cave paintings and the bones of wild animals.

✚ 209 D4
🕐 Daily 9–5 💲 Moderate

13 Campeche

Sunsets are spellbinding at Campeche, a fortified city on the west side of the Yucatán peninsula now looking to hit the big time. Extra funding has smartened up what was ten years ago a rather run-down state capital notable for its seafood restaurants, colonial architecture and for being the first place the Spanish set foot in Mexico. Even now, with UNESCO World Heritage status as a colonial fort, the town doesn't overwhelm tourists with attention, preferring to let them fall for the place in their own time. The Spanish began building the city's seaward fortifications in the 17th century after years of pirate raids. There's a sound-and-light show, conjuring up the battles between the pirates and Campeche's citizens, at

8pm on Tuesdays, Fridays and Saturdays at the Puerta de Tierra (the Land Gate). You can walk or cycle along the seafront (*malecón*), a popular place from which to watch the sunset, but the focal point of Campeche is its colonial Plaza Principal. There's often live music on Sunday evenings, when the plaza is a social whirl.

On one side of the plaza the Franciscan Catedral de la Concepción dates from the 17th century and has a handsome interior. Four blocks southeast of the plaza, the Ex-Templo de San José is an outstanding baroque church, its facade covered in blue and yellow Talavera tiles. Learn more about the Mayan people at the Baluarte de Soledad, on the *zócalo*. This bulwark of the old city

Left: The Ex-Templo de San José, Campeche

Edzná's impressive buildings cluster around the central Gran Plaza

walls (most sections have been demolished and used for building materials) contains a museum of Mayan relics. Or see a Mayan site for yourself at **Edzná**, a large area of ruins some 55km (35 miles) southeast of Campeche. The ruins include a pyramid, the Templo de los Cinco Pisos, irrigation canals and further buildings yet to be excavated. Edzná dates back to 600 BC and was abandoned in the 15th century.

➕ 208 C4
Tourist Information
✉ Ruis Cortines, Plaza Moch Couuh
☎ 981 811 9255 ⏰ Daily 9–3, 6–9

🔟 Río Bec sites

In the southeast corner of the Yucatán, close to Chetumal, there is a collection of Mayan archaeological sites that have been labelled Río Bec. The building techniques are cruder than those of the Puuc region – blocky towers without interior chambers

Becán, once capital of the Río Bec area

were built instead of elegant pyramids – but they are an interesting day trip from Chetumal. The sites are **Xpujil**, dominated by three crumbling towers characteristic of Río Bec architecture; **Becán**, from the late Classic period and notable for its defensive fortifications and moat; and **Chicanná**, west of Becán. Chicanná's highlight is the mouth-shaped entrance – complete with fangs – of one of its temples. All three sites can be toured from Chetumal, with several tour operators offering daytrips.

Xpujil
🚩 209 D3 ⊠ 100km (62 miles) west of Chetumal 🕐 Daily 8–5 🎟 Inexpensive

Becán
🚩 209 D3 ⊠ 15km (9 miles) west of Xpujil 🕐 Daily 8–5 🎟 Inexpensive

Chicanná
🚩 209 D3 ⊠ 12km (7 miles) west of Xpujil 🕐 Daily 8–5 🎟 Inexpensive

🔢 Calakmul

Calakmul is remote but rewarding. The Mayan archaeological site and UNESCO-designated Biosphere is best reached via Highway 186 from Chetumal. It is thought that Calakmul was one of the most influential bases of power in the Mayan empire for up to 1,000 years and it was certainly the largest Mayan city, with 6,500 buildings yet to be recovered from the jungle. A handful of the city's pyramids are accessible and you can also see the Gran Acrópolis, a large ceremonial space. Mayan relics collected at Calakmul are on display in the archaeological museum in Campeche.

The 728,460ha (1.8-million-acre) Reserva de la Biosfera Calakmul is a vast wilderness covered in tropical jungle and full of wildlife, including jaguars, monkeys and 250 species of birds.

🚩 209 D3
⊠ 213km (132 miles) southeast of Campeche ☎ No telephone; www.calakmul.org 🕐 Daily 8–5
🎟 Inexpensive

A spider monkey in the Calakmul Biosphere Reserve

Where to... Stay

Prices

Expect to pay for a double room per night:
$ under US$50
$$ US$50–150
$$$ over US$150

CANCÚN

Ritz-Carlton $$$

Apart from the marble-lined interiors, the wide range of sports facilities, beachfront access and revitalizing spa, the Ritz-Carlton has one particular attraction not matched by its rivals in Cancun: an excellent culinary school, which opened December 2006, with classes held Monday through Satruday. All rooms have views of the Caribbean, and with seven bars and eateries, there are plenty of places to find inspiration.

➕ 209 F5 ✉ Retorno del Rey 36, Zona Hotelera ☎ 998 881 0808; www.ritzcarlton.com

Sunset Lagoon Hotel & Marina $$$

The Sunset Lagoon, with its charming Mediterranean-style architecture, is located closed to the heart of the Hotel Zone and some of the best shopping malls and nightclubs. Facilities include water sports, swimming pool with slide, spa, beauty salon, bars, restaurants and open-air theater. The rooms, some with whirlpools, are gracefully decorated and have views of the Laguna de Nichupté or the gardens. You will see some of the most spectacular sunsets in Cancun here.

➕ 209 F5 ✉ Boulevard Kukulcán Km 5.8 ☎ 998 881 4500; www.sunsetlagoon.com

COZUMEL

Presidente Intercontinental $$$

Hit hard by Hurricane Wilma, the Intercontinental used the opportunity for a complete revamp. The 1970s-built resort has jumped several rungs up the style ladder; it now looks new and offers fewer rooms and more suites. There's also a new scuba training center, making it popular with divers and their families, who can also laze on the resort's beautiful beach. Accommodations are elegant, comfortable and spacious, with modern services such as wireless internet. Note that prices have also edged upward.

➕ 209 F5 ✉ Carretera Chankanaab ☎ 987 872 9500; www.intercontinentalcozumel.com

ISLA MUJERES

Hotel Na Balam $$

This lovely beach hotel has been designed in a sophisticated *palapa* style. It is set in a lush tropical garden with hammocks under the palm trees, a pool, a bar and a restaurant which offers Maya, vegetarian and fusion cuisine. Standard rooms have a king- or two queen-size beds and a private terrace or balcony.

➕ 209 F5 ✉ Calle Zazil Ha 118 ☎ 998 877 0279; www.nabalam.com

MÉRIDA

Hotel Caribe $

The Hotel Caribe occupies a converted 19th-century convent in central Mérida, just a block from the main square. It has a quaint colonial atmosphere and is ideal as a base for touring the city. There are great views of the cathedral from the rooftop sundeck, which has a pool. The rooms are basic, but clean and comfortable, and most have air-conditioning. The restaurant serves Yucatecan and international cuisine.

➕ 209 D5 ✉ Calle 59 No 500 ☎ 999 924 9022; www.starwood.com

Where to...
Eat and Drink

Prices
Expect to pay per person for a meal, excluding drinks:
$ under US$10 **$$** US$10–20 **$$$** over US$20

While the dining scenes in Playa del Carmen and Cancún are dominated by loud bars and restaurants serving an approximation of Mexican food, you can taste the real deal in Mérida. The city has a strong culinary tradition and is a good place in which to seek out some of the region's distinctive, local specialities.

CANCÚN

▼▼▼ Lorenzillo's $$

Lorenzillo's is famed for its seafood specialities, served in a *palapa* (palm-thatched building) overlooking the lagoon. The lobsters come from the restaurant's own farm so you don't need to worry about depleting the Caribbean. There are several house recipes for the lobsters, but the restaurant also offers pasta and meat. Service is attentive and families with children are made very welcome. Reservations are recommended during the peak season.

➕ **209 F5** ✉ **Kukulcán Boulevard Km 10** ☎ **998 883 1254;** www.lorenzillos.com.mx
⏱ Daily 12–12

PLAYA DEL CARMEN

▼▼ Hotel Deseo $$$

This is not the place to be if you want to have an early night – there's lounge music piped all over the hotel at all hours. The roof is perfect for relaxing or grabbing a quick nap and the strictly minimalist rooms have large windows overlooking the heart of Playa del Carmen. The hotel is located just a short walk from the beach. Children are not permitted at the Deseo.

➕ **209 F5** ✉ **Lote Hotelero 6, Desarollo Playacar** ☎ **984 873 4500;** www.royalhideaway.com

▼▼▼ Occidental Royal Hideaway Resort & Spa $$$

The Royal Hideaway may not be the most luxurious hotel on the Riviera Maya, but you need never leave the comfortable confines of this all-inclusive resort. The award-winning hotel has 200 rooms, which each feature marble bathrooms, air-conditioning, wireless internet access and vast beds. If you venture outside you can try the spa treatments, take tennis lessons or have a go at watersports like kayaking, snorkeling, sailing, windsurfing and water polo.

➕ **209 F5** ✉ **Avenida 5, Calle 12** ☎ **984 879 3620;** www.hoteldeseo.com

UXMAL

▼▼ The Lodge at Uxmal $$$

The Lodge blends Mayan and European architectural styles to great effect and has been built using materials native to the region. the rooms are individually decorated with ethnic ceramics, textiles and artwork, and the suites have private Jacuzzis. The restaurant's changing menu caters to all with its mixture of regional cuisine, Mexican classics and international dishes.

➕ **209 D4** ✉ **At the main entrance to the archaeological site** ☎ **987 976 2031**

series of cavernous, American-style malls packed with outlets that you might find north of the border: the best of the malls is La Isla Shopping Village at Km 12.5 on Kukulcan Boulevard, but most offer a similar selection of retailers. Close to the biggest hotels in the Zona Hotelera you will also find abundant expensive boutiques selling everything from Cuban cigars to jade jewelry – prices are high here. Items particular to the Yucatán include hammocks and guayaberas, the Cuban-style shirts popular with young and old.

In Cancún, the small shop in the folk art museum, **La Casa del Arte Popular Mexicano** (Boulevard Kukulcan Km4, tel: 998 849 4332, www.museoartepopularmexicano. org, open daily 9–9), is the best place in the city to buy Mexican handicrafts. The owners have selected masks, ceramics, textiles and ornaments from the most

Where to...
Shop

Shopping in the Yucatán is a case of sorting the wheat from the chaff – in the tourist areas of Cancun and Playa del Carmen there are scores of souvenir shops peddling poor, mass-produced examples of Mexican crafts, in addition to the over-sized sombreros. There's one exception: the La Casa del Arte Popular Mexicano in Cancun.

However, in the rest of the region there are numerous local markets and small craft shops were items of a higher quality can be found. In the holiday hotspots of Cancun and Playa del Carmen you should expect to bargain with the shopkeeper or stallholder; their prices are marked up and they may be happy to sell something for up to half the asking price. Cancun's shopping scene is dominated by a

Puerto Madero $$

Sizzling steaks and seafood are the main attractions at this buzzing restaurant on Cancun's main thoroughfare. The Argentine-themed restaurant occupies a waterside location in the Marina Barracuda, with fine sunset views from the raised terrace. After enjoying a steak (there are seven kinds) or seafood ranging from tuna and swordfish to lobster tails, you can retreat to the bar's comfortable leather chairs.

➕ 209 F5 ⊠ Kukulcán Boulevard Km 14 ☎ 998 885 2829;
www.puertomaderocancun.com
⊙ Daily 1pm–1am

MÉRIDA

Los Almendros $$$–$$$

Get a taste of Yucatecan cooking at this well-known restaurant overlooking Parque Mejorada, east of the zócalo. Yucatecan cuisine has been influenced by northern and southern Europeans over the years

(the Dutch were trading partners in the 19th century) and you might be able to detect their influence in some of the dishes served at this traditional restaurant, where the servers wear folk costumes.

➕ 209 D5 ⊠ Calle 50 No. 493,
Parque Mejorada ☎ 999 928 5459
⊙ Daily 12–3, 7–11

PLAYA DEL CARMEN

La Cueva del Chango $–$$

Breakfast, lunch and dinner are all treats in this exotically decorated restaurant. The breakfast menu offers the choice of starting the day in a western or Mexican style, with fresh-baked breads, granola, fruit or queso fresco. Lunch consists of generous salads and Mexican specialties. The emphasis is on natural, fresh foods and La Cueva even brings a little of the jungle to town with its own nursery gardens.

➕ 209 F5 ⊠ Calle 38 ☎ 984 873 2137 ⊙ Mon–Sat 8am–11pm, Sun 8am–2pm

skilled artisans across Mexico. They also hold frequent exhibitions of local work and contribute to local festivals. The shop is located on the second floor of the Embarcadero building.

La Isla Shopping Village

(Boulevard Kukulcan Km 12.5, Zona Hotelera, tel: 998 883 5025, www.laislacancun.com.mx), just opposite the Sheraton Hotel, is Cancún's glitziest shopping mall. It is located at the northern end of the lagoon and has an array of stylish boutiques, a disco, restaurants, a cinema and a marina. It's an entertaining place to explore but prices are inflated.

Widely regarded as the best place in Mérida to buy crafts, though not the cheapest, the state-run **Casa de las Artesanías** (Calle 63 No. 503a, tel: 999 928 6676, open Mon–Sat 9–8, Sun 9–2) specializes in Yucatecan items made by Yucatán artisans. The range of items, from ceramics to textiles, is updated regularly.

Where to...
Be Entertained

If you like all-you-can drink deals, swish bars and super-sized nightclubs, you'll love the nightlife in Cancún and Playa del Carmen. Cancún's nightlife is typified by Senor Frog's, a long-time fixture on the Zona Hotelera's drinking circuit with a seating capacity of 1,500.

Many of the upscale hotels, such as the Hyatt Cancún Caribe, on Boulevard Kukulcán have jazzy lounge bars or ballrooms.

Activities in the Yucatán tend to be based around the sea; fishing, diving and watersports like windsurfing, jetskiing and waterskiing are major attractions on the Riviera Maya, although the diving industry suffered after the damage wreaked by Hurricane Wilma in 2005. Game-fishing trips depart from the islands of Cozumel and Isla Mujeres. Scuba diving operators are back on their feet, but the damage to the reefs of Isla Mujeres will put off advanced divers.

Senor Frog's

This restaurant-bar turns into a raucous nightclub later at night, with DJs, karaoke and a waterslide that drops revellers into the lagoon. It is a good place to start a night out in Cancún.

✉ Boulevard Kukulcan Km9.5, Zona Hotelera, Cancún ☎ 998 883 1092; www.senorfrogs.com 🕐 Daily noon–3am

Los Dos Cooking School

Learn to cook delicious Yucatecan specialties in this live-in cookery school and guesthouse. Chef and founder David Sterling guides gastronomes through typical Yucatán menus in a wide range of packages, all in English.

✉ Calle 68 No. 517 (corner 65 and 67), Col. Centro, Mérida ☎ 999 928 1116; www.los-dos.com

Hidden Worlds

With many of the reefs suffering from human interference or hurricane damage, diving and snorkeling in the Yucatán's underground *cenotes* is an exciting alternative. Hidden Worlds offers first-time and experienced divers the chance to explore these underwater caves.

✉ Highway 307, north of Tulum ☎ 984 877 8535; www.hiddenworlds.com.mx

Walks & Tours

1 Mexico City's Centro Histórico

Walk

On this walk you'll enter the historic heart of this Latin American metropolis, passing the continent's largest cathedral, art galleries and remnants of ancient civilizations.

DISTANCE 1.6km (1 mile) **TIME** 2–3 hours
START/END POINT Zócalo 🔲 210 E2

The immense Catedral Metropolitana is the largest and oldest cathedral in Latin America

1–2

Standing on the north side of the vast Zócalo, with the **Catedral Metropolitana** (▶43) facing you, turn left down Avenida 5 de Mayo. This broad boulevard, lined with shops and restaurants, is one of the capital's main thoroughfares, linking the Zócalo with the Alameda. You're heading toward the Casa de los Azulejos, but look for some of the street's landmarks too, such as the grand La Nueva Bar Opera where Pancho Villa fired a bullet into the ceiling before being assassinated in 1923.

The impressive tiled facade of the Casa de los Azulejos

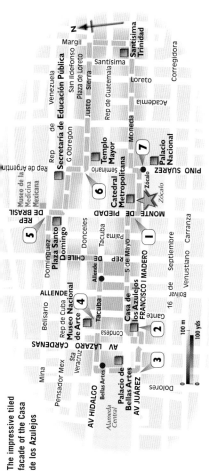

2–3

Turn left down Condesa; on the corner of Francisco I Madero the **Casa de los Azulejos** (▲ 52) is notable for the beautiful Talavera tiles on the exterior. Turn right immediately and resume walking toward the southeast corner of the Alameda on Francisco I Madero.

3–4

With the elegant **Palacio de Bellas Artes** (▲ 51) on your right and the large expanse of the **Alameda** (▲ 51) on your left, turn right and walk to the northeast corner of the Alameda, then turn right onto Avenida Tacuba. This is a much less stately street than 5 de Mayo, with street vendors, a Metro station and a market toward the far end. However, it does have several important art institutions along it.

The Palacio de Bellas Artes houses a museum, theater, cafeteria and excellent bookshop on the arts

4–5

The first is the **Museo Nacional de Arte** with its large collection of Mexican paintings, drawings, sculptures and ceramics from the 16th century to 1950, shortly after you pass the north-south street of Condesa. Next to it, the restaurant **Los Girasoles** (▶ 56 and right) is a good place to stop for lunch. Continue along Tacuba and turn left onto Republica de Chile, a shop-lined street, after the Metro station. Then turn right onto Belisario Dominguez, past the **Plaza Santo Domingo**, a historic square surrounded by 18th-century buildings, including the Antigua Aduana (former Customs House) on the east side, the Mexican baroque Convento de Santo Domingo (1737) on the north side and the old Edificio de la Inquisición (Inquisition Building) at the northeast corner.

5–6

At the corner of Belisario Dominguez and Republica de Brasil, turn right. On the corner the **Museo de la Medicina Mexicana** is closed for renovations. Continue along Brasil until you come to the Secretaría de Educación

Right: An equestrian statue of Carlos IV of Spain stands outside the Museo Nacional de Arte

Taking a Break

There are places on the route to stop and have a bite to eat, including **Los Girasoles** restaurant on Plaza Manuel Tolsá (▶ 56).

Above: The lavish belle epoque interior of Bar La Opera, on Avenida 5 de Mayo

Pública (Ministry of Education), where you will turn left onto Republica de Cuba and then right onto Republica de Argentina, where street stalls sell pirated CDs. This is a bustling area, so keep a hand on your bags. You're now zig-zagging toward the Templo Mayor.

6–7

The unprepossessing **Templo Mayor** (➤ 44–45), former capital of the Aztec Empire, greets you at the corner of Donceles. Excavations are ongoing, but at the moment, from a distance, it closely resembles a pit, surrounded by concrete walls on one side and a government building on the other. Continue right, past the Templo Mayor and the Plaza de Loreto, then take a right down Margil and another right down Zapata, after Republica de Guatemala, leaving the baroque church **Santísima Trinidad** on your right. This road will bring you back to the east side of the Zócalo. As you re-enter the square the **Palacio Nacional** (➤ 46) is on your left.

The **Templo Mayor (Great Temple)** was unearthed by accident during construction of the metro

2 Espiritu Santo Island, Baja

Kayak

DISTANCE 20km (16 miles) **TIME** Allow three days
START/END POINT Cone Beach, Espiritu Santo ✚ 198 B2

Espiritu Santo (Island of the Holy Spirit), in the Sea of Cortéz, 32km (20 miles) offshore from La Paz, is a marvelous place to explore – but only a restricted number of operators have permits to visit the island owned by the Nature Conservancy. The most usual way of seeing the island is to kayak from one end to the other over three days. In the winter (the weather is too hot in the summer) prevailing winds mean that tours start from the southern tip of the island at Cone beach and travel up the west side of the island to the sea lion colony at the northern tip (on a fragment of rock off Isla Partida).

1–2

The first day entails just 6km (4 miles) of paddling – a relaxed kayaking pace is 3km (2 miles) per hour, leaving plenty of time for

taking in the sights. Day one finishes at **Playa Coralito**, a small, quiet beach with a stand of mangrove on the other side of a ridge.

Kayaking is the best way to see the island

2–3

The next day, set off from Coralito to kayak the 9.5km (6 miles) to **Candelero** or **Musteno** beaches, two of the most attractive beaches on the island. There are caves at Musteno after a climb up the rocky hillside past Espiritu's largest residents: the organ pipe and cardon cacti. The cardon cactus is pollinated by bats so the flowers open at night.

Tour operator

Book in advance with Baja Outdoor Activities (tel: 52 612 1255636; www.kayakinbaja.com). No kayaking experience is necessary; a safety drill on day one involves exiting the kayak underwater. Tents, sleeping mats, all food and drink, equipment and transfers are included. You will need to bring sandals to wear in the water (stingrays, sea urchins); sun block, a hat and a water bottle.

Left: Looking out over Playa Coralito

Below: Sunset over the Sea of Cortéz from the Bay of Candelero

The Sea of Cortéz

The Sea of Cortéz, the narrow but deep channel of water between the Baja peninsula and mainland Mexico, was described by Jacques Cousteau as "the world's aquarium." It's one of the most diverse marine areas in the world, containing 31 marine mammal species (one third of the world's whale and dolphin species), 500 species of fish and more than 200 bird species. It's also a very fragile ecosystem, under pressure from developers on both sides of the sea. This is why Espiritu Santo, a 9,430ha (23,300-acre) island 32km (20 miles) offshore from La Paz at the southern end of Baja, was bought by the Nature Conservancy for $3.3m in 2003.

Other less visible inhabitants include rattlesnakes, a small, indigenous wildcat and squadrons of pelicans, dive-bombing the bays for fish.

Espiritu Santo

The west coast of Espiritu Santo is a series of sandy coves divided by rocky headlands; visitors can camp on one of the island's 20 deserted beaches. When you're not paddling you can go snorkeling among tropical fish and sea lions or hike into the rocky interior of the island. Espiritu Santo was inhabited by Indian tribes, and the grassy mounds behind the beaches are not dunes but middens containing prehistoric items; archaeologists prefer visitors not to walk on them.

3–4

The third day takes you across the open water between Espiritu Santo and Isla Partida. **Playa Partida** is one of the island's best beaches and is a popular mooring for yachts. Finish the tour of Espiritu with an afternoon snorkeling with sea lions at the large colony on **Isla Partida** before returning to La Paz in a motorboat.

3 San Miguel de Allende

Walk

DISTANCE 1.6–2.2km (1–2 miles) **TIME** Allow 2–3 hours, including browsing time
START/END POINT Jardín Principal ☐ 205 E3

San Miguel de Allende (▶95) is a joy to discover on foot – not least because driving down the narrow streets would be a futile exercise and you would miss all the smart art galleries tucked behind heavy wooden doors. This walk takes in several of the town's ever-increasing number of galleries, while also passing most of the major attractions.

1–2
Start the walk in **Le Jardin**, the leafy square in the center of San Miguel's historic core. San Miguel's wealthiest families built their homes facing onto the plaza in the 17th and 18th centuries, with more houses radiating

Left: The backstreets of San Miguel
Center: The Royal Convent of the Immaculate Conception

outwards along the streets. The square is now lined with ironwork benches with locals reading newspapers and pigeons bathing in the fountains at each corner. The central bandstand is ringed by orange trees. Cross the square to the pink parish church of the **Arcangel St Michael**. Turn right down Umaran then take the next left down Jesus. **Galeria Le Noir**, a

contemporary art gallery, **Ambar**, displaying sculpture, fossilized amber and jewelry, and **Galeria 4D**, specializing in handmade jewelry, are three of the most interesting galleries on Jesus.

2–3
Turn right down Nadrante before turning left down

Hernández Macías. At the foot of the hill, the **Caracol Collection** displays a wide range of Mexican crafts. Follow this road around the corner and past the bazaar on the right. Keep right.

3-4

At the junction turn left to see the copper pots and pans in **Artesméxico Galería Carlos Muro** and a good view of the dome of the Temple of the Immaculate Conception, one of the largest in Mexico. Otherwise turn right up Zacateceros. This street is lined with shops and galleries selling wrestling masks, *guayaberas* (shirts), pottery and art – at slightly cheaper prices than the center. Follow the road up the hill and facing you is the **Temple of the Immaculate Conception**, with an amazing Gothic interior and altar to the left.

4-5

Walking past the Temple (turn right at the junction) you can stop for refreshment at El Campanario restaurant on the right. Turn left

down Hernández Macías. On the left is the **Royal Convent of the Immaculate Conception**, opposite the Plaza Colonial. The convent was built at the same time as the church on the same plot; the construction budget was 40,000 gold pesos. Inside the grounds, peaceful tropical gardens, including lime trees, surround a fountain. There are cafés inside the Plaza Colonial and the Convent.

5-6

Turn tight onto Mesones with the **Angela Peralta Theater**, named after the opera singer,

Left: One of San Miguel's intriguing galleries
Right: The impressive dome of the Temple of the Immaculate Conception

on the corner. Built in 1875, it remains an important venue for shows; the neoclassical facade was added 1914 to 1916. The **Galería Izamal** (▶ 105) opened in 1991 and was one of the first galleries in San Miguel. Continue up Mesones. You can stop at the charming, wholefood café El Tomate on the right for a snack. Turn left down Pepe Llanos to the **Oratorio de San Felipe Neri** and the Civic Plaza, where a clothing and craft market

is held. The Oratorio is the foundation of Catholicism in San Miguel de Allende. Its present structure is largely the same as it was in the 18th century, with a baroque facade featuring five saints guard-

ing the unusual ornamental columns. Prior to the Jardin Principal, the **Civic Plaza** was the administrative center of San Miguel, its buildings holding the town's Royal houses, the granary and the jail.

The Churrigueresque-style Oratorio de San Felipe Neri, near the Plaza Cívico

6–7
Turn right on Nunez then left up San Francisco to the **Calvary Sanctuary** at the top of the hill. After this, turn right down Correos, which will take you back to your starting point in Le Jardin, the social hub of life in the city.

Taking a Break
There are plenty places on the route to stop and have a bite to eat, including El Campanario restaurant and the wholefood café **El Tomate** (below).

The Riviera Maya

Drive

DISTANCE 285km (177 miles) **TIME** Allow 1 day
START/END POINT Cancún ⊞ 209 F5

This drive starts in Cancún (▶ 156–157) and follows the Yucatán shore south on the multilane Highway 307 to Tulum. Here you can divert inland to visit Cobá, a Mayan city still hidden in the jungle. With the coast on your left during the drive south through the state of Quintana Roo, the landscape on your right will be a flat, scrubby plain, but the farther you go from Cancún, the less development there will be. You can make a fuel stop at Tulum's gas station before turning inland. Signposting is generally good, but be vigilant for erratic drivers and traffic police who stop speeding motorists.

The crystal clear water of the Xel-Há ecological resort is ideal for snorkeling

1–2

Pick up a rental car from one of the international firms at Cancún airport and take the Riviera Maya's Highway 307, signposted from the airport. Drive 20km (12 miles) south of the airport to **Puerto Morelos**, a down-to-earth fishing village with pristine, uncrowded beaches that hasn't been inundated by tourists. Those who come mostly arrive in order to take the car ferry across to **Cozumel** (▶ 157). There's excellent snorkeling offshore and a large botanic garden, the Jardín Botánico Dr. Alfredo Barrera, where you can see many Yucatán species, including monkeys, parrots, orchids and cacti. The garden is on the south side of the village and you can walk there from the village center.

the pedestrianized zone and is packed with bars and restaurants. Avenida Juárez has a more naturally Mexican ambience.

4–5

Leaving Playa del Carmen, continue south on Highway 307 to **Xcaret** (▶ 166), a Mayan theme park which has a stunning beachside setting. Attractions include archaeological replicas, evening extravaganzas and the chance to swim with dolphins. It is popular with day trippers from Playa del Carmen.

A moment of peace and quiet on the beach at Playa del Carmen

2–3

Return to Highway 307 and continue south. On the left, Playa Paraíso and Punta Maroma are two excellent beaches. A further 14km (9 miles) south, **Tres Ríos** is one of the area's most authentic eco-parks. The park underwent a revamp in 2006 and reopened in mid-2007. It is based around the jungle and mangrove ecosystems of the area and in addition to animal and plant exhibits, offers a wide range of activities including snorkeling and horse-back riding.

3–4

Rejoining Highway 307, head south to **Playa del Carmen** (▶ 156–157), a smaller version of Cancún. Playa del Carmen, like Cancún, has been rigorously exploited by developers, with familiar brands at every turn. But it's more manageable in scale than Cancún, more laidback and easier on the wallet. If you visit the beach, turn north and walk along the shore to Playa de Cocos, where a strip of beach bars looks out to sea. Avenida Quinta is the main street in

Taking a Break

Stop halfway in Playa del Carmen for lunch at La Cueva del Chango (▶ 173) or, if you're not ready to eat yet, refuel with a coffee from Java Joes. If you stop at Aktun Chen's caves, there's a small restaurant serving ice-cold drinks and light meals. And there are restaurants at the eco-parks of Xel-há and Xcaret.

5–6

Further south is **Akumal**, "place of the turtles" in Mayan, a smaller, more exclusive beach resort. Look for the turnoff on the left side of the road. It could have been called "place of the shipwrecks" as several Spanish galleons are thought to have sunk offshore. Akumal is one of the older resorts on the Riviera Maya and the hotels along the beach-front are more low-key than those in Cancún. There's good snorkeling in the Ya Kul lagoon, north of Akumal.

6–7

Shortly after returning to Highway 307, look out for a sign to **Aktun Chen**, 4km (3 miles) south of Akumal. The limestone Yucatán

The waters around Akumal, once famous for its turtles, teem with marine life

peninsula is riddled with innumerable underground cave systems (the sinkholes are called *cenotes*). The eco-park of Aktun Chen is based around one such cave system, which has an underground river. There are frequent tours underground (taking 75 minutes), so

you will have to time to see the caves before continuing south. In the third cave there is a 12m-deep (39-foot) *cenote*, surrounded by 5-million-year-old stalactites and stalagmites. Serious scuba divers will also want to visit **Nohoch Nah Chich** (signposted Cenote Dos Ojos), which also lies south of Akumal. It is the second largest underwater cave system in the world, extending 60km (45 miles).

7-8

Back on Highway 307, the next stop is a slice of beach paradise: **Xcacel**, a white-sand beach that has been the object of a tussle between conservationists and developers. The beach was a key nesting site for sea turtles, but increased usage by people is driving them away. Just south of Xcacel, the eco-resort of **Xel-Ha** (▲ 166) is a man-made lagoon with tropical fish, adventure activities, a spa and Dolphin World. The park's entrance is directly to the left from Highway 307.

8-9

The final stop on the Riviera Maya, although there is an option to continue inland, is **Tulum** (▲ 158–159), a truly exciting climax to the drive. The highlight is the Mayan ruins north of the main settlement, with a temple and pyramids overlooking the turquoise sea and white sand beaches. It's a dramatically beautiful setting, largely uncompromised by hotel development farther down the coast. The tallest building is El Castillo, but none of the constructions match mid-Mayan masterpieces such as Chichen Itzá. You can stay overnight in **Tulum**.

9-10

Alternatively get back in the car and turn inland at the crossroad that leads to **Cobá** (▲ 166–167), one of the lesser-known archaeological sites and one of the most intriguing. Still obscured by jungle, Cobá was once a city of up to 50,000 people; you can get a view of the extent of the ancient city from the top of the 42m-high (138-foot) Nohoch Mul pyramid, the tallest in the Yucatán. If you do include Cobá on this excursion, you might also like to continue along the same road northwest to **Valladolid** (▲ 167), a large colonial city. From Valladolid you can take Highway 180-D directly back to Cancún.

Left: Nohoch Mul, Cobá, offers great views of the jungle from the top
Right: Valladolid's Cathedral of San Gervasio, built with stones from ancient Mayan ruins

Practicalities

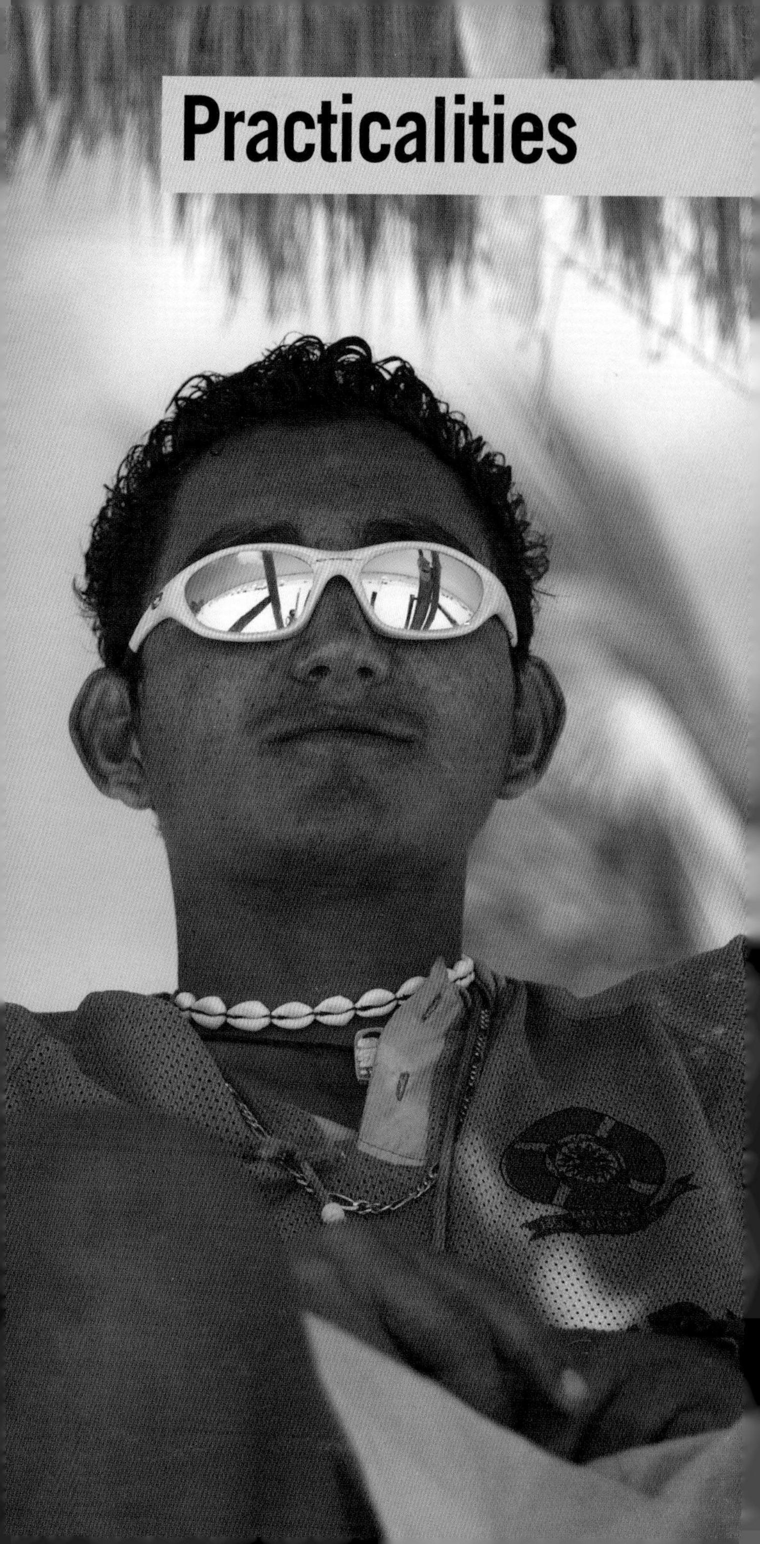

Website
● Official website of the Mexico Tourist Board, in English and other languages: www.visitmexico.com

In the UK
Mexican Tourism Board
Wakefield House
41 Trinity Square
London EC3N 4DJ
☎ 020 7488 9392

In the US
Mexican Tourist Board
400 Madison Avenue
Suite 11C
New York, NY 10017
☎ 212/308-2110

BEFORE YOU GO

WHAT YOU NEED

	Some countries require a passport to remain valid for at least six months beyond the date of entry – contact their consulate or embassy or your travel agent for details.	UK	Germany	USA	Canada	Australia	Ireland	Netherlands	Spain
● Required ○ Suggested ▲ Not required △ Not applicable									
Passport/National Identity Card (American citizens will also need their passport to return to the U.S.)		●	●	●	●	●	●	●	△
Visa (regulations can change – check before you travel		▲	▲	▲	▲	▲	▲	▲	▲
Tourist Card		●	●	●	▲	●	●	●	●
Onward or Return Ticket		●	●	●	●	●	●	●	●
Health Inoculations (tetanus and polio)		▲	▲	▲	▲	▲	▲	▲	▲
Travel Insurance		○	○	○	○	○	○	○	○
Driver's Licence (national)		●	●	●	●	●	●	●	●
Car Insurance Certificate		○	○	○	○	○	○	○	○
Car Registration Document		●	●	●	●	●	●	●	●

WHEN TO GO

Mexico City

☐ High season   ☐ Low season

JAN	FEB	MAR	APR	MAY	JUN	JUL	AUG	SEP	OCT	NOV	DEC
19°C	21°C	24°C	26°C	24°C	23°C	23°C	23°C	23°C	21°C	20°C	19°C
66°F	70°F	75°F	79°F	75°F	73°F	73°F	73°F	73°F	70°F	68°F	66°F

☀ Sun   ☁ Cloud   🌧 Wet   ⛅ Sun/Showers

In such a vast country, the weather is usually determined by where you are and, more pertinently, your altitude, than by the time of year. The tropical lowlands of the **Yucatán** tend to have higher rainfall throughout the year than the arid deserts of **Baja** and **northern Mexico**. However, there are some rules. The peak season tends to be over the winter months because this is when temperatures and rainfall are at their lowest. The rainy season begins in the south and works its way north from May onward. Toward the end of the rainy season (September, October, November) **hurricanes** can strike the Caribbean coast. Temperatures are also at their highest during the rainy season. In the winter, temperatures can fall very low in the highlands, even during the day. Take a warm jacket and a hat.

In the US
Mexican Tourism Board
1880 Century Park East
Suite 511
Los Angeles, CA 90067
☎ 310/282-9112

In Canada
Mexican Tourism Board
1610-999 West Hastings
Street, Suite 1110
Vancouver, British
Columbia V6C 2W2
☎ 604/669-2845

In Germany
Mexican Tourism Board
Taunusanlage 21
Frankfurt-am-Main
D60325
☎ 69 71 03 38 95

GETTING THERE

By Air Mexico City is an 11- to 12-hour flight from London; Cancún is a slightly shorter trip. There are 60 airports in Mexico and most of the major cities receive international flights. Most visitors from America can fly to resorts such as Cabo San Lucas or Puerto Vallarta direct from the U.S., or with just one change at Mexico City. Guadalajara and Puebla are increasingly popular alternatives. All have money-changing facilities, taxis, restaurants and duty-free shops.

By Land Arriving in Mexico overland from the U.S. is a popular and relatively easy option. There are a large number of border crossings and you can usually walk or drive across. You need Mexican automobile insurance to bring in your own vehicle. Most border crossings now have long-distance bus terminals, so you can easily get to your destination from the border. You can also cross by land from Guatemala and Belize.

By Cruise Ship Cruise ships from all around the world dock in Mexican ports. Destinations such as Acapulco, Cozumel, Ensenada and Puerto Vallarta are most popular. Contact a travel agent or a website such as www.cruiseweb.com for details and schedules.

TIME

 Mexico straddles two time zones. Most of the country is 6 hours behind GMT (the same as U.S. Central Time), but the far west (Baja) is 7 hours behind (on Pacific Coast Time in the U.S.).

CURRENCY AND FOREIGN EXCHANGE

Currency The currency in Mexico is the **peso**. It is often represented by $, the dollar sign, which can cause confusion.
There are 100 centavos in one peso and the peso comes in denominations of 20, 50, 100, 200, 500 and 1000 peso notes. The exchange rates will vary but expect to get about 10 pesos to one U.S. dollar.

Exchange The safest way to carry currency is by traveler's checks, although not all currency exchanges (*casas de cambio*) will take them now. You may need to use an international bank to exchange **traveler's checks**. It is advisable to use **dollar traveler's checks** issued by well-known names such as American Express. Outside cities and tourist areas it may be harder to change **euros**, **pounds sterling** and other currencies. Tourist hotels will also change money (traveler's checks or cash) but the exchange rate will not be as favorable as banks or the *casas de cambio*. The most convenient method of payment is by credit or debit card. Note that when you draw money out of foreign ATMs your bank may charge a fee. It is better to draw out one large sum of money rather than several small sums. You will need to know your PIN number. **Credit cards** are widely accepted in Mexico but are not likely to be accepted in markets, local restaurants and small shops.

TIME DIFFERENCES

GMT	Mexico City	USA New York	Germany	Netherlands	Australia
12 noon	6am	7am	1pm	1pm	Sydney 10pm

WHEN YOU ARE THERE

CLOTHING SIZES

UK	Rest of Europe	Mexico	USA	
36	46	46	36	
38	48	48	38	
40	50	50	40	
42	52	52	42	Suits
44	54	54	44	
46	56	56	46	
7	41	41	8	
7.5	42	42	8.5	
8.5	43	43	9.5	
9.5	44	44	10.5	Shoes
10.5	45	45	11.5	
11	46	46	12	
14.5	37	37	14.5	
15	38	38	15	
15.5	39/40	39/40	15.5	
16	41	41	16	Shirts
16.5	42	42	16.5	
17	43	43	17	
8	36	36	6	
10	38	38	8	
12	40	40	10	
14	42	42	12	Dresses
16	44	44	14	
18	46	46	16	
4.5	37.5	38	6	
5	38	38	6.5	
5.5	38.5	39	7	
6	39	39	7.5	Shoes
6.5	40	40	8	
7	41	41	8.5	

NATIONAL HOLIDAYS

1 Jan	New Year's Day
5 Feb	Constitution Day
24 Feb	Day of the National Flag
21 Mar	Anniversary of Benito Juárez's birth
1 May	Labour Day
5 May	Anniversary of Mexican victory against French at Puebla
16 Sep	Independence Day
12 Oct	Celebration of Columbus's discovery of the New World
20 Nov	Revolution Day Conception
25 Dec	Christmas Day

OPENING HOURS

○ Shops   ● Post Offices
● Offices   ● Museums/Monuments
● Banks   ● Pharmacies

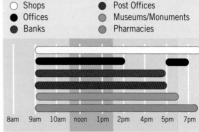

8am 9am 10am noon 1pm 2pm 4pm 5pm 7pm

☐ Day   ☐ Midday   ☐ Evening

Shop hours are typically 9am–8pm.
Office hours are Mon–Fri 9–2, 4–7.
Banks open 9am–5pm on weekdays, but branches in major cities may stay open for a further two hours and on Saturday mornings.
Post offices are generally open Mon–Fri 9–6, Sat 9–1.
Pharmacies are open Mon–Fri 9–8, Sat 9–1, but there should be one 24-hour pharmacy in town. Many **museums** and **attractions** close on Mondays. Their opening hours will vary.

POLICE, FIRE AND AMBULANCE 080

GREEN ANGELS (TOURIST PATROL) 55 5250 8221

FOR OTHER CRISIS LINES, SEE LOCAL PHONE BOOK

PERSONAL SAFETY

- Avoid walking alone in unlit streets at night.
- Be very careful when you draw money out of ATMs.
- Certain areas of Mexico, particularly the less visited, are affected by bandits.
- Avoid driving at night.
- Don't hail taxis in the streets of the capital.
- Use the first-class or deluxe bus services. There have been reports of buses being held up or hijacked.
- Women traveling alone should exercise particular caution. If you are unduly hassled by someone in the street most Mexicans would come to your aid.

Police assistance:
 113 from any phone

TELEPHONES

Most public phones take phone cards (Ladatel), widely available from shops and kiosks in various values. Mobile (cell) phones will work in Mexico if they are a tri-band phone with international roaming enabled. Avoid making long-distance calld from hotels: taxes increase costs.

The country code for Mexico is 52. Cities and regions have their own three-digit code and the rest of the number is usually seven digits.

International Dialling Codes
From Mexico to:

UK:	00 44
USA / Canada:	00 1
Irish Republic:	00 353
Netherland:	00 31
Australia:	00 61
Germany:	00 49

POST

There are *correos* (post offices) in most towns and cities. Stamps are also sold in shops and hotels. Overseas mail is slow but generally reliable, and is a better service than internal post. For anything urgent or of value, use a courier service.

ELECTRICITY

The power supply is the same as the U.S.: 120v, 60Hz. Most plug sockets are the two flat pronged variety. International adaptors are available in airports and most electrical items, including phone chargers, will work in Mexico.

TIPS/GRATUITIES

Tipping is not expected for all services and rates are lower than those elsewhere. Carry some low denomination peso notes with you. As a general guide:

Resort restaurants	10–15 percent
Porters/Bellboys	10–20 pesos per bag
Tour guides/drivers	50 pesos
Fuel station attendants	5 pesos
Taxis	Not necessary, or round up to nearest 5 pesos

UK
☎ 55 5242
8500

USA
☎ 55 5080
2000

Germany
☎ 55 5283
2200

Netherlands
☎ 55 5258
9921

Spain
☎ 55 5380
4383

HEALTH

Insurance It is essential to take out reliable travel insurance when visiting Mexico as emergency hospital treatment can be very expensive. For minor ailments pharmacists give good advice, or contact a local doctor through your hotel.

Dental Services Mexican dentists have a very good reputation. If you need emergency dental treatment, ask at your hotel for a recommendation.

Weather To avoid sunstroke, use a high-factor sunscreen, wear a hat and drink lots of water. It is sensible to avoid the heat of the midday sun. Malaria has been eradicated from cities and tourists areas in Mexico but may be present in rural areas. Take advice on whether you need anti-malaria medication for your trip.

Drugs Bring any prescription medicines you require with you. Prescription medicines are also widely available in *farmacia* (pharmacies) across Mexico. Also bring a basic first-aid kit: mosquito repellent, anti-histamine cream for insect bites, a general antibiotic and pain-relief tablets. The liberal use of lime juice apparently acts as a deterrent against bacteria.

Safe Water Avoid drinking unpurified water; this includes ice cubes, mixers in drinks and brushing your teeth in the hotel. *Agua purificada* (purified water) or bottled water is widely available and is the best way to minimize the chance of illness.

CONCESSIONS

Students/Youths There is little available in the way of reductions for students, as most youth discounts are for Mexican citizens. Children under the age of 12 get reductions on domestic flights and sometimes free beds in their parents' rooms.

Senior Citizens Again, discounts apply solely to Mexican nationals.

TRAVELING WITH A DISABILITY

Facilities for visitors with a disability are severely lacking in most areas of Mexico, but many of the major museums have made significant progress with access. Airports and hotels are also improving fast and have wheelchair ramps and adapted toilets. Be aware of uneven sidewalks (pavements) and roads, which are often in a poor state of repair.

CHILDREN

Children are warmly welcomed almost everywhere in Mexico. Baby-changing facilities are limited.

TOILETS

Public toilets are generally unpleasant. Always carry your own toilet paper. Used toilet paper should be placed in the receptacle provided, not flushed down the toilet. Failing to observe this custom blocks the drain or pan.

CUSTOMS

The import of wildlife souvenirs sourced from rare or endangered species may be either illegal or require a special permit. Before purchase you should check your home country's customs regulations.

USEFUL WORDS AND PHRASES

Spanish is the language used throughout Mexico, although in large resorts English is also widely spoken. If traveling to smaller places it is essential to know a few basic phrases. Mexican Spanish has slight differences in vocabulary and usage from Castilian Spanish, but otherwise it is very similar. Accents change throughout this vast country, and in some areas you will hear local indigenous languages such as Náhuatl, Maya or Zapotec.

GREETINGS AND COMMON WORDS

Hello. Good morning **Hola. Buenos días**
Good afternoon **Buenas tardes**
Good evening/night **Buenas noches**
Goodbye **Adiós**
See you later **Hasta luego**
Yes/no **Sí/non**
Please **Por favor**
Thank you **Gracias**
It's a pleasure/you're welcome **De nada**
That's all right **Está bien**
Excuse me, can you help me? **¿Disculpe, me padrí ayudar?**
I don't speak Spanish **No hablo español**
Do you speak English? **¿Habla inglés?**
How are you? **¿Cómo está?**
I don't understand **No entiendo**
I don't know **No lo sé**
Please speak more slowly **Por favor hable más despacio**
Please repeat that **Por favor repita eso**
What does this mean? **¿Qué significa esto?**
What is the time? **¿Qué hora es?**
Hello, pleased to meet you **Hola, encantado/a**
My name is **Me llamo**
What's your name? **¿Como se llama?**
I live in **Vivo en**
Where do you live? **¿Dónde vive usted?**
Can you write that for me? **¿Me lo puede escribir?**

NUMBERS

1	**uno**	16	**dieciséis**
2	**dos**	17	**diecisiete**
3	**tres**	18	**dieiocho**
4	**cuatro**	19	**diecinueve**
5	**cinco**	20	**veinte**
6	**seis**	21	**veintiuno**
7	**siete**	30	**treinta**
8	**ocho**	40	**cuarenta**
9	**nueve**	50	**cincuenta**
10	**diez**	60	**sesenta**
11	**once**	70	**setente**
12	**doce**	80	**ochenta**
13	**trece**	90	**noventa**
14	**catorce**	100	**cien**
15	**quince**	1,000	**mil**

ILLNESS AND EMERGENCIES

Help **Socorro**
I don't feel well **No me siento bien**
I have had an accident **Tuve un accidente**
Could you call a doctor? **¿Podría llamar a un médico?**
Stop thief! **Al ladrón!**
I have been robbed **Me han robado**
Where is the police station? **¿Dónde está la comisaría?**
I have lost my passport/wallet/purse/hand-bag **He perdido me pasaporte/la cartera/el monedero/la bolsa**

GETTING AROUND

Where is the information desk/timetable? **¿Dónde está el mostrador de información/el horario?**
Can I have a single/return ticket to…? **¿Me da un boleto sencillo/de ida y vuelta para …?**
I'd like to rent a car **Quiero alquilar un coche**
Is this the way to…? **¿Es esto el camino par ir a…?**
I'm lost **Estoy perdido**
Please take me to… **Me lleva a…, por favor**

DAYS/MONTHS

Monday **lunes**
Tuesday **martes**
Wednesday **miércoles**
Thursday **jueves**
Friday **viernes**
Saturday **sábado**
Sunday **domingo**
January **enero**
February **febrero**
March **marzo**
April **abril**
May **mayo**
June **junio**
July **julio**
August **agosto**
September **septiembre**
October **octubre**
November **noviembre**
December **diciembre**

MENU READER

a la brasa flame-grilled

a la plancha grilled on a griddle

aceitunas olives

aguacate avocado

agua mineral con gas/sin gas sparkling mineral water/still mineral water

al horno baked/roasted

almeja clam

arroz rice

arroz con leche rice pudding

asado roast

atún tuna

borracho cooked with wine

café coffee

calamares squid

caldo de pollo chicken-based broth with vegetables, seasoned with cilantro (coriander)

camarones shrimps

cangrejo crab

cazón dogfish

ceballo onion

cerveza beer

ceviche raw fish in lime juice with tomatoes, onions, spices and chilis

chalupas fried tortillas, shaped like a boat, with sauce and salad

chícharos peas

chicharrón pork crackling

chilaquiles rojos small fried tortillas with red tomato sauce

chilaquiles verdes as above with green tomato sauce

chiles en nogada stuffed peppers with white almond sauce and red pomegranate seeds, echoing colors of Mexican flag

chilorio loin of pork in chili sauce

chivo goat

chorizo/salchicha sausage

chuleta chop or cutlet

coco coconut

cordero lamb

costillas ribs

dorado dolphin (fish)

duraznoz peaches

enchiladas rojos fried tortillas filled with chicken and red *mole*, sprinkled with onion and cream

enchiladas verdes as above with green tomato sauce

enfrijoladas fried tortillas with a bean-based sauce, with cheese, cream and onion

ensalada de nopales cactus-leaf salad

fajitas anything rolled up in a flour tortilla, but strictly should contain skirt of beef

flan crème caramel

fresa strawberry

frijoles beans

frito fried

granada passion fruit

guacamole mashed avocado and green tomatoes, with onion, cilantro and sometimes chili

guayaba guava

hamburguesa hamburger

helado ice cream

hígado liver

higo fig

hongos/champiñones mushrooms

huachinango red snapper

hueva egg

huevos a la mexicana scrambled eggs with chili and tomatoes

huevos ahogados hard-boiled eggs in a tomato-based sauce

huevos motuleños fried eggs in a sauce of peas, tomatoes, cheese and fried banana

huevos rancheros fried eggs and diced chili in a tomato sauce on top of a tortilla

jamón ham

jugo de fruta fruit juice

jurel yellowtail

langosta lobster

leche milk

lechuga lettuce

lomo tenderloin

mantequilla butter

manzana apple

mermelada jam

mero grouper

mixiotes chicken or rabbit wrapped in maguey leaves

mole a chili-based sauce, used to accompany cooked chicke or turkey

naranja orange

nopales young leaves of the prickly pear cactus

ostra oyster

palmito palm heart

pan bread

papas fritas french fries

papaya pawpaw

pato duck

pavo turkey

perro caliente hot dog

picadillo minced beef with tomatoes and vegetables

piña pineapple

plátano banana

poché poached

pollo chicken

puerco pork

pulpo octopus

quesadillas doubled-over tortillas, heated, slightly crisp, filled with one or more of chicken, cheese, green peppers, spinach, chorizo, nopal

queso cheese

rábano radish

refrescos soft drinks

relleno stuffed/filled

res beef

robalo bass

sandía watermelon

sopa de tortilla tomato-based soup with shredded tortillas

tacos rolled up tortillas, usually filled with beef or chicken

tamales meat and chil sauce wrapped in corn dough and then in maize or banana leaves and steamed

tamarindo tamarind

té tea

ternera veal

tocino bacon

torrejas bread soaked in honey and fried

trucha trout

tuburón shark

vino tinto/vino blanco red wine/white wine

zanahoria carrot

Atlas

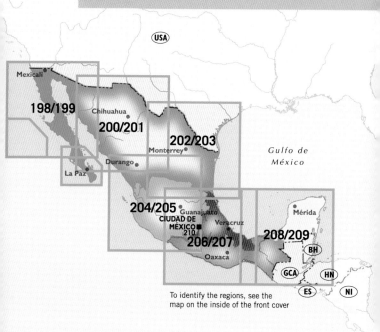

USA

Mexicali

198/199   Chihuahua

200/201

202/203

Monterrey

Durango

La Paz

Gulfo de
México

204/205   Guanajuato
CIUDAD DE
MÉXICO   Veracruz
210

Mérida

206/207   **208/209**

Oaxaca   BH

GCA   HN

ES   NI

To identify the regions, see the
map on the inside of the front cover

Regional Maps

▬▬▬ Major route	☐ City
▨▨▨ Motorway	▫ Town/village
▨▨▨ National road	✈ Airport
─── Regional road	▣ Featured place of interest
─── Other road	▪ Place of interest
─·─·─ International boundary	National park
─··─ Regional boundary	

198–209
0 ————— 100 km
0 ————— 50 miles

City Plans

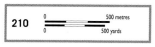

─── Main road/minor road	Important building
─── Railway	Park
▣ Featured place of interest	● Metro

210
0 ———— 500 metres
0 ———— 500 yards

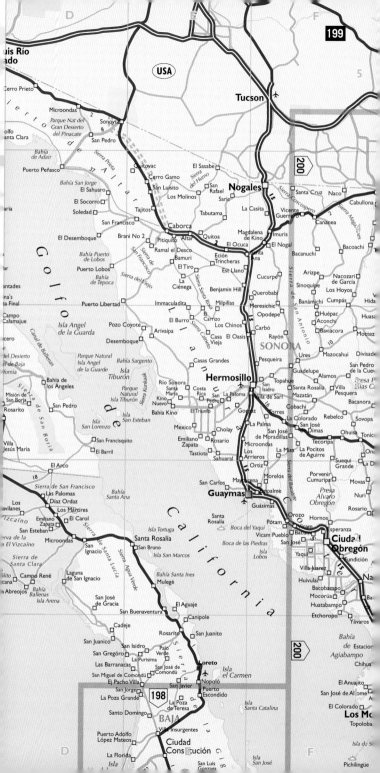

5

USA

Tucson

Luis Río
ado

Cerro Prieto

Microondas 2
Sonoyta 8
San Pedro

Parque Nat del
Gran Desierto
del Pinacate

Golfo
nta Clara

Bahía
de Adair

Puerto Peñasco

Quitovac

Cerro Gamo

San Luisito

Tajitos

El Sasabe

El Sahuaro
El Socorro
Soledad

San Francisco

El Desemboque

Brani No 2

Pitiquito

Ramal el Desco

Bamuri

El Tiro

La
Ciénega

Puerto Lobos

Bahía Puerto
de Lobos

Bahía
de Tepoca

Puerto Libertad

Immaculadita

El Burro

El
Carrizo

Los Chinos

Casa
Vieja

El Oasis

Rayón

Casas Grandes

Arivaipa

Desemboque

Pozo Coyote

Río Sonora
Santa
Maria
Costa
Rica

El Triunfo

La Palma

La Ciénega

Benjamin Hill

Querobabi

Meresichic

Opodepe

Carbó

SONORA

Pesqueira

Ures

Guadalupe

Mazocahui

Divisade

San Pedro
de la Cueva

Topahue
Santa Rosalía
Villa
Pesquera

Bacanora

Mazatán

Cobachi

Rebelco

Sovopa

Ohuisa

Toni

La D

Isla Angel
de la Guarda

Canal de Ballenas

Parque Natural
Isla Angel
de la Guarde

Parque
Natural
Isla Tiburón

Bahía Sargento

Isla
Tiburón

Isla
San Esteban

Bahía Kino

Isla
San Lorenzo

San Francisquito

El Barril

Mexico

Cholay

Emiliano
Zapata

Rosario

Tastiota

Sahuaral

Los
Arrieros

La Misa

La Pocitos
de Aguirre

Suequi
Grande

Movas

Nuri

Rosario

Bahía de
los Angeles

San Pedro

Misión de
San Borja
Rosarito

Sierra de San Borja

Villa
Jesús Maria

El Arco

18

Sierra de San Francisco

Las Palomas
Diaz Ordaz

Los
avilanes

Emiliano
Zapata
San Esteban

El Carol

Microondas

Los Mártires

San
Ignacio

Santa Rosalía

San Bruno

Isla Tortuga

Bahía
Santa Ana

Isla San Marcos

Bahía Santa Ines

Mulegé

Sierra de
Santa Clara

erva de la
a El Vizcaíno

lito
ana

Campo René

Abreojos

Bahía
Ballenas
Isla Arena

Sierra Agua Verde

Laguna
de San Ignacio

San José
de Gracia

San Buenaventura

El Aguaje

Canipole

Cadeje

Rosarito

San Juanito

San Juanico

San Gregório

Las Barrancas

San Miguel de Comondú

Ej Pacho Villa

San Jorge

La Poza Grande

Santo Domingo

San Isidro
La Purisima

Palo
Verde

San José de
Comondú

San javier

La Poza
de Teresa

198

Loreto

Nopoló

Puerto
Escondido

Isla
el Carmen

Isla
Santa Catalina

BAJA

Puerto Adolfo
López Mateos

La Florida

Villa Insurgentes

Ciudad
Constitución

San Luis
San José

Isla

Pichilingue

Isla de S

California

Calamajué

Cocero

del Desierto
al Baja
fornia

ntados

na's
ta Final

Golfo

de

California

Sierra del Bacatete

200

Sierra del Viejo

Sierra de San Francisco

Bahía de
los Angeles

199

Parque Nat del
Gran Desierto
del Pinacate

Sierra Prieta

37

Sierra
del Humo

Sierra del Viejo

San Rafael

Sarie

La Casita

Tabutama

Caborca

Quitoa

2

El Ocuca

Altar

Santa
Ana

Ramal el Desco

Ción
Trincheras

Est Llano

Magdalena
de Kino

Imuris

El Nogal

Cucurpe

Milpillas

Sierra Santa Rosa

Nogales

1.5

Santa Cruz

Naco

Vicente
Guerrero

Cananea

Sierra Coscospero

Bacoachi

Cabullona

Sierra Mazatán

Arizpe

Nacozari
de García

Sinoquipe

Los Hoyos

Banámichi

Cumpás

Huépac
Aconchi

Baviácora

Mottez

Huas

Hid

Bacanuchi

Sierra de San Antonio

San Isidro

Villa de Sarí

Goguaz

Torres

La Colorada

San José
de Dimas

Tecoripa

San Pedro

La Paloma

Hermosillo

Kino,
Nuevo

El Triunfo

San José
de Moradillas

Microondas

Ortiz

Morelos

Maytorena

Empalme

San Carlos

Guaymas

Guásimas

Pótam

Orozco

Vícam

Hornos

Porvenir
Cumuripa

Presa
Alvaro
Obregón

Boca del Yaqui

Vícam Pueblo

San José

Boca de las Piedras

Isla
Lobos

Yaqui

Esperanza

Ciudad
Obregón

Na

Fundición

Villa Juarez

Huivulai

Bacobampo

Mocorúa

Huatabampo

Etchoropo

Yávaros

Bahía
de Estación
Agiabampo

Chihua

El Anuajito

San José de Al

El Colorado

Topolobar

Los M

200

Presa
Elías Ca

Nacori

10

Sahuaripa

La
Misa

Baroyeca

Onar

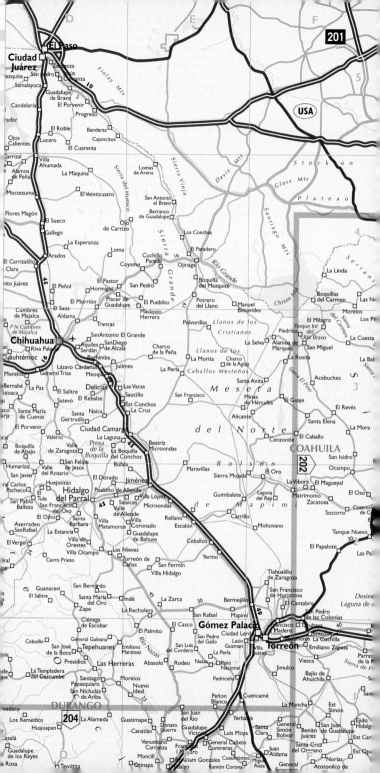

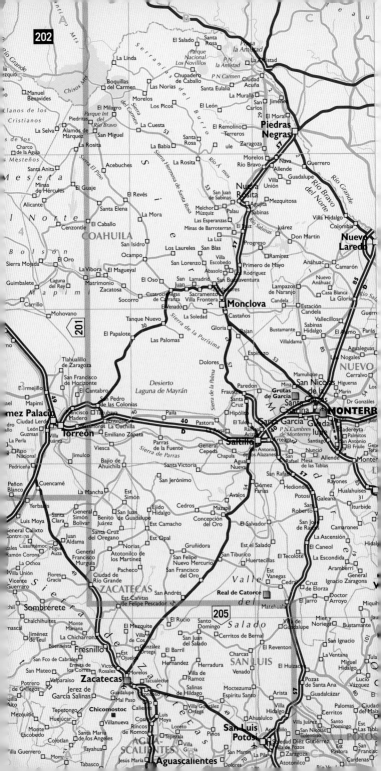

207

207

Campeche

Hampolol
Seybaplaya
Haltunchén
China
Tixm
Sihoch
Champotón
Santa C
Chencán
261
Pixtun
Xcabacab
Sabancu
Pi
Chekubul
Chicbul
Ciudad del Carmen
Puerto Real
Dieciocho
Zacatal
de Marzo
Escár
Laguna
Nuevo
de Términos
Mamante
Mat
Campechito
180 Atasta
División
Frontera
del Norte
221
Tupilco Puerto Chiltepec
Alvaro
El Vapor
Sánchez
Ceiba
Obregón
Buenavista
Magallanes
Paraíso
Barra
Tecolutilla
Palizada
Candelaria
de Tonalá
El Espino
Nacajuca
Jonuta
Monclo
Agua Dulce Alemán
San Joaquín
Salsipuedes
Nueva
Aleman
Cunduacán
TABASCO
186
El Triunfo
Coahu
180
Villahermosa
La Venta
Cárdenas
El Limón
Bonito
Ciudad Pemex
Chablé
San Pedro
La Reforma
Tepetitlán
Balancán
La Revancha
Las Choapas
Pueblo
Hidalgo
Filisola
Huimanguillo
Nuevo
Macuspana
Tulipán
Tenosique
Francisco
Astapa
Jalapa
Catazajá
203
de Pino Suárez
Rueda
Mezcalapa
Tacotalpa
Libertad
La Palma
El Chichón
Chontalpa
195
Salto
Gregório
Río
de Agua
Palenque
Méndez
Chancalá
El Nara
Pichucalco
Teapa
197
Raudales
Ixtacomitán
Agua Azul
Río Usumacinta
de Malpaso
Ostuacán
Amatán
199
Yajalón
Tzinteel
Pueblo
Tapilula
Veijo
Tecpatán
Temo
Copainalá
Pueblo
El Bosque
Chilón
Presa
Apic Pac
Nuevo
Ocosingo
Yaxchilán
Nezahualcóyotl
Iztotól
Lacanjá
Cañón del
Bochil
Tenejapa
Altamirano
Bonampak
Sumidero
Soyaló
Santo
Cintalapa
San Tomás
Tuxtla
Chiapa
Teopisca
de Figueroa
do Corzo
San Cristóbal
El Vergelito
Gutiérrez
Suchiapa
de las Casas
Amatenango del Valle
Las Cruces
Benito
Iquipilas
CHIAPAS
Las Margaritas
Nuevo
Juárez
Santa
México
Venustiano
Las
80
Comitán de
P N Lagunas
Isabel
Domingo
Zaragoza
Carranza
Rosas
Domínguez
de Montebello
Chahóma
San Francisco
Tzimol
Santo Domingo
Villa
Brillante
Pujiltic
Tzizcao
Lagunas de
190
Flores
Revolución
La Trinitaria
Montebello
U Hidalgo
Arriaga
Mexicana
Presa
Santa Inés
de Zaragoza
Paredón
Buenavista
La Concordia
San Antonio
San Pedro
de la Angostura
Jaltenango
Tapanatepec
Tonalá
de la Paz
Puerto Palomas
Tres Picos
Chicomuselo
El Jocate
Frontera
Puerto Arista
Custepec
Comalapa
200
Pijijiapan
Silepec
El Carmen
Mapastepec
Motozintla
Acacoyagua
Escuintla
de Mendoza
Acapetagua
Va Comalitlán
Union
Huixtla
Juárez
Cacahoatán
Tapachula
El
Mazatán
225
Carmen
Frontera
Puerto Madero
Hidalgo

Bahía de Campeche

Ría Ce
Parque N
Celestún
Chunch
La Costa
Tank

tepio
tepio
e Laguna
de Catemaco
drés Tuxtla
tzacoalcos
Cosoleacaque
Minatitlán
de Morelos
El Juile Tenochtitlán
Medias Aguas
Vasconcelos
Istmo
Jesús Carranza
de
Tehuantepec
Lázaro Santa María
Cárdenas Chimalapa
San Miguel
Chimalapa
Santo Domingo
185
Juchitán
de Zaragoza
San Mateo
a Cruz
Golfo
de
huantepec
l

Sierra de La

Minas del Norte de Chiapas

Sierra Madre de Chiapas

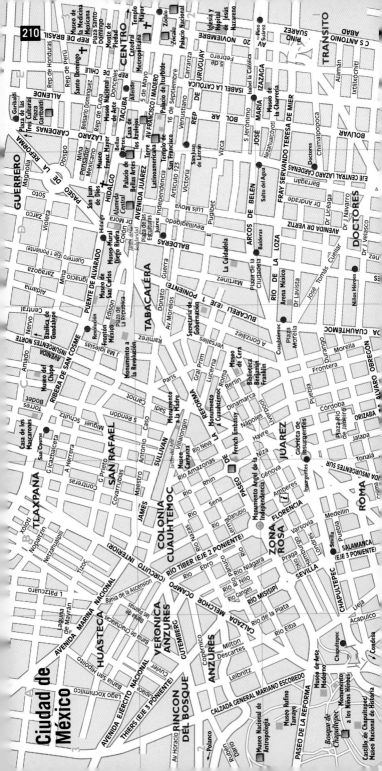

Ciudad de México

Picture Credits

The Automobile Association would like to thank the following photographers, companies and picture libraries for their assistance in the preparation of this book.
Abbreviations for the picture credits are as follows - (t) top; (b) bottom; (c) centre; (l)
left; (r) right; (AA) AA World Travel Library.

Front and back covers: (t) AA/C Sawyer; (ct) AA/P Wilson; (cb) Robin Barton;
(b) AA/C Sawyer. Spine: AA/R Strange.

Alamy © Wolfgang Kaehler/Alamy 2(4), 59, © Luc Novovitch/Alamy 70, © Danita
Delimont/Alamy 170b; **Robin Barton** 180t, 180b, 181l, 181r, 182l, 182c, 182r, 183l,
183r, 184l, 184r; **Corbis** © Fred Prouser/Reuters/Corbis 12t, © Cyril Iordansky/
Reuters/Corbis 12c, © SERVIN HUMBERTO/CORBIS SYGMA 13tl, © Douglas
Kirkland/CORBIS 13tr, © Bettmann/CORBIS 22t, © Danny Lehman/CORBIS 22b;
EMPICS Sport/PA Photos 23t.

The remaining photographs are held in the Association's own photo library (AA WORLD
TRAVEL LIBRARY) and were taken by **P Baker** 11tr; **S Day** 16(6); **F Dunlop** 8b, 15tr,
15br, 63t, 63b, 71, 146; **L Dunmire** 60, 62t, 64, 65t, 65c, 65b, 66, 67b, 175, 193t;
C Sawyer 2(1), 2(2), 2(3), 5, 6, 8t, 9tr, 10tcr, 10b, 11tl, 11tcr, 12/3b, 15tl, 15bl, 17, 20,
21c, 23b, 24(3), 25, 33, 34/5, 35t, 36, 38b, 39b, 40, 43, 44, 45t, 45b, 46, 48, 49t, 49b, 50,
52t, 52b, 53t, 85t, 85b, 86t, 86b, 87t, 87b, 88, 88/9, 93b, 94t, 95b, 96t, 99t, 101t, 101b,
108, 111c, 111b, 114t, 114b, 115, 116t, 116c, 116b, 117, 120l, 121, 122, 123t, 124t,
131bl, 131br, 132t, 133b, 134t, 134b, 136, 140, 141t, 143b, 152, 153t, 153b, 155b, 156t,
156b, 157t, 162t, 162b, 163, 164, 166t, 167, 168t, 168b, 169, 176, 177b, 178l, 178r, 179,
186, 188r, 189, 193bl, 193br; **R Strange** 3(1), 3(2), 3(3), 6/7, 9tl, 9tcl, 9tcr, 9b, 10tl, 10tr,
11br, 12b, 14l, 14r, 16(1), 16(2), 16(3), 16(4), 16(5), 16/7, 18, 19, 21tl, 21tr, 21b, 24(1),
24(2), 34, 37t, 37b, 38t, 39t, 41t, 41b, 42, 47t, 47b, 53b, 72t, 72 (insert), 77t, 77b, 83, 84,
89, 90, 91t, 91c, 91b, 92, 93t, 93c, 94b, 95t, 96b, 97, 98b, 99b, 100,107, 109t, 109b,
110t, 111t, 112, 113t, 113b, 118, 120r, 123b, 124b, 129, 131t, 132b, 133t, 135t, 135b,
137,138t, 138b, 139b, 141b, 142, 143t, 145t, 145b, 154, 157b, 159, 160/1, 161, 164/5,
166c, 166b, 170t,177t, 185, 188l; **P Wilson** 3(4), 10tcl, 11tcl, 11bl, 24(4), 51, 61, 62b,
67t, 68, 69, 72c, 72b, 73, 74, 75, 76, 98t, 110b, 119, 139t, 144t, 151, 155t, 158, 165, 187.

Every effort has been made to trace the copyright holders, and we apologise in advance
for any accidental errors. We would be happy to apply the corrections in the following
edition of this publication.

SPIRAL GUIDES

Questionnaire

Dear Traveler

Your comments, opinions and recommendations are very important to us. So please help us to improve our travel guides by taking a few minutes to complete this simple questionnaire.

Send to: Spiral Guides, MailStop 66, 1000 AAA Drive, Heathrow, FL 32746–5063

Your recommendations...
We always encourage readers' recommendations for restaurants, nightlife or shopping – if your recommendation is added to the next edition of the guide, we will send you a FREE AAA Spiral Guide of your choice. Please state below the establishment name, location and your reasons for recommending it.

_____

_____

_____

_____

_____

Please send me AAA Spiral _____
(see list of titles inside the back cover)

About this guide...
Which title did you buy?

_____ **AAA Spiral**

Where did you buy it? _____

When? m m / y y

Why did you choose a AAA Spiral Guide? _____

_____

_____

_____

Did this guide meet your expectations?

Exceeded ☐　　Met all ☐　　Met most ☐　　Fell below ☐

Please give your reasons _____

_____

_____

_____

continued on next page...

Were there any aspects of this guide that you particularly liked?

_____

_____

_____

_____

_____

Is there anything we could have done better?

_____

_____

_____

_____

_____

About you...

Name (Mr/Mrs/Ms) _____

Address _____

_____

_____ Zip _____

Daytime tel nos. _____

Which age group are you in?

Under 25 ☐ 25–34 ☐ 35–44 ☐ 45–54 ☐ 55–64 ☐ 65+ ☐

How many trips do you make a year?

Less than one ☐ One ☐ Two ☐ Three or more ☐

Are you a AAA member? Yes ☐ No ☐

Name of AAA club _____

About your trip...

When did you book? m m / y y   When did you travel? m m / y y

How long did you stay? _____

Was it for business or leisure? _____

Did you buy any other travel guides for your trip? ☐ Yes ☐ No

If yes, which ones? _____

_____

Thank you for taking the time to complete this questionnaire.
